Communicating with Orcas researched information with a spiritual aspect. Mary Getten brings together her knowledge working as a whale naturalist and her ability to telepathically communicate with the whales to offer a nicely balanced picture of these ancient beings.

—Patty Summers author of *Talking with the Animals*

Communicating with Orcas is a most enlightening work. Mary has done an excellent job of developing communications between orcas and humans. The orcas are sharing their extreme wisdom with Mary and others. I have enjoyed this book, as well as learning a lot as I read. I do hope that many more humans can learn from sea-going mammals.

—John E. Upledger, D.O., O.M.M., President and Medical Director of The Upledger Institute, Inc., Palm Beach Gardens, Florida

A fascinating glimpse into the possibilities of animal-human communication, Mary Getten's *Communicating with Orcas: The Whales' Perspective* is both inspiring and thought-provoking.

—Brenda Peterson, *Build Me an Ark: A Life with Animals*

Mary Getten weaves a story of deep communication and understanding between humans and orcas. Her work shakes cultural concepts of evolution and awareness in animals, including humans, and imparts fascinating information directly from the orcas themselves.

—Penelope Smith, founding animal communication specialist, author of *Animal Talk* and *When Animals Speak*, editor of *Species Link* magazine

COMMUNICATING

── *with* ──

ORCAS

THE WHALES' PERSPECTIVE

Mary J. Getten

HAMPTON ROADS
PUBLISHING COMPANY, INC.

Excerpt reprinted with permission of the publisher from *Killer Whales* by John K. B. Ford, Kenneth C. Balcomb, and Graeme M. Ellis. © University of British Columbia Press 1995. All rights reserved by the publisher.

Excerpt reprinted with permission. Hoyt, E. 1992. *The Performing Orca: Why the Show Must Stop.* Whale and Dolphin Conservation Society, Bath, UK, pp. i to ix, 1 to 104.

Excerpts from *Whale Tales* © Whale Tales Press, Friday Harbor, WA. Used by permission.

Cover design by Frame25 Productions
Cover art by Glenn R. McGloughlin through Shutterstock.com
Typesetter: Frame 25 Productions
Hampton Roads Publishing Company, Inc.
1125 Stoney Ridge Road
Charlottesville, VA 22902

434-296-2772, fax: 434-296-5096, e-mail: hrpc@hrpub.com, www.hrpub.com

If you are unable to order this book from your local bookseller, you may order directly from the publisher. Call 1-800-766-8009, toll-free.

Library of Congress Cataloging-in-Publication Data

Getten, Mary J.
  Communicating with orcas : the whales' perspective / Mary J. Getten.
    p. cm.
  Summary: "Getten, a naturalist and animal communicator, relates her conversations with the Orca whales in 'J-Pod,' a family of whales that live in the waters off Washington State. Getten uses her abilities to uncover what the whales think about various topics"--Provided by publisher.
  ISBN 1-57174-466-5 (alk. paper)
  1. Killer whale. 2. Human-animal communication. I. Title.
  QL737.C432G48 2006
  599.53'6--dc22
                            2006005104

ISBN 1-57174-466-5
10 9 8 7 6 5 4 3 2 1
Printed on acid-free paper in the United States

ACKNOWLEDGMENTS

This book could not have been written without the cooperation and insight of many whales. I am thankful for each orca's contribution and acknowledge the immeasurable joy that the wild and captive whales give to millions of people each year.

My deepest gratitude goes to Granny, the leader of J pod, who graciously took me into her world and answered all my questions. This is really her book. She was the inspiration and a coauthor in every sense. Granny's generous gifts of time, information, patience, and love created this work. I am also thankful to her son, Ruffles, for his help and support.

I would like to express my love and appreciation to Raphaela Pope for joining me in this adventure. Her participation gave me the courage to continue these interviews and established a wonderful friendship. I am grateful to Elizabeth Morrison and George Denniston who coached, encouraged, and edited this material during its evolution. Their support kept me going, along with my many friends (you know who you are) who commented on material and pushed me to continue. Thanks also to Ashley Anderson and Natalie Herner for the use of their photos.

Special thanks go to Richard and Sabryna Bach for introducing this material to Hampton Roads. I also extend my gratitude to everyone on the staff at Hampton Roads, especially to Bob Friedman for agreeing to publish this book and editing it.

My heartfelt appreciation goes to Penelope Smith, Jeri Ryan, Carol Gurney, Beatrice Lydecker, and all the animal communicators who blazed the way for my colleagues and me. They opened hearts to the truth about animals and built the road to acceptance that we are now able to walk.

And finally, a special thanks to Jane Goodall who inspired me to pursue whatever I want in life regardless of the protocol or what the world thinks. She dissolved the walls that had kept women out of careers in science and research and became a shining example for generations of women. Thank you, Jane.

Contents

INTRODUCTION

Everything in this book is true—the names, the places, the events, the people, the whales, and their words. The whale communication sessions were tape-recorded and meticulously transcribed word by word. Each incident on the water is an actual event that I experienced. I have taken some liberties with the order of these conversations, and who said what to whom, but the words remain intact. Truth is important to me, so I have done everything possible to be accurate.

The truth is that all animals are intelligent, spiritual, emotional, thinking beings. Our ancestors knew this, and we are rediscovering their knowledge. As we look at animals with a different perspective, we ponder their inner lives. What do they think about? Do they have hopes and dreams? Are we driving them mad or making them sick?

When I was in school, I dreamed of living in the jungle and assisting Jane Goodall in her chimpanzee studies. I devoured each new story in the *National Geographic* and savored it again and again. I wanted to dive deeply into the lives of wild animals and understand them from the inside out.

My life took another path and I never made it to the Gombe, but eventually my love for wild animals was rekindled—not with jungle animals, but with the creatures of the sea. After working for four years with seals and sea lions in a California rehabilitation center, I moved to Washington state and began leading whale-watch trips in the San Juan Islands.

Lucky me. I spent thousands of hours in the company of wild orcas—killer whales. I saw them hunt, travel, sleep, play, and romance. I interpreted their behavior for passengers on whale-watch cruises but was frustrated with our limited knowledge of these fantastic creatures. The literature was sadly lacking.

Researchers have studied orcas since 1970, but most of our questions are still unanswered. What do they think of us? Is pollution harming them? Why do whales beach? Who fathers the calves? Where do they go in the winter? The list is endless. Orcas spend only 5 percent of their time at the surface, where we can see them. What are they doing the other 95 percent?

Fortunately, I had taken my first class in telepathic animal communication in 1988. I knew that animals could speak to us, and once I started communicating with whales, there was no turning back. I now had the ability to do "research" with whales that required no equipment, grants, permits, degrees, or facilities. I could ask the whales anything, about any facet of their lives. My only limitation was knowing what to ask.

In 1996, I enlisted the help of another animal communicator to investigate the lives of orcas from their perspective. Raphaela Pope didn't know a thing about whales and wouldn't be influenced by her personal beliefs or knowledge of them, but she was a good telepathic animal communicator. She had spent years talking to people and their pets, helping them understand each other better. Once she encountered my orca friends, she too was intrigued by the secrets they held. Through telepathic interviews we were able to better understand these magnificent beings. Together, we set out to learn about orcas—from their perspective.

Raphaela and I spent more than a year interviewing whales—wild and captive orcas. This is the story of that adventure: two women who dove deeply into the sea and met Granny, the matriarch and leader of J pod, a group of orcas that frequent the waters of Washington. Granny opens up her world and answers all of our questions with style and humor; so does Ruffles, Granny's son and the oldest male in the community; and so do four captive whales who tell us about life in a tank.

To truly understand orcas, or any species, we must talk to them directly. Through observation and traditional research, we can make assumptions, but they are just that. Like humans, each whale is an individual, and what is true for one is not true for all. Understanding orcas is an endless process, and our project is just the beginning. It became an incredible journey of insights and surprises. Some days it was hard to believe we were actually talking to whales, probing the depths of their knowledge and investigating their emotions. The rest of my life seemed so normal. Other days, well. . . .

WHALES 101

As I drove into the little town of Friday Harbor, delicious, cool morning air blew through the open windows of my car. Here on San Juan Island, in the pristine waters of the Pacific Northwest, even the hottest summer day is fresh and invigorating. Today, a few clouds drifted across a clear blue sky, and Mount Baker, snow-covered and majestic, glowed in the morning sunshine.

It's going to be a fine day on the water, I thought. It was July 2, 1997, a year after Raphaela and I had begun our orca communication project, and the tourist season was in full swing. Friday Harbor, the largest town in the San Juan archipelago, is the center for whale-watching, whale research, and whale mania.

I glanced across at Shaw and Brown Islands above the hundreds of masts, fishing vessels, and whale-watching boats moored at the Friday Harbor Marina. The eight o'clock ferry from Anacortes on the Washington mainland was just arriving, late as usual, I noted. I hurried down the main dock to the *Western Prince*.

Mary on the Western Prince

1

Dew still clung to the railing as I stepped aboard. The captain, Bob Van Leuven, was washing the windows and getting the 47-foot cruiser ready for our trip. He moved easily around her white-and-turquoise deck, his blonde hair shining in the early morning sun. This was his twelfth year as her owner and operator, and my seventh year as her naturalist. Whale-watching was a passion for Bob, as it was for me. Neither Bob nor I had ever missed a day or a cruise.

The smell of fresh-perked coffee floated out of the galley. I stuffed my lunch into the little fridge and headed for the wheelhouse, where I filled in the log and adjusted my binoculars. As "Queen of the *Western Prince*," I loved informing and educating passengers about the area and the wildlife we encountered. There were many exciting and remarkable creatures here, but most people came for one thing only—whales. These weren't just any whales. They were killer whales, and the orcas of the San Juan Islands are among the best-known and most loved creatures in the entire world.

This morning, instead of the usual collection of tourists, we were taking out a charter group, students from John Carroll University in Cleveland, Ohio. I liked school charters, especially groups with a fairly good knowledge of whales. They asked interesting questions. Their professor, Mark Bodamer, was an old friend of mine. His students had all read my book *The Orca Pocket Guide,* so my talk would have to be a bit more creative than usual. They already knew the basics of orca life.

I went out to the railing as my group thundered down the dock. They looked like bright, curious kids—my favorite kind. Mark appeared from the crowd wearing a huge grin. "Mary, it's great to see you," he called. "Are we going to have whales today?"

There it was, the eternal question—the same question I've been asked hundreds of times each week for the past seven years. "I sure hope so," I replied brightly. I knew from the *Western Prince*'s excellent whale-spotting network there were definitely whales in the area, but I've learned never to make promises.

I went on, "It looks like we have a pretty good chance right now, but then you never know about these guys. They can take off without warning, so I never say for sure until I see the whites of their eye patches." Two of the girls giggled and rolled their eyes. So much for my repartee.

The students climbed aboard and we shoved off. It was truly a glorious day. The sun reflected brightly off the smooth water and there was barely a ripple on the surface. I got on the loudspeaker. "Good morning, everyone. I'd like to welcome you aboard the *Western Prince*. My name is Mary, and I'll be your naturalist today."

I continued with information about the life vests, snacks, binoculars, and most importantly the bathroom. I told them that I would give them as much information as I could about the various wildlife we encountered. Before I even finished the general information, I spotted a bald eagle sitting low in a tree near the shoreline. She was beautiful, and we stopped to talk about her and get a closer look.

As soon as we left the eagle, several students made their way to the wheelhouse. They were bubbling with excitement and couldn't wait to tell me what they had done the night before. Early in the evening, they had attended a presentation on orcas given by Peter Fromm, local author of a book called *Whale Tales*. The students had fallen into conversation with Peter afterwards and had mentioned that they were going whale-watching with me the next day.

Peter and I have known each other for years. When we first met, I was working in the research department of The Whale Museum in Friday Harbor, helping researchers study the orcas of the San Juan Islands. He told the students that I had developed an unusual skill—the ability to communicate telepathically with animals. I was supplementing my scientific knowledge of whales by talking to them directly. He let them know about my relationship with Granny, who was one of the whales we would be looking for today. Unfortunately, he had given me quite a billing to live up to!

I wondered about the students' reaction. There are people to whom animal communication seems absolutely normal, and others who find it so far out they can scarcely believe I am serious. Where would these students fall?

Sally, a slim blonde from Kansas, told me that she was very excited about the possibility of communicating with orcas. Though she had never seen a whale, she had felt an indescribable bond with the farm animals she knew as a child and was certain that they understood her.

She told me that immediately after Peter's presentation, she had organized about a dozen students to try to communicate with the whales. They decided to attempt it near the water, so they walked down to the dock in the dark. When they reached the end of the dock, they gathered in a circle and sat down. Hands held high, palms facing forward, they quieted themselves and sent energy into the center of the circle.

When their force field was almost visible, a student named Brian began his appeal to the whales. "Orcas of this area, please hear our call. We are students from Ohio who have traveled far to see you. We have great respect for you and sincerely hope that you will show yourselves to us tomorrow."

Brian now told me that he was a bit skeptical about the possibility of telepathic communication but felt it was worth a try anyway. He was fascinated with whales. The previous winter in Hawaii he had had a very striking encounter while on a whale-watch trip. A huge humpback had breached right next to his boat, and he had looked straight into its mammoth eye before the creature crashed back into the sea. The consciousness that had stared back at him was unquestionable and compelling.

Next, Barbara, a sweet girl with a Southern drawl, had spoken. "We have only love for you and wish you no harm. Please show us something of your lives so that we may understand you better." Each student took a turn, speaking his truth to the whales with respect and love. Most of them had never seen a whale in the wild, although many had experienced cetaceans in marine parks.

When everyone had spoken, they held hands in silence and sent rays of love to the orcas. Silently they had made their way back to their rooms and drifted off to sleep, each one hoping that the message had been received.

By the time the students finished their story, the hair was standing up on the back of my neck. I had goose bumps everywhere and my hands automatically crossed over my heart. I was filled with joy that these students had made such a sincere and heartfelt effort to communicate with the whales. Now they were here, ready to meet the whales in person.

"You've done very well," I told them. "I'm sure the whales got your message. They are very receptive to our thoughts, particularly when they are sent with such love and reverence. If they are able to come meet you today, I'm sure they will."

"Why couldn't they come?" asked Brian.

"Well, it depends on what they are doing. Orcas spend most of their time either traveling and looking for food or eating. When they find fish, they feed until they are full. If the whales are somewhere else feeding today, they may simply not be able to appear."

I recalled the first time I had asked Granny if she could arrange to meet the *Western Prince* on a certain day. She had replied, "We don't make decisions like that. I can't tell you where we'll be on a given day. We are part of nature's flow and balance. If there are fish present, we may be there. We do not plan ahead. We live in the moment."

By this time there were eight students crammed into the wheelhouse, all full of questions about how I communicate with whales and what they have to say. Melissa asked if I had always been able to communicate with animals.

"Yes and no," I told her. "Telepathic communication is a natural skill that we all have, but like most people I had forgotten it. Fortunately there are some great teachers who can help. I started studying animal communication in 1988, so I've been working at it for some time."

"How do you actually do it? Do you hear words or what?" she pressed. Melissa told me that she had an old dog back home in Chicago. She was sensitive to his needs and usually understood what he wanted, but she also wanted to tell him how much he meant to her before it was too late. She wondered if she could learn how to communicate with him.

"First, you must get really quiet and centered inside. I find a deep place within me where everything is silent. Then I mentally call out to the animal, and most of the time I get an answer. Sometimes I hear words, but at other times I may see pictures. Often a feeling or knowing comes to me in answer to a question. Once in a while, I get bodily sensations. One time, Ruffles, an adult male orca, showed me what it was like to eat a fish."

"That's really wild. I wish I could talk to whales," she said.

I explained to Melissa that this innate ability lies dormant in all of us. "If you want to develop your telepathic communication skills, the best place to start is with a good teacher who will show you techniques for quieting your mind and provide practice and validating experiences to get you started. Learning telepathic communication is a little like studying a foreign language. You can do it, but it takes time to develop your abilities."

Wayne from Texas spoke up. "Last night, Peter said you are particularly close to a whale named Granny. What do you talk to her about?"

"We talk about anything and everything. I'm trying to get a complete picture of Granny's life. I've known her for seven years now. She is the leader of J pod and a very old and wise whale. I've found that Granny has a unique perspective and really wants to share her thoughts with all of us.

"I spend hundreds of hours with these orcas every summer and see remarkable things, but most of their world is hidden from us. We really know so little about them. I wanted to ask Granny directly about her life and especially about those things we cannot study, like her feelings. Does she have hopes and dreams? How does she feel about us? Is she angry about the captures and the killing?

"I'm also really concerned about her environment. Is there enough food? How are the contaminants we pour into the water affecting her? My list of questions is endless.

"I am working on this project with a friend who has been a professional animal communicator for many years and even teaches classes on how to communicate with animals. We have asked Granny and some other orcas everything we can think of about their lives. Hopefully, we've asked the right questions. It's tricky to know what to ask an individual who lives in such a foreign land."

Wayne's forehead wrinkled. "I never thought of it that way. Do you talk to the whales on your trips and ask them to come over to the boat?"

"That's an interesting question, and one that's been difficult for me. These whales are my friends. I love to see and talk to them, but I don't take advantage of our friendship. So the answer is no. When I'm on the water, I'm here to educate people about the whales. Sometimes Granny and her pod cruise over to say hi, but it's her decision."

Brian wanted to know if the whale-watch boats bother the orcas. That was probably one of the first questions I had asked Granny, and I knew her reply by heart. She has told me that the love and reverence that come to her from the people on the whale boats is a joy to receive. She doesn't really like the noise, but she's adjusted to it.

About an hour out of port, we spotted some whales. It was only ten o'clock and already 15 boats were escorting them north in Haro Strait, between Vancouver Island and the San Juans. There were several Canadian inflatables jammed with tourists, three boats from Friday Harbor, a passenger ferry from Seattle carrying more than 200 people, and six kayaks.

It was almost the Fourth of July, the busiest boating weekend of the summer, when the whales are a primary focus. By this afternoon it would be a madhouse out here with close to 100 boats around the whales. I shuddered thinking of the afternoon trip yet to come, but I had whales ahead and needed to identify them.

There are approximately 90 resident orcas that frequent the waters of Washington and southern British Columbia. They live in family groups known as J, K, and L pods. I wanted to find out which pod was here this morning so I could talk about various individuals and habits. I watched intently with my binoculars trying to get a good look at the large male near the front of the group.

Males are easier to identify because their dorsal fins, which are twice the size of females', often have distinctive characteristics. The water was still calm, but the boats were causing a lot of wakes, and I was having trouble seeing the big male's saddle patch, the grayish-white area on the body right behind the dorsal fin. Many patches have a unique pattern that identifies an individual. Some whales have distinctive nicks or cuts in their fins. At times you need to see both the fin and the patch to make a positive identification. That was the case this morning.

I could see three males and about ten females and subadults, but I didn't know how many more whales were behind or ahead of this group. It looked like part of L pod, the largest family, but I would have to positively identify an individual to be sure. I focused my binoculars on the large male. He had a big nick in the back edge of his dorsal fin about halfway down. This was definitely an L pod whale, but I couldn't tell if it was Dylan or Mega. They both have a big nick, so I would have to see the saddle patch to be certain.

Scanning the water, I saw the tip of his dorsal fin again breaking the surface. I focused my binoculars, and just before the patch appeared, a boat blocked my view. Damn, I missed him. The sleek black figure slid out of sight. I hoped he would come up again soon. Traveling orcas in this area tend to surface and breathe three to five times in succession and then stay down for about three minutes before the sequence starts again. Now he was on the other side of the passenger ferry from Seattle.

Five seconds passed, ten, 15, and I knew he was down. Swiftly I scanned the surface for another whale. There was a male over by a Canadian whale-watch boat. A quick look at the bulbous dorsal fin told me it was Leo. I spoke into the mike: "The large male over by the black inflatable is L44, known as Leo. He was born in 1974 and is a mature adult. This group of whales we are watching is part of the L12 subpod, an extended family of about 17 whales. I don't know yet if they are all here, but I'll tell you about as many of them as possible."

Leo's mom, Olympia, was a few yards away from him with his sister Spirit and her two calves. We had three generations in tight formation. I love encountering a family traveling close together. It gives me an opportunity to explain about orcas' tight social structure while I point out differences in sexes and sizes.

I talked about this group as long as we were in a good viewing position. That turned out to be about ten minutes. Six or seven more boats had joined the flotilla since we had arrived, and the area had become crowded and chaotic. Federal regulations require that boats stay 100 yards from the whales, and it was getting difficult to do this while maneuvering around all the traffic.

The whales were moving north at about five miles per hour. They were spread out over about a mile and were simply traveling, not feeding or playing. A young woman with dark hair knocked on the wheelhouse window. "When do they breach?" she asked.

"Whenever they want. We don't see that every trip. It's totally up to them, and we never know when it's going to happen. Keep watching; maybe you'll be lucky."

Captain Bob was listening intently to the radio. "We might have whales coming around the south end of San Juan Island," he said. "I'm hearing some fishermen on the radio. I doubt if anyone is with them. Should we go?"

I stared out the window for a moment considering the options. We had whales right in front of us and could spend two hours with them if we stayed here, but it wasn't the experience I wanted to give these kids. With so many boats crowding around, it was unlikely the whales would come close to us.

But if we left these whales and went to look for the others, it would take at least 30 minutes to get there, maybe as much as an hour. It was possible that we might never even find them. They could easily take off across the strait and head for Port Townsend or Sequim. If that happened we would end up with nothing except a boat full of angry, disappointed teens.

It was a big gamble, but my gut said that we should go.

We left L pod and headed south in Haro Strait. Vancouver Island was visible across the water and the buildings of Victoria glistened in the distance. It took about 40 minutes to get to False Bay, on the south end of San Juan Island. Bob and I constantly scanned the surface for fins or blows.

I began to get worried. We should have seen them by now. Had they turned around? There weren't even any boats in the area. I was beginning to doubt the wisdom of my decision when I spotted something ahead and to our left. Yes! It was a dorsal fin.

As I watched I could see a tiny fin next to the adult. It was a mom and her calf. Suddenly, blows appeared in the distance behind them. The whales were coming straight at us. "There they are!" I shouted at Bob. He cut the engines, and we slowed to a stop. I announced that we had whales dead ahead, and everyone rushed to the bow.

There were about 15 females and subadults spread out over a two-mile area. I couldn't identify anyone at this distance, but many of the saddle patches were "open," a distinctive pattern that I recognized.

"It looks like K pod," I said to Bob. He nodded. Two females were swiftly approaching the boat on the left side. They surfaced right next to us, and I clearly saw their saddles and fins. It was Kiska and her daughter Raggedy who tail-slapped three times as she went by. Cheers rose, cameras clicked, and the weight on the deck shifted as everyone ran from the bow to the stern.

There still wasn't a boat in sight, but more whales were coming, three on the right and two on the left. Another female and two juveniles were about 300 yards away, near the shoreline. It was hard to know where to look. Without warning a female came flying out of the water no more than 100 yards from the boat.

"Breach!" I screamed into the microphone, "At two o'clock." Everyone rushed to the right side. They were laughing and clapping, whooping and hollering. "Keep watching that same area!

Sometimes they do it twice." As if on cue, this beauty hurtled skyward in full view of everyone. The roar from the students was deafening.

"I got it!" a small girl on the bow shouted, holding her camera high.

"Yes, yes!" her friend yelled as they jumped up and down, hugging each other. I couldn't stop grinning. The female surfaced again about 250 feet behind the boat still moving west.

While everyone crowded the stern watching her leave, I concentrated on the water in front of us. I was searching for Taku, the only adult male in this pod, but there were no large dorsal fins in sight. Suddenly another 12 whales appeared, heading straight for us. There were two males in the group. "This is more than K pod," I said to Bob. "It looks like we have the Js, too!"

When the students had told me about their whale communication session the night before, I had hoped that Granny would hear them and respond. I love this whale so much and wanted to share her with the students. My heart pounded as I lifted the binoculars. The sun was directly in front of me, and it was impossible to see any dorsal fins or saddle patches at this angle. I was desperate to see if Granny was in this group, but I couldn't identify anyone. I snatched the microphone.

"We've got another group of whales coming straight at us, and I think it's J pod." Stampeding buffaloes couldn't have made more noise as the crowd shifted back to the bow. The whales, now lined up side by side, were heading directly for our bow. We sat dead in the water. It was a spectacular sight. Their blows were backlit by the sunlight, and sparkles glinted off their smooth black skin as they surfaced. They were coming closer and closer. Now we were surrounded. They were on the left, on the right; the lead whale was diving directly under the bow.

And then I saw her. Granny was on the left, two whales away from the boat. "Granny!" I shouted out the window. "That's Granny on the left, the female with the little scoop out of her dorsal fin. And there's Ruffles, her son, down on the end. He has the very wavy dorsal fin. That's where he got his name. This is J pod, so we have two pods here right now!"

There was mass pandemonium on deck. Whales were going by on both sides; the students screamed and ran back and forth. I sprinted to the stern and strained to see Granny as she surfaced again. A juvenile erupted from the water in a full breach. Another tail slapped. We were all crowded together on the back deck watching as the whales traveled farther and farther away. Everyone was laughing and talking at once.

Brian bounded up to me breathing heavily. "That was unbelievable!" he exclaimed. "Did you see that breach? Man, I never thought we'd get to see them so close. This was awesome!"

"Yeah, they're beautiful, aren't they? I'm so glad you got to see Granny. It's hard to believe she's in her mid-eighties, isn't it? She looks so strong and fit."

A group had gathered around us, and I told them that scientists think Granny was born around 1911. It is very difficult to determine the age of an adult whale, so scientists make estimates by looking at the ages of her children. Or if we get lucky, the whale may be identified through its markings in historic photos. It's possible that Granny appears in a picture from the 1940s with a calf.

Granny and Lummi, the leader of K pod, are considered to be the oldest whales in the whole community and are approximately the same age. Scientists have only been studying orcas for about 30 years, so they do not know how long these whales can live. They think the average female lives to about 60, but no one knows what the maximum life span could be. That will take another 50 to 70 years of observation and research.

"Lummi should be around somewhere with her son Taku, but we haven't seen them yet."

Blows erupted on the right, taking us by surprise. We had stopped looking for whales and were engrossed in our conversation. We ran to the side of the boat. It was Granny's granddaughter, Samish, and her three-year-old calf, Riptide, along with Princess Angeline and her four-year-old, Polaris. Both moms brought their calves right up to the rear deck and stopped.

There was dead silence except for the sound of the four whales breathing. The shrieks and screams had stopped. We stood transfixed by their presence. They were only a few feet away and lay motionless on the surface. Water droplets rolled down their smooth backs, the sun reflecting off them. An explosive "Pooo" sounded with each exhale, followed by a hollow hiss as their huge lungs filled with air. As they breathed on the surface, we looked into their blowholes. Then with a dip of their heads, the four orcas dove and left our sight.

No one spoke. They were awestruck. Eager eyes looked to me for an explanation.

"They heard your call last night," I said. "They got your message, and it made these two moms feel safe enough to bring their calves over to meet you." A collective sigh went up from the crowd, and smiles broke out everywhere.

"When you approach animals with love and reverence, they respond to you. Don't forget to thank them tonight."

"We won't. This was the most incredible experience of my life!" Sally exclaimed. "Do you really think they heard us?"

"Yes, I do. This was very unusual. In seven years on the water, I have never seen two moms bring their calves over and lie on the surface. Events like this happen so rarely that I can only attribute it to your sincere communication last night. You did a great job."

There were no more whales up ahead, and it was time to get back to port. The Js and Ks were now heading up Haro Strait, most likely trying to catch up with L pod. Bob fired up the engines and took off. The students settled into their seats, some talking and laughing while others sat silently gazing into the distance. I knew that an experience like this might alter some of their lives, and I was happy to have played a part.

I returned to the wheelhouse with a profound sense of satisfaction and love for these orcas, deeply grateful for their presence. The sight of Granny swimming by was still with me. Most of our communication had taken place when we were not in physical contact, and the full impact of her magnificent physical form had overwhelmed me. How could I possibly be talking to this incredible being?

WHEN MARY MET GRANNY

My first meeting with Granny took place on a foggy morning in May of 1991. I had arrived early at Lime Kiln Lighthouse, a whale research lab on the west side of San Juan Island, and sat down to begin my data entry work. Engrossed in the computer, I suddenly had the feeling that someone was watching me.

As I looked out the window behind me, dorsal fins appeared from the mist. I ran outside to the rocks and saw about a dozen whales going by, some very close to shore. They were traveling slowly, just moseying along heading north. I stood alone on the rocks, peering around the lighthouse to watch them as long as possible.

Without warning, a female orca came straight up out of the water directly in front of me only 20 feet away. The huge black-and-white body rose silently from the depths, water cascading down her shiny, taut skin. Half of her body was exposed. The stillness was shattered by her explosive exhale. She hung motionless, gazed at me for a few seconds, and then slid quietly back into the water.

Ashley Anderson

Granny

My feet were glued to the rocks. What was that? Why did that whale look at me? Then I found myself shouting, "Oh my God. Did you see that? She looked at me!" No one appeared to answer my call or share this incredible moment with me. I was alone—just the whale and me.

I ran to the other side of the lighthouse in time to see my whale surface and noted a little scoop out of her dorsal fin and her solid saddle patch. She surfaced again and then disappeared. I stood there for a long time in the swirling fog trying to make sense of the encounter.

I had seen and felt a consciousness in this whale that I had not expected. She had regarded me and made a connection. There was no doubt of that in my mind.

My data entry work for The Whale Museum had begun recently. The lighthouse is used as a research station because the resident orcas pass this spot frequently in the summer months. They go by so often and so close to shore that it has been dubbed "Whale Watch Park."

Lime Kiln Lighthouse sits in pristine surroundings on Haro Strait. Tall Douglas firs and red-barked madrone trees cover the grounds right to the rocky shoreline. Harbor seals and river otters play in the kelp beds while Dall's porpoises frolic and feed in the swift currents of the strait. Vancouver Island shines across the water. I have also seen minke and gray whales from the lighthouse, but the big attraction is always orcas.

Still a bit dazed, I went into the lighthouse and grabbed *Killer Whales,* the orca identification guide, and scanned the pictures looking for the marks I had just seen on this whale. I soon identified her as J2, the whale popularly known as Granny.

What was her life like? How does she live? Where does she go and with whom? Is she happy? I had never been that close to an orca before and was completely astonished at her size and beauty. It was amazing that she had been right in front of me, looking into my eyes. Was she as interested in me as I was in her? Did she know I was there, or was she just spyhopping to see what was happening at the lighthouse?

The impact that Granny and her family would have on my life began almost immediately. My encounter with her galvanized my interest in orcas and pushed me into high gear. I wanted to learn everything about them, but found only about a dozen books. Orca research was a fairly new field, and little had been published at that time.

It had only been about 25 years since the first orcas were captured for aquariums. Beginning in 1965, each year more and more whales were captured in the waters of Washington and British Columbia. Public outcry and concern for them led the Canadian government to begin a study in 1970 to determine the population and the impact that the captures might be having on it.

Biologist Mike Bigg headed the team that took a census up and down the British Columbia coast. His team also started following the whales, recording their vocalizations and photographing them. Dr. Bigg discovered that he could identify individual whales by their unique markings, and his photo-identification technique revolutionized cetacean research. In *Killer Whales*, which Dr. Bigg wrote with John Ford, Graeme Ellis, and Ken Balcomb, it says, "The minimum information that we try to obtain from an encounter with a pod is the identity of all individuals present. We also attempt to determine the sex and traveling companions of each animal, and to make a tape recording of their vocalizations for studies of the different sounds made by each pod. Many other kinds of data can be collected, such as travel routes, group mixing, dive times, feeding activities, travel speeds, times spent on various activities, interactions with fishing operations, and so on."

The study expanded into Washington in 1976 with a census by the Center for Whale Research. Scientists on both sides of the border were now gathering many types of data. New and historic photos of orcas were collected from naturalists and the general public. Although this research yielded much information, the 1994 edition of *Killer Whales* says it best. "One might expect that after 20 years of field research we would understand all of the important features of the life history and ecology of killer whales in British Columbia and Washington. This, however, is far from the case. We and our colleagues have assembled a considerable amount of detailed information on certain aspects of the whale's biology, but answers to some fundamental questions have eluded us. Where are the whales in the winter and what is their diet? Who are the fathers of the calves that we have seen born during the study?"

From that day forward, I studied orcas and spent as much as time as possible observing them from the lighthouse. My effort paid off when later that summer I was hired as a naturalist on a whale-watch boat. Now I was able to follow the whales for hours instead of just seeing them as they passed the lighthouse.

The orcas most commonly seen in Washington are known as the southern resident community. J, K, and L pods comprise this breeding group of approximately 90 whales. They live in a home territory year-round that extends from southern Washington to the midpoint of Vancouver Island and includes the inland waters of Puget Sound and Georgia Strait. These whales are primarily fish eaters. During the summer months they travel through the San Juan Islands following salmon migrating to the Fraser River in Vancouver, British Columbia.

The resident whales live in a matrilineal society. Each pod is an extended family of subpods, immediate family groups of a mother and her children, both sons and daughters. While it is common among mammals for daughters to remain with their mothers, it is highly unusual for sons to do so.

Granny is the matriarch and leader of J pod. Later, when I had begun communicating with her, I asked about her position as leader. She said, *"Leadership to some extent is a human concept. In our society it is very simple. Those with the most experience help and serve by making decisions. I cannot remember a time when the oldest female has not held the leadership position. It is perfectly logical that the pod benefits most from the wisdom and experience of the elder."*

Whenever we encountered J pod on my whale-watch trips, I looked for Granny. She became the focus of my stories. Her immediate family group provided an opportunity to observe four generations—aunts, uncles, and cousins—all living and traveling together.

Pods are extremely stable groups. We have never known a resident whale to leave its own pod and join another. An orca is born into a pod and remains there for life. I found that J pod members were rarely separated by more than a few miles and kept in touch vocally, making calls back and forth beneath the surface. Their primary focus was food, but when they had eaten well, there was always time for play.

In the early 1990s, Granny was accompanied by two adult offspring: Ruffles, a male estimated to be in his early forties, and Sissy, a female in her late fifties. Later Granny told us that she had given birth to another calf many years ago that had died at about five.

Researchers have found that most females lose their first calf, and there is almost a 50 percent mortality rate for orca infants. Sissy was the mother of Samish, an adult female. Samish gave birth to her first calf, Capricorn, in 1987, when she was 13 years old. Unfortunately, Capricorn died of unknown causes in 1991. Three years later, Samish gave birth to Riptide.

By concentrating on Granny and her family, I was able to learn more about their particular habits and patterns. This allowed me to give passengers insight into their world and tell them things they would never know through short observation.

For example, Granny is a wonderful baby-sitter. The first time I saw her alone with her four-year-old great-grandson, Capricorn, the rest of the pod was out in the strait, fishing. Granny and Capricorn were playing in a kelp bed near the shore, tail-slapping and rolling over one another. I wondered why Capricorn's mother, Samish, wasn't nearby and hoped that nothing had happened to her. We watched Granny and Capricorn play for about 20 minutes, and then our boat moved out into the strait, where we found Samish fishing with her uncle Ruffles. I realized that Granny had been baby-sitting!

I've often encountered Granny with one or two little ones close by with no mom in sight. She frolics and plays with them like a youngster, never letting on that she is nearing 90.

J pod is seen more in the San Juan Islands than any other group. During the summer they travel together within their territory looking for food and socializing with their cousins in K and L pods. In the winter, J pod passes through the islands at least once a month, and they appear again on a regular basis from late April through October.

The more I got to know orcas, the more they captivated me. Their magnificent size and graceful movements are absolutely awesome, and the explosive sound of a whale's blow was enough to cause ripples on my skin. I wanted to be as close to them as possible and see lots of action.

Most of the people on my whale-watching trips were awestruck like me. Almost everyone who sees these animals soon acquires a strong desire to be physically close to them and to see them out of the water. Orcas have a mystery about them that makes them even more attractive. They spend roughly five percent of their time at the surface, and even then we see only about a third of their bodies. They are hidden from our view most of the time.

What are they doing down there? What do they really look like? How big is that body? Where do the fins attach? What is their tail like? The mere presence of orcas elicits excitement and wonder. There is so much we cannot see and don't know about them that our analytical minds run wild.

As I continued working as a naturalist through the summers of 1991, 1992, 1993, and 1994, my love for these whales increased. It was still exhilarating to be near them, but I wanted to relate to them on a deeper level. Even though I saw them on a weekly and sometimes daily basis, it seemed as if I barely knew them. How could I bridge the gap between our worlds?

I didn't realize it yet, but the key was right in my hands. It would be several more years before I found the courage to use it.

I began physically calling to Granny out loud. Whenever she appeared, I ran to the deck or leaned out the wheelhouse window and yelled, "Hey, Granny!" I called to honor her and let her know I was there. I knew that she heard me and understood my greeting from the sense of joy and peace that flowed through me after this ritual. Granny and I enjoyed this relationship for several years before we began to speak telepathically.

When I first moved to the San Juan Islands in 1991, I immediately became a volunteer with two wildlife organizations: Wolf Hollow Wildlife Rehabilitation Center and the Marine Mammal Stranding Network. Wolf Hollow is an organization that treats all types of injured and orphaned wildlife, from hummingbirds to deer. The Marine Mammal Stranding Network is completely devoted to dead and live stranded marine mammals: whales, dolphins, porpoises, seals, and sea lions.

Through the Marine Mammal Stranding Network, I continued my work with seals and sea lions that had begun in California. At the same time, I was learning more about the diverse wildlife of the islands. In the San Juans, the live strandings are mostly harbor seal pups that have been orphaned or separated from their mothers. It is heartbreaking to find a tiny little bundle of fur, 25 percent below its birth weight, still alive and looking for its mother. If a pup meets certain federal guidelines, it can be moved to a treatment center. If not, it must be left on the beach to die.

In 1994, after investigating strandings in San Juan County for three years, I became a coordinator of the Stranding Network. My job also included training volunteers and conducting public education. At the same time I took an administrative job at Wolf Hollow. As my interaction with seals and other wildlife intensified, I became increasingly aware of the gulf between us. These animals were sick and hurting, but they could not tell us what was wrong. It was difficult to watch a fox writhe in pain, and I was faced with my inadequacy in understanding animals. This frustration, combined with my intense yearning to know and understand Granny and her family, renewed my interest in telepathic communication.

My first exposure to animal communication had been in 1988, during my time as a volunteer at The Marine Mammal Center in Sausalito, California. This hospital for seals and sea lions treats hundreds of animals each year. I found it frustrating when we didn't know what was wrong with an animal or where it hurt. Then I heard about telepathic communication and was ecstatic! By learning how to talk to animals, I could provide a wonderful service to our patients at the center.

I took a class with veteran communicator Penelope Smith. I was very enthusiastic in the beginning, talking to everyone about animal communication, but most people gave me a queer look and changed the subject. In the 1980s, this ability was either unheard of or was regarded with great skepticism. My disappointment at its lack of acceptance overcame my desire to learn, and I put this skill away. It was easier to slide back into the "normal" world that considers animals less evolved or intelligent than humans, without feelings or awareness.

Looking into Granny's eyes on that day in 1991 opened me again to the truth that all animals are sentient beings. They are conscious, feeling, and thinking individuals. She had peered into my eyes and, without a word, conveyed that message.

How I wish I'd taken that opportunity to communicate telepathically with her. We could have begun our relationship years earlier, but for many reasons it didn't happen. At that stage, my thinking about whales was strictly scientific. I spent my time working with biologists and was immersed in their world and ways of thinking. I hadn't even thought about telepathic communication for several years.

However, by 1994, my desire to learn was so deep that disapproval and skepticism no longer held me back. The world had also changed in the intervening years and telepathic communication was now being discussed in many circles. So I took another class in animal communication from Penelope Smith and then enrolled in a weekend course with another teacher. I practiced fervently, consulting with harbor seals, eagles, and other patients at Wolf

Hollow, with varying results. I talked to cows on the side of the road, to neighborhood dogs, and to birds in the forest.

Eventually, I talked to Granny.

I didn't gather up the courage to contact her until about a year after I began communicating with other animals. It's not surprising that it took me so long. What do you say to such a magnificent creature? This would be my first conversation with a whale, and I had no precedent to follow. Although I had a burning desire to learn about Granny and her family, my insecurities held me back.

Whales are different from other animals. Many people have attributed mystical abilities to them. Some people consider cetaceans more advanced than humans. I was intimidated by the thought of contacting such a being. I felt small and insignificant and didn't want to intrude or get off to a bad start.

I was also plagued by thoughts of my first deliberate communication with an animal. It had occurred at the 1988 workshop I attended at Penelope Smith's house. When the time came for us to talk to an animal, Penelope sat me down in front of her cockatiel, Pirouette.

I knew nothing about birds. Mammals were my passion, and I had no interest in delicate little avians. Truthfully, I was a little frightened of them, yet here I was face to face with a cockatiel, and it was time for us to talk.

I looked into her little bright white face, admiring the crest of yellow feathers on her head and the orange dot on her cheek. Drinking in her features I relaxed and thought, "This won't be too tough. She seems nice enough." So I began to think about what to say to her.

This is where it all went downhill. I didn't have a clue what to say to a bird. You would have thought that I'd spent my entire life locked in a closet. Not a single question appeared. Time ticked by and I knew I had to do something, so I kept repeating, "Hello, Pirouette. Hello, Pirouette. Hello, Pirouette."

Finally, I stopped for a moment to think of something else to say, and clear as a bell I heard Pirouette say, *"Can't you say anything but hello?"*

I was mortified and certain that this two-ounce bird thought I was stupid. Shame enveloped me, and I shut down. I sat looking at the ground, failure written all over my face. There I was, a human, a member of the dominant species on the planet, and I couldn't even think of a single thing to ask a bird.

Penelope thought it was hysterical. Laughing, she came over and said, "Pirouette loves to talk to people and is terribly frustrated. You never gave her a chance to speak." I was embarrassed and felt even more certain that I should avoid birds from now on.

My reluctance to communicate with Granny was fueled not only by the Pirouette experience, but also by my occupation. I was a naturalist, a scientist. I was afraid that the scientific community would meet telepathic communication with skepticism and ridicule. Since I made my living as a naturalist, I couldn't afford to be considered foolish.

Moreover, I still thought of myself as an amateur communicator. I wasn't confident of my abilities. What if I made a fool of myself and alienated Granny? All these fears contributed to my putting off our telepathic meeting.

Finally, one sunny day in the summer of 1995, I mustered up my courage and went to Whale Watch Park. I found a quiet spot away from everyone. Orcas had been passing the lighthouse frequently, and there was a good chance they would go by.

This time it was going to be different. I had written down a list of questions to ask Granny, and I mulled them over as I ate my sandwich. Before long I could see fins in the distance, heading my way. I grabbed my binoculars to identify someone. Was it J pod? I wanted to see Granny before I made contact. There was a large male near the front, and within seconds I had identified him as Ruffles. I didn't see Granny near him, so I closed my eyes and centered myself, trying to get calm and peaceful. My heart was pounding loudly. I checked again with the binoculars, and this time I spotted her close to the lighthouse with three females and a calf. They were taking their time.

I felt like Dorothy as she stood in front of the great Oz, small and in awe of this being. I took a deep breath, closed my eyes and again went inside. When I reached that place of calm where communication happens, I called out mentally, "Granny, are you there?"

Without hesitation I heard, *"Yes, dear, I'm here."*

My stomach turned to butterflies but I went on. "Granny, my name is Mary, and I work on one of the whale-watch boats, the *Western Prince*. I'm the blonde woman who yells at you when you come near. Do you know who I am?"

"Yes, certainly, my dear. I have been waiting for your contact. It is good to speak to you." The sweetness and immediacy of Granny's response calmed my fears. I didn't shut down as I had with Pirouette. In fact, I felt my heart opening up in Granny's presence.

"Would you be willing to answer a few questions for me?"

"Yes, of course, go ahead."

"Granny, how is the fishing? Are you finding enough food?"

"Well, it isn't what it used to be. There are less fish, and we have to travel farther, but we are not suffering. They are still sufficient."

"How is the new baby in your family? Is it doing well?"

"Oh yes, this youngster is the joy and delight of our family. We are so happy to have him."

We continued for about ten minutes. I can hardly even remember what we talked about. It was casual and normal, like a telephone conversation with a friend I hadn't talked to in a few months. Then I asked, "Granny, would you be willing to talk to me again?"

"Certainly, whenever you wish."

"Watch for me on the water, okay? I'll continue to shout when I see you."

"I will do that."

"Thank you, Granny."

"You are most welcome."

Slowly I came back to physical reality and opened my eyes. Sunlight danced upon the gentle waves in front of me, but the whales were gone. They had traveled north out of my sight. I was bursting with joy. Granny had spoken to me, and she had been gracious and kind.

Why had I waited so long to communicate with her? Her comment, *"I have been waiting for your contact,"* was wonderful but perplexing. How did she know I was going to contact her? I lay back in the grass and dreamed of the possibilities as wispy clouds floated across the sky.

After this communication, I continued to call out to Granny from the boat and took the time to chat with her occasionally, but I was careful to keep it to myself. Once in a while Granny told me something that was contrary to scientific belief. For example, she told me they sometimes eat harbor seals, although researchers believe that J pod eats fish exclusively.

Incidents like this were always disconcerting. Was I hearing things wrong, or were the researchers off base? I couldn't talk to anyone about these discrepancies without telling them I got the information telepathically from Granny. There wasn't a single scientist that I knew who would be willing to engage in such a conversation.

I also didn't want to mix the communication with my naturalist work. If people knew that I could talk to whales, they might make unreasonable demands of me. Orcamania was in full swing that summer. *Free Willy II* had just been filmed in the San Juans, and tourists by the thousands were coming to see the whales. Knowing where the whales were at any given moment was a carefully guarded secret in the whale-watch industry. I didn't want to impose on Granny or the other whales by requesting their presence at my boat or in any way abusing their friendship.

I took more animal communication courses during the next year, improving my telepathic communication and keeping my whale talks secret. This was my situation in the summer of 1996, when Raphaela came to Friday Harbor.

MEETING OF THE MINDS

I met Raphaela Pope at an Interspecies Counselor course given by Penelope Smith in January of 1996. An interesting group of people from around the country with varying degrees of expertise in telepathic animal communication had gathered at Penelope's home in Marin County, just north of San Francisco. Raphaela had not planned on attending but found herself registered through a misunderstanding and decided to show up at the last minute.

I had heard about the course only a few weeks before it began. When I called, Penelope informed me that there was only one space left and I would have to meet several requirements including getting testimonials from clients and writing documents before I could be accepted into the course. I scrambled to pull it all together and was admitted.

As everyone gathered at the workshop, Penelope discovered there was an extra person she hadn't expected. Sue's registration and payment had been lost in a terrible fire at Penelope's home, so the class had really been full when I called. I felt lucky to be included but didn't realize then that the workshop would change my life.

I had registered hoping to determine whether I was skilled enough to start a practice as a communicator. It had been six years since I had taken my first class in animal communication, and I was still insecure about my abilities. It was a wonderful course, and after the five days I knew I was ready. What I didn't know was that the universe had lined things up for Raphaela and me to meet and that our collaboration would take us to fantastic inner realms with the whales.

On the last evening Raphaela and I were seated together at dinner. We had a rousing conversation about animals and spirituality, discovering that we enjoyed each other's company and had much in common. Raphaela lived with her husband in Berkeley. By day, she was a case management nurse, but in the evenings she did animal consultations on the phone. I was eager to learn from her how to balance two very different occupations, knowing that I would be doing that myself very soon. I promised to stay in touch with her and looked forward to continuing this new friendship.

I was surprised and delighted when Raphaela called me about six months later. As it usually happens, we had both gone back to our lives after the workshop and had forgotten about keeping in touch. Now she was calling to say she was coming to San Juan Island on vacation and would like to get together. She wanted to see the whales with me, and I was delighted. There is no greater gift than giving someone her first experience with orcas. It is an awe-inspiring moment that can be emotional and profound.

I was very excited about seeing Raphaela and renewing our acquaintance, but I also had an ulterior motive. It had been impossible for me to talk to scientists about the discrepancies in our information. Hopefully, I could convince her to speak to Granny and get independent confirmation about the information I had been receiving.

The day before we were due to meet, I made a quick trip over to the mainland for some supplies. As I parked on the ferry, I noticed that the car in front of me had California plates. It had been a long day, so instead of going upstairs into the lounge, I reclined my seat and took a nap.

As the boat approached Friday Harbor, I awoke and rearranged myself. There in front of me was Raphaela, furiously trying to open her car door. She had locked the keys inside! I couldn't believe that with 150 cars on the boat, she was parked right in front of me. What were the chances?

I jumped out to help, and in her panic, she barely recognized me. We waved down a ferry worker who popped her car door open just as the traffic in front of her began to move. Raphaela shouted, "I'll call you in the morning," and waved goodbye as she sped off the ferry.

The next day she called early. After a good laugh about her dramatic entrance to Friday Harbor, we decided to have lunch before the whale-watch cruise. We met in the Downrigger at a table overlooking the harbor. It was great to see her again, and I was bursting with excitement to tell her about my conversations with the whales. I poured my story out. Raphaela was fascinated. She had always admired whales but had never had the chance to speak with one.

"Raphaela, there are some questions I'd like you to ask Granny if we see her today. I just don't trust myself completely, and I really need some validation. Are you willing to check in with her?" I asked.

"Willing? Let me at it!" she exclaimed. "What an opportunity. I'd love to talk to a whale."

I pulled a small list from my pocket and handed it to her. "There's just a few questions here, and then you can ask whatever you like. I'll let you know which whale she is if we're lucky enough to see her. Oh, I really hope you get to meet Granny. She is so incredible."

Raphaela laughed. "My gosh, I'll be happy to see any whale, and if I get to talk to one, too, all the better."

It was an unusually hot, sunny day, and the *Western Prince* was crowded with passengers from around the world. I seated Raphaela on the bow in an excellent viewing position. I told Captain Bob what we were doing, and he added a question to the list, too.

Raphaela sat quietly enjoying the seals and eagles that we stopped to see. Even though I was busy with my naturalist duties I could watch her from the wheelhouse. When three Dall's porpoises appeared and rode our bow wake, she squealed with delight and hung over the edge until a perfectly placed exhalation covered her face with mist. Her brown eyes danced as she turned to me in the wheelhouse window, her face dripping with seawater.

We were in Speiden channel, heading toward Haro Strait, when I spotted whales in the distance. I hoped it was J pod. As soon as I announced that we were approaching whales, the bow was swamped with passengers. Instead of rushing forward with the rest of the passengers, Raphaela closed her eyes and centered herself in the midst of the chaos.

I was in the wheelhouse looking for a whale to identify. The orcas were about a quarter of a mile away when a lone female separated herself from the group and began swimming straight toward the *Western Prince*. My heart pounded. Could it be Granny? I knew that Raphaela was trying to reach her telepathically. Surely this couldn't be happening. I was mesmerized as she swam to the bow. Yes, it was Granny!

Family Group

I picked up the microphone and began talking. "This is Granny, the leader of J pod and one of the oldest whales in the community. Scientists think she was born in 1911. That makes her 85 years old! Doesn't she look great? You can identify her by that little scoop out of her dorsal fin. Granny is about 22 feet long and weighs around four tons. She has an adult son and daughter, a granddaughter, and a great grandchild."

Granny swam a slow circle completely around the boat so everyone could see her. When she finished, she swam back to the pod. It was an electrifying moment. The passengers were unaware of the direct communication I knew was taking place, but they were entranced by Granny's proximity. Everyone was laughing and applauding.

I couldn't wait to hear about their conversation. As the *Western Prince* slowly followed Granny to the rest of the pod, I ran to the bow and asked, "Did you get her?"

"Oh yes," she replied dreamily with a big smile on her face.

I didn't know if Raphaela had obtained the information I had requested, but I could see one thing—she had fallen in love with Granny.

We spent about a half-hour with J pod. Ruffles, the largest male, chased a salmon directly under the boat, prompting cheers from the passengers. I swear he does that on purpose. Four females worked a small school of salmon together while their youngsters cavorted and played. By the time we left, everyone on board was beaming and talking together about what an outstanding trip it had been.

I was delighted that my friend had met Granny and gotten to see her whole family. After the trip we settled ourselves on a bench in the park overlooking the harbor. Raphaela's grin spoke volumes. I could see that she had been impacted by her encounter with Granny, and my curiosity could not be contained.

"Okay, I want the whole story," I said. "Every last word. What did she say?"

"It was so exciting," she began. "When you announced that there were whales up ahead, I looked but couldn't see much. You know how bad my eyesight is. Anyway, I decided to just settle down and get into my telepathic space. I figured I'd see them soon enough.

"So, I called out, 'Granny, where are you?' and immediately I heard, *'Dead ahead.'* My eyes flew open and there she was swimming toward the boat. I couldn't believe her size, and she was heading straight for us! I thought my heart was going to burst!

"It was really hard to take my eyes off her, but I knew I had to continue, so I closed my eyes and asked, 'Granny, how is your life?' I was afraid she might let me have it about how we've ruined her home and filled it with pollution and taken all her fish, so I steeled myself while I waited. Instead, in a very sharp and humorous way she replied, *'Good. How is yours?'*

31

"She caught me totally off guard and I muttered, 'Fine, thanks.' I was so surprised by her wry response that I needed to look at your list just to know what to ask. So I went right for your biggest question, 'Do you ever eat harbor seals?'"

"Yes, sometimes the seals give us their bodies when it's necessary, but not often."

"What did she mean, 'when it's necessary?'" I demanded.

"I don't know," Raphaela whined. "I didn't even think to ask her. I was just trying to get through my list. She really had me ruffled. I felt like a small child talking to a queen. What a presence! She carries such a feeling of greatness that I was a little intimidated. Anyway, I noticed that she was swimming a complete circle around the boat and I thought, 'That's interesting, I wonder why she's doing that?' Immediately an answer shot into my head."

"I am doing this for your pleasure."

"Even though she said 'your,' I knew she meant everyone on the boat. She really understands how thrilling it is for us to see her. I felt that she was totally aware and knew exactly what would please us the most. I am so impressed with her!"

"Did you ask her about the boats?" I inquired. Captain Bob wanted to know if the whale-watch boats were affecting them adversely. He and I had talked about this quite a bit and were very concerned about our impact.

She nodded. "I asked her if the man-made noises interfered with their communication."

"Granny said, *'Of course. The constant noise diminishes receptivity. We get relief at night. We adapt, as do you.'* She surprised me. I really thought she would be complaining."

"I find these whales to be incredibly tolerant," I told her. "It doesn't surprise me at all."

"Then I asked her how she felt about the people and the boats. Granny paused a moment like she was trying to formulate the correct response and said, *'We sense your hunger to know us and be in touch with us. We give you this contact out of love and service for our planet. Know and understand your connections and mutual dependence on our planet. Love it. Protect it. Your exis-*

tence depends on it. You are children of the beloved earth, sky, wind, and water. When you detach, you die. There is a wave of changing consciousness on the planet. It is part of our mission to foster it by sharing our presence with you.'

"I was in such awe that my mind just went blank. Finally I asked, 'What message do you have for humanity?'"

"I just gave it," she replied.

"At that point I figured I just better say goodbye. Granny wasn't at all what I expected."

"What did you expect?" I asked.

"I don't know. I guess I thought that I'd get some sort of mystical dreamy quality, not this razor-sharp intellect. I've heard about these whales for many years, but I just wasn't prepared for her presence. Her words were direct and clear, almost purposeful. Her awareness was beyond anything I've ever encountered with another animal. Thank you so much for asking me to talk to her."

We sat quietly, watching the boats come and go from the harbor, lost in our thoughts about Granny. My mind was filled with speculation about her life, and I longed to know her secrets. An explosion of insight lit the way.

"How would you feel about doing some more communicating with the whales?" I asked.

"I would absolutely love to!" she exclaimed. "What do you have in mind?"

Everything was coming together in my brain, little pieces zooming in from all directions to complete the picture. "Let's investigate the lives of these orcas through interviews. We can ask them about every facet of their lives and really get to know them. There are so many things we don't know about them that I think it would be fascinating."

"Oh, wow. That would be amazing," she replied. "But I don't know anything about whales. How will I know what to ask?"

"That's the beauty of it," I whispered. "We can work together. I know what to ask, but if I do all the asking, my answers will be suspect since I already know so much about the whales. You, on the other hand, know nothing, so you have no preconceived ideas. I can formulate the questions, and you can communicate with Granny."

"Don't you want to do some of the communicating?"

"Sure, but only about subjects I don't have an opinion on. That way our information will be objective. I think this could work. Are you interested?"

Raphaela jumped up off the bench. "Are you kidding? Of course, I'm interested! When do we start?"

"I wish we could begin tomorrow, but you're taking off, aren't you?"

"Yeah, I'm going to Lopez Island tomorrow and then making a stop in Seattle on my way home. I'll be back in Berkeley in about ten days. Oh dear! How are we going to do this?"

I thought for a moment. "I can get a few days off in early August. Why don't I just come down to Berkeley, and we can start our interviews there? We don't have to be here to talk to them," I replied.

"You're right. We can get together anywhere and still communicate with them. Oh, this is so amazing. I can't believe we're actually going to do this."

"I've wanted to crawl into these whales' heads for five years now. I can't tell you how grateful I am that you've come along. I just don't have the courage or the confidence to do this alone," I confided.

"Well, you don't have to. I'd love to work with you," she exclaimed.

I saw Raphaela off at the ferry the next morning after breakfast. We were both so excited that we'd hardly slept, but we weren't tired. In fact, we were energized by the prospect of meeting these whales on a telepathic level and all that might involve.

Telepathy is the universal language that all animals use. It is direct mind-to-mind communication and doesn't require physical contact to accomplish. Animals use telepathy to communicate with each other all the time. I love watching two horses in a field have a nonverbal connection that results in snorts and squeals. They have just spoken telepathically, and one of them didn't like the exchange.

Humans were not excluded when telepathic abilities were bestowed upon the earth's creatures. There are numerous references in literature to indigenous people who communicated with animals. Often these folks were also in touch with nature spirits and even the elements. Today, we occasionally hear about a tribe who still maintains this connection with all living things.

All humans are born with this ability, but in the "civilized" world we have lost these skills through socialization. As babies, we communicate with our parents telepathically, especially our mothers. Most mothers will admit that they always know what their baby needs, but as children begin to speak, they are highly praised for this new skill. Many parents unknowingly ignore their children's telepathic requests and respond only to speech. This teaches the child that they must now speak to get their needs met. Slowly, their telepathic "muscles" wither.

Children who maintain their telepathic abilities are usually not supported in our society. A small child who tells her mother that the cat says it needs a drink is met with disapproval and informed that the cat can't talk. Children are told that it is just their imagination and not real. Eventually, they stop using this skill and embrace the beliefs of the culture.

Telepathic information comes in many forms, and I'm convinced that we all experience it daily. Most people just fail to recognize or acknowledge it. It's a lot like being a satellite dish. The communicator receives a download of information from the animal, which must then be filtered and interpreted. Who you are, and how developed your different telepathic channels are, determine how the information is expressed. The good part is that when the information comes through your filter, it gets translated into whatever language you speak. So, you don't have to be fluent in German to understand a dog in Germany. Even though whales don't speak human languages, we are able to interpret the information that is telepathically transmitted and explain it in words.

It's a wonderful universal system that allows us to speak with any creatures.

There are at least four ways we receive telepathic information: pictures, hearing, feeling, or a sense of knowing. The most common way to receive telepathically is through mental pictures. Most humans automatically picture something when they speak about it, so receiving pictures is quite natural. Many dog owners report that their animal companions read their mental pictures and run to the door as soon as they think about taking them for a walk. British scientist Rupert Sheldrake researched this subject for five years and presents his findings in *Dogs That Know When Their Owners Are Coming Home.* He studied many different animals that read thoughts or mental pictures and found this ability also in cats, horses, parrots, and other critters.

Animals often communicate with pictures. During consultations I always receive pictures, ranging from an elaborate movie to something as simple as seeing one body part that hurts. Pay attention to the pictures that pop into your head and see what kind of telepathic information you are receiving every day.

I also hear information from animals when I speak to them. It varies from animal to animal, but sometimes it's just like a conversation with a person. Once in a while an animal will show me what it hears, such as in the case of a lost animal. I try to hear from their perspective to determine if they are inside or outside, near a freeway, or in the woods.

Telepathic communication also comes in the form of feelings, both physical and emotional. When I tune in to a cat, I can often tell if it's happy, sad, depressed, or content. Occasionally, I can feel the animal's physical problem in my own body. Feelings are easily transmitted, especially when they are intense.

Intuition or a sense of knowing is the form of telepathy that is most difficult to accept. When this kind of information appears, people question its validity because it can't be experienced through our other senses. Explaining how you know is impossible—you just do. Yet this form of telepathy is just as legitimate as the others.

Everyone has the ability to receive telepathic information in all these ways; however, most people are strongest in one or two areas. Most of my whale conversations to date had involved pictures and sound. These seemed to be the strongest, but I wondered now what we might encounter in the months to come. The prospect of experiencing life as an orca through Granny's eyes was beyond my wildest dreams.

DIFFICULTY AT THE BEGINNING

I stepped off a plane at the Oakland airport on August 5, 1996. The terminal was packed, and I searched the anxious faces until I spotted Raphaela waving wildly from the back. "Mary, over here!"

We laughed and talked loudly as we wove through the city traffic to her hilltop home in Berkeley. "How is Granny?" she asked.

"Terrific. I saw her yesterday. The Js and Ks were having a party."

"Oh, you're so lucky. I wish I could have been there."

"You don't have it so bad," I reminded her. I gazed appreciatively at the variety of plant species that abounds in the Bay Area, such a contrast to the endless firs and cedars of the islands. It was nice to be back in California.

After Raphaela's encounter with Granny, I was delighted that she was becoming as enthralled with the whales as I was and that we could relate to them in the same way. I had felt isolated in a town full of whale fanatics who didn't share my view of who these creatures were or how they should be treated. They loved the whales and were constantly trying to protect them but assumed that they knew what the whales wanted.

Natalie Herner

Distinctive saddle pattern

"We need to regulate the boats around the whales," they shouted. "They don't have enough to eat." I loved the whales too but felt we should ask the orcas directly what they wanted or needed, instead of deciding we knew best.

The smell of eucalyptus engulfed me as we wound up her narrow street. Raphaela's house was perched on a hillside between other homes, but they were difficult to see through all the vegetation. Her garden was a mass of colors, and I stopped to smell the stargazer lilies on my way to the front door. The sun's warmth on my head kept me from going inside for a few moments. I love the heat, and even in the summer I feel cold in the islands. It was close to eighty degrees in the garden. I was in heaven.

A large golden retriever met me at the door. She pushed her nose into my hand, as her rear end swung rhythmically from side to side.

"This is Tootsie," Raphaela said, beaming. Tootsie looked into my eyes and immediately sized me up as "someone who may drop bits of food."

I set my bags down and stroked her head. "Hi, Tootsie, it's a pleasure to meet you." Her plumed tail was buffing the wooden floor. I knelt down and gave her a hug.

Over Tootsie's shoulder I spotted a beautiful tawny-colored cat peeking around the corner from the dining room. "Sophia, this is Mary. She's going to be staying here for a few days."

Sophia approached tentatively and then offered her head for a rub. "Hi, Sophia. I love kitties. Would you like to sleep with me tonight?" She purred contentedly as I petted her. We looked adoringly into each other's eyes and instantly became friends.

Raphaela took me upstairs to my bedroom. It was filled with birds! I enjoyed the brightly colored budgies and Dax, a mini macaw, but I was uneasy with Sancho, a small green parrot called a caique. She eyed me intently, bobbing her little head up and down. I could tell she was trouble and got her message loud and clear: "Give me a chance and I'll tear you to shreds!"

Introductions completed, we went downstairs to the living room. Raphaela and I sat down, looked into each other's eyes, and burst into laughter. "I am so excited to start this project I can hardly contain myself," she exclaimed.

"I know. I feel the same way, too. It's as if I've been preparing to do this for lifetimes. I think something really big is about to happen."

"Yes, I agree," she said. "I feel like I'm being prompted from 'beyond' to get this information. I've never experienced anything like this."

"I'm a little nervous," I admitted.

"Oh, me too! I have no idea what to expect. Are you ready to start?"

"You bet," I said. "I've got my notebook all ready. Why don't you tune in with Granny first, and I'll take notes. We can switch when you get tired."

We settled into two cozy chairs in the living room. Tootsie spread out on the couch. Raphaela centered herself and said, "Granny, are you there?" I sat poised with a pen and notebook ready to take down every word.

Granny immediately replied, *"Yes, I am here."*

"Granny, my name is Raphaela, and I talked to you when I was out on the *Western Prince* with Mary last month. Do you remember me?"

"Yes, my dear. I remember you."

My God. This is so amazing, I thought. Granny was right there, available when we called. How does she hear us? Why does she remember Raphaela? Does she remember everyone who comes to see her?

"Granny, Mary and I would like to ask you some questions. Would you be willing to talk to us?"

"Certainly. That would be fine," she replied.

"We would like to ask you about your life. We want to know what it's like to be an orca, and we're hoping you will help us understand."

"This is a very good idea. Many people are interested in our lives. I have seen the number of people coming to see us multiply tremendously in recent years. Our conversations could increase

understanding between our species. This is a contribution I am happy to make."

I was so fascinated with Granny's dialogue that I forgot to take notes. When I remembered, I found it impossible to keep up.

"Can you stop for a minute? I can't possibly write everything down. It's moving too fast." This wasn't going to work. I was determined to record every single word to ensure that the material had integrity and clarity. I didn't want to misinterpret or incorrectly record anything. It could all be important!

"I have a tape recorder upstairs we can use," Raphaela said.

Tape recorder rolling, we started again. We had no idea of the limits of this communication and needed answers to practical questions. Raphaela asked, "Granny, can you talk to both of us simultaneously?"

"Yes, I can. Telepathic communication is well suited to our capabilities. It is the form we use the most."

So, they DO speak telepathically. I thought so. If Granny can speak to both of us at once, how many whales might she be able to converse with? Could a whole pod talk simultaneously?

"Will you be able to give us three or four hours of telepathic communication a day in the weeks that we will be working?"

"My time is unlimited."

Unlimited time, what a concept! Everyone I knew complained bitterly about not having enough time, and I found it difficult to even schedule lunch with a friend. My world had very distinct boundaries that kept me boxed in. Granny's seemed wide open and unfettered.

"Granny, can you be in the San Juans from September 19th to the 25th? I'll be there with Mary then and would like to see you."

"Decisions are made in each moment, not in advance. We are in flow with nature. Fish may bring us there. But don't worry; even if we are gone you can still enjoy our beautiful home. I need not be there to communicate with you."

When we began the first session, Raphaela connected with Granny telepathically, asked her questions, and then relayed the answers. She spoke the questions and answers aloud so they could be recorded. I sat nearby listening to the exchange and keeping an eye on the tape recorder. Before long, I couldn't contain myself and started interjecting questions.

"Ask her if they eat herring. Are the salmon disappearing?"

Raphaela stopped and asked Granny my questions, then continued with her own inquiries. Within minutes I broke in again. This back and forth with two people asking questions became difficult. Raphaela had to think of questions to ask Granny, listen to me, and interpret Granny's responses all at the same time.

"I think I need a break," she said. "Why don't you take over for a while?"

"Okay, give me a minute to get settled." I went deep inside and found my place of quiet where communication takes place. "Granny, it's Mary. Raphaela's tired. Are you willing to continue talking to me?"

"Certainly," she said.

"Do you have a concept of how old you are?" I asked.

"I am old and ancient and have traveled these waters long. How long, you ask? Time is not as relevant to us as it is to you. The ebb and flow of our lives is natural, not like the schedules you keep. Your lives are built around time. We flow with what is happening from moment to moment."

We had thought that we might try to record her autobiography, so I decided to start asking her about the early years. "Granny, tell us, please, what it was like when you were a calf."

"This was a wonderful time in my life. I spent my days with my mother and played with other youngsters in the pod. We traveled our territory and fished."

"Did you learn how to breach?" I asked.

"Oh yes, all calves learn how to breach and play on the surface."

"How did you spend your days?"

"We played and rested and fished. Sometimes we came upon other pods, and it was very exciting meeting other whales."

"Did anything dangerous or special happen?"

"Not that I can recall."

"How did things change as you got older?"

"*I spent less time with my mother and more with other family members. I learned how to fish and was more independent.*"

Hmmm. This line of questioning wasn't producing much information. I guess I had expected to hear a story similar to a human's: "I graduated from Stanford, where I met my husband. We married and traveled for three months in Europe . . ." Where were the markers, the events that divide human lives?

I jumped ahead to later in her life. "What happened when you were a teenager?"

"*Oh, I traveled and fished.*"

It was quickly becoming apparent that an orca's life is fairly similar from one year to the next. "Raphaela, I'm starting to think that the autobiography idea isn't going to work. It seems as if the daily life of an orca doesn't change much over time. It's mostly swim, swim, swim, play, play, play, eat, eat, eat! When does something else happen?"

"Yeah, I was just thinking the same thing. I'm also not sure we're going about this the right way. I keep wanting to break in and ask questions."

"I know what you mean," I said. "Maybe I should just connect with Granny and be the communicator. You can take the role of interviewer. It would be much easier if I didn't have to think of follow-up questions and keep track of what we wanted to ask. It's hard to bounce back and forth."

"That's a good idea," she said. "I'll interview Granny through you, and when we switch, you can do the same."

We started again with our new interview format. Things went much more smoothly, and the conversation flowed naturally. Sometimes the communicator would stop and ask a question, and often she gave her own comments or described pictures and feelings that occurred. Telepathic communication is a rich experience of images, sound, and feelings. Words alone cannot accurately convey the message.

It wasn't long before we began to encounter other problems; for example, quantitative questions. Humans usually think in terms such as how long, how far, and when. We place great importance on time. Granny didn't seem to think that way. Whales live very much in the present, dwelling neither in the past nor the future, and of course they don't use our system of numerical years. We kept trying to establish "when" something occurred, but Granny was often unable to tell us in terms we could understand. Her mind didn't work the same way as ours. Time just wasn't relevant to her.

We wanted to place her in the historical context of the San Juan Islands. Scientists don't know when Granny was born. They estimate that it was in 1911, but we hoped to prove her age by asking her about recorded events. Before my trip to Berkeley, I had talked to several people about time markers that we could question her about. Captain Bob had suggested the fish traps that were used in the early 1900s. If she remembered them, perhaps we could determine how old she was at the time.

For this session I set up the telepathic link, and Raphaela asked the questions.

"Many years ago there were fish traps in the area known as the Salmon Bank. Do you remember this?"

Granny stated, *"Yes, I remember the fish traps. There were many of them in that shallow area."*

"Granny, did you have any children at that time?"

"I had one calf during the time of the traps, a male who died quite young."

I got the impression that the traps were present for six to eight years. I thanked her and said that we would use the fish traps as a time indicator and might ask her if things happened before or after the traps.

We were very excited about this information and hoped that we could pinpoint Granny's age through it. Disappointment set in, though, when I checked the information on the fish trap industry and found that it existed in Puget Sound and the San Juans from 1899 to 1934. It was unclear exactly when and how long the traps at the Salmon Bank were present. I hadn't researched it enough. We also didn't know what these traps looked like, so it was possible that Granny was referring to other structures she remembered. The fish traps were useless.

We tried using the eruption of Mount St. Helens in 1980 as a time marker and asked Granny if she remembered it.

"Yes, we remember that volcanic event quite well. Incredible sonic waves came through the water. We are quite familiar with this type of wave, which is created by activity in the seafloor. I remember a big event, where continuous sound came for quite some time and we could feel much movement of the earth."

After that we often asked, "Was that before or after the eruption of Mount St. Helens?" This line of questioning became quite tedious, and Granny found our constant time questions annoying. Her irritation became clear later that day when Granny was talking about reintroducing formerly captive whales to the wild and said, *"It would take quite a while. . . ."* Instantly we both thought, "How LONG?"

Raphaela howled as Granny said, *"Don't ask me that!"*

I was totally shocked to find that I had heard her before the words came out of Raphaela's mouth. Actually what I heard was, *"Don't start. Don't even start with the time stuff."* We broke out in uproarious laughter. We were in a state of elation and wonder. I knew that we were not just making this up. We were both hearing the same thing independently. When we calmed down, we realized that Granny doesn't like time questions because they don't apply to her life.

I found it very interesting that neither of us had verbalized "How LONG?" Granny was apparently able to hear our thoughts and respond without our intending to communicate with her. This occurred frequently in our sessions. I was also surprised that I had heard Granny when she was communicating with Raphaela. I hadn't experienced this phenomenon before. This ability to listen in when the other person was communicating became a common occurrence in our sessions, especially when the subject was emotional or the whale really wanted to express something. Raphaela confirmed that it occasionally happens with clients when she is doing consultations.

Things weren't moving along in the way I'd hoped. There wasn't an easy way to chronicle things without obsessing over time markers, and it could be that Granny was remembering the big quake in Seattle during the 1960s instead of Mount St. Helens. There was no way for us to know for sure!

"There has to be a better way," I said. "What if we made a list of all the things we wanted to know about and then asked Granny?"

"I think that could work," she said, "but it's difficult to know where to start. The cetacean world is so different from ours that I'm unsure of the right questions to ask. It's a bit like being an interspecies anthropologist."

So we wrote down every subject we could imagine: their physical bodies, sex, whale-watching, social interactions, feeding, territory, death, spirituality, problems, children, whales in captivity, and their interactions with humans. It was a place to start, and we could add on as new subjects appeared.

We changed our approach and shifted from looking at Granny's life through the lens of time to investigating subject matter. Each session we picked a subject and then queried Granny at length about it. Invariably her answers prompted a whole new line of questioning. It was nearly impossible to stick to a subject, so our conversations were far reaching and ever changing. We never knew where she would take us.

Raphaela and I soon learned that we needed to work on our interview skills. Granny was exceptional at remembering which questions we had asked, and unfortunately, we had a tendency to forget and repeat ourselves. It was not unusual for her to start a response with *"As I have said in the past. . . ."*

We also had a bad habit of asking too many questions at once. Swept away in excitement, question after question rolled out. One day, I was on my fifth sentence without stopping when Granny sweetly said, *"You ask many questions at once, my daughter. Start with the simplest."* Within minutes I was at it again. This time she broke into laughter and said, *"Way too many questions. Start with one.*" As long as we didn't pester her about time, she was patient and usually found our enthusiasm amusing rather than annoying.

Communicating with a mind of such depth was wondrous. I was beginning to get a glimpse of what it was like to be a whale. I marveled at her deep calm. There wasn't a trace of anxiety or worry anywhere. When I was communicating with Granny I felt as if I were floating on a cloud, wrapped in a soft warm blanket. She exuded love, kindness, and acceptance. She treated me as if she were *my* Granny and often referred to us as "my dear" or "my daughter" with great warmth and tenderness.

She was willing to take us into her world and tell us whatever we wanted to know, to share her knowledge of the deep. Because of her unfathomable level of consciousness, when I finished a session as communicator it would take me more than five minutes to be fully back in the present. I had to return from an altered state. I felt blessed just by talking to her, and it was a tremendous joy to be in her presence.

LET'S GET PHYSICAL

When I catch a glimpse of Granny's sleek, glistening body moving elegantly through the water, I find it hard to believe that orcas and other whales once lived on the land, or at least their ancestors did. Cetaceans evolved from a land mammal related to today's even-toed ungulates: sheep, cattle, camels, and their relatives. Their remote ancestors ventured back into the sea about 55 million years ago. It was a bold step that resulted in a gorgeous group of animals. The cetaceans are graceful and fluid, pure poetry in motion.

Polar bears are making this same adventurous transition from land to sea animal at this very moment. I was startled the first time I encountered a picture of a polar bear in a book about marine mammals. I didn't know that they were an evolutionary work in progress.

They still look like other bears but have changed to such a degree that many scientists now consider them marine mammals. Their feet are becoming webbed, and their teeth are now better at biting than grinding, an adaptation made in their shift from omnivore (other bears eat roots, berries, and leaves as well as fish and meat) to carnivore. The polar bear is still more closely related to bears than to other marine mammals, but it spends most of its time near the sea and sea ice and subsists almost entirely on arctic marine animals, mostly seals. While we tend to think of evolution as something that happened a long time ago, the polar bear shows that it's continuing today.

Scientists have not yet been able to establish the origin of the two different types or suborders of whales: Mysticeti, or baleen whales, and Odontoceti, or toothed whales. Some scientists believe they diverged from a single common ancestor and marched down separate evolutionary paths. Others think they converged from two independent groups, becoming more alike as time went on. Although modern techniques such as genetic karyotyping and protein analysis are bringing scientists closer to the truth, this question is still unresolved.

All cetaceans have the same basic streamlined shape, but there are numerous physical and social factors that separate them into two distinct types. The mysticetes or baleen whales are generally large—some very large. Whalers hunted them because their huge size made them lucrative targets. Many are also slow moving so they were easy targets. There are ten species of baleen whales: the blue, fin, sei, Bryde's, minke, humpback, gray, right, bowhead, and pygmy right whale.

Blue whales are the largest creatures to ever inhabit the planet, even bigger than the dinosaurs. They can grow to a length of 100 feet, and their mouths are big enough to hold an elephant with room to spare!

Strangely, the huge baleen whales subsist on the tiniest of food—minute animals called zooplankton. Some are only the size of a pinhead, while krill, the largest, are no bigger than your little finger. A blue whale can eat three tons of krill every day! Instead of having teeth, these whales sport a large strainer made of baleen plates that hang from the roof of their mouth and filter their tiny prey from the sea.

The mysticetes do not echolocate or dive deeply and females are usually larger than males. They have two blowholes, just as we do. They are often solitary and do not live in family groups like Granny and her relatives. Large aggregations gather during their annual migration between their summer feeding areas and the winter calving and breeding grounds. The gray whales travel 5,000 miles one way to reach their special place. A thriving whale-watch industry has grown around the gray whale calving lagoons in Baja, Mexico, and the humpback calving grounds in Hawaii.

Granny belongs to the Odontoceti or toothed whale groups that are generally smaller than the baleen whales. There are more than 65 species of toothed whales, including the dolphins and porpoises. The largest is the sperm whale, which can reach 60 feet in length. Moby Dick was a sperm whale, a creature that dives to the bottom of the sea to eat giant squid. Scientists have tracked them to nearly two miles beneath the sea! It is totally dark at that depth, and they must rely solely on their excellent echolocation abilities to capture their prey. All toothed whales use echolocation.

Echolocation is a marvelous ability that is found in very few animals. To "see" what is in its environment, an orca sends out a series of high-pitched, intense clicks. The clicks travel through the water as sound waves. When they meet an object, an echo returns to the whale and is received through the lower jaw, which is filled with a fine oil. The sound travels through the oil to the ear.

These clicks are created by implosive movements of air in the whale's nasal passages, then focused and projected into the water through the "melon," a large pocket of fat on their forehead. They are able to control the rate of clicking and its frequency at will.

While the mechanics of echolocation are fascinating, what follows is even more incredible. For each sound, the whale must remember the frequency, analyze the sound, and compare it to the memory of other sounds, searching for subtle differences. This information allows the animal to create a mental or sound picture from the echoes it receives. Their analysis is so highly developed that they are able to discriminate between almost identical objects.

Orcas are very large by toothed whale standards, but only about a third the size of sperm whales. Odontocetes use their teeth to consume mainly fish and squid, although some orcas feed primarily on seals, porpoises, and other whales. Unlike most mammals, toothed whales have only one blowhole. It is believed that the other blowhole evolved into the complex structure now used for echolocation.

Toothed whales are very social animals, live in family groups, and tend to stay within a home range year-round, as our resident orcas do. Their males are generally larger than females—the opposite of baleen whales.

When I finished describing the differences between toothed and baleen whales, Raphaela shook her head. "It's amazing how different they are," she said. "Let's ask Granny about their evolution. I would love to clear up a long-standing question in the scientific community."

I agreed but wasn't so sure any information we got would clear up the scientific question. My skepticism told me it might not be taken seriously. Still, I was quite willing to find out what Granny had to say on the subject. I asked to be the communicator for this session.

I settled down and tuned in to Granny. When I was ready, Raphaela asked her if she knew the origin of the two types of whales.

Granny replied, *"I believe that we all came from one source. We have ancient memories of all whales being more alike than we are now. We orcas get urges and feelings to engage in migration, which is no longer appropriate for us. I believe that this urge goes back millions of years when the family of whales was slowly separating into different groupings."*

I was surprised to hear that they had urges to migrate. These orcas have lived in their home territory for thousands of years. You'd think that those feelings would have vanished long ago. I began to wonder about some of my own urges. Did my love of the forest originate with my ancient ancestors, the chimpanzees? I certainly feel most at home surrounded by trees. I wondered how many of my feelings were established in me long before my ancestors walked upright.

Raphaela next asked, "How do you account for all the separate species of whales, and how different they are?"

"I can't say why the humpback has winged flippers, but look at your own species. I have seen many distinct humans. There are those with dark skin, others with small eyes. You have races that are tiny and others that are big; some tend to be round while others are slender.

"It is even more obvious with cetaceans. We have had more time to change and grasp our individuality, and it is still changing. Life does not stop—evolution continues. Changes in body characteristics and shapes are constantly, slowly shifting. It is hard to observe in one lifetime, but things have changed tremendously in your species in just the past few centuries. Think back and observe what has happened to body form."

Granny now showed me a picture of a huge basketball player, an obviously contemporary figure, standing next to a skinny little man with a handlebar mustache who seemed to be from the nineteenth century. The difference in body size and shape was astonishing. I thought about the variety of shapes and sizes I see on my whale-watching trips—everything from tiny Japanese women to huge Nordic men.

"These changes are not unusual. In the sea, evolution has been doing its magic, changing us for millions of years. You on the land have not reached this degree of differentiation. The human races might have become as individual as the whales, except that now you travel and breed throughout the planet. The mixing of your gene pool that is occurring may actually create a whole new race."

I liked Granny's description of "evolution doing its magic." It certainly did a fabulous job with orcas. They are absolutely magnificent creatures in many ways, but it is their physical characteristics that we know the most about since they are most easily studied by scientists. And physically, they are awesome!

Our first detailed physical knowledge of orcas came from whaling stations. Before I began to study orcas I imagined that only the larger whales had been victims of whaling, but I discovered with shock and dismay that orcas too were hunted. They were slaughtered in the North Atlantic between 1938 and 1967, and large numbers were taken in the southern hemisphere in the late 1970s and early 1980s. Thousands of orcas were killed in these commercial operations. As the whales were cut up and processed, research biologists studied some of them. Scientists at the whaling stations looked thoroughly into each body system, made measurements, and weighed each organ.

There are limits, though, to what you can learn in this way, and scientists who conduct research on orcas in the wild have taken the study much further. They have observed how orcas use their bodies in action, and studied the differences between individuals. They have also mapped territories and recorded activities and social behavior.

Captive animals in marine parks have also given us a great deal of information. Scientists have been able to take blood and urine samples, X-rays, and yearly measurements and perform physical examinations. We have also learned about their sleep patterns, their communication, and their ways of acquiring knowledge.

So what have scientists managed to learn about orcas so far? Let's start with their biological classification. Orcas belong to the order Cetacea, the suborder Odontoceti, and the family Delphinidae, the dolphins. Many other toothed whales are also in the dolphin family, but orcas are the largest members. People are often surprised to learn that orcas are technically dolphins and wonder why we call them whales. The term "whale" is given to any cetacean that is more than 12 to 13 feet in length. Their scientific name is *Orcinus orca*. The English translation of *Orcinus* is "belonging to the realms of the dead" and *orca* means "a kind of whale."

Orcas are found in all oceans of the world. They are tremendously versatile animals, inhabiting seas from the ice pack in polar latitudes to tropical regions and are generally seen within 500 miles of continental coastlines. There are large concentrations of orcas in the waters of Japan, Iceland, Norway, Antarctica, British Columbia, Washington, and Alaska, and they are seen occasionally in other parts of the world as well.

Orcas are easy to recognize. You might not be able to tell a fin whale from a blue, but once you've seen an orca, or even a picture of one, you will always recognize them. They are shiny black with an oblong white patch above each eye. Orcas also have an extensive white patch that runs from the chin through the belly and extends up the flanks. Behind the dorsal fin is a grayish marking called the saddle patch. In orca calves, the white markings may have an orange tinge for up to one year.

Dr. Mike Bigg, one of the authors of *Killer Whales*, discovered that each orca has a unique saddle patch pattern and often distinctive cuts and nicks in the dorsal fin that can be used to identify it. He found this by studying photographs of the animals, a technique now known as photo-identification. In the field, we identify individuals by looking at the dorsal fin and saddle patch and comparing them to photographs if we are not familiar with the markings. That's how I identified Granny that first day at the lighthouse.

Granny's saddle patch is solid and not at all distinctive but she has a little nick scooped out of her fin, halfway down the rear edge. Her fin is also less curved than many females'. Researchers now think that orcas can also be identified by the unique shape of their eye patches, although this would be impossible in a field situation. The differences can only be recognized on photographs in which the whales have the grace to stand still. Humpback whales are identified by unique markings on the underside of their tail flukes, but this area is always white on orcas.

The orca's most obvious feature is the dorsal fin, which is tall enough to be seen at great distances. Whale spotting is done visually, not with underwater radar or sonar, as so many people believe. We simply look for their fins in the water. The fins of females and juveniles stand up to two and a half feet high and curve to the rear. Adult males reign supreme in the fin department. Their dorsal fins stand up to five feet in height and are shaped like a triangle with little or no curve to the rear. Their impressive size elicits "wows" from the crowd every time. Ruffles has a very large and distinctive fin that looks wavy from the back. The pectoral fins on the front of his body are broad and paddle-shaped. Like the dorsal fin, a male's pectoral fins and tail flukes are much larger than a female's.

Even though orcas are dolphins, they do not have a long beak like Flipper. The front of their head, known as the rostrum, has a small cone-shaped snout and Flipper looks tiny by comparison. Male orcas are larger than females, up to 30 in length, and weigh as much as ten tons. Granny is about 22 feet long and weighs around four tons, which is about average for a female. Orca calves are seven to eight feet in length and weigh 400 to 500 pounds at birth.

There are three types of orcas found in the Pacific Northwest: resident, transient, and offshore. Granny's family and K and L pods make up the southern resident community. There is also a northern resident community of more than 200 whales that range north from mid-Vancouver Island through British Columbia into the southern tip of Alaska. More than one hundred transient orcas also pass through this area as they traverse their home range, which runs from Alaska to mid-California. They are seen in small numbers at all times of the year. We don't really know how many offshores there are since they are so rarely encountered.

Residents and transients have been studied extensively, but the offshores are still very mysterious. These three types could be considered different races. They are physically quite similar (although there are some differences), but they differ in their range, behavior, social structure, food, and communication.

Both transient and resident orcas can be found within the same territory but are rarely observed interacting with each other. They appear to be segregated. Preliminary genetic analysis indicates that these two groups have not interbred for hundreds of thousands of years and should perhaps be classified as separate subspecies.

Resident orcas like Granny and her family live in groups of five to 60 individuals and stay within a home range of about 500 to 600 miles. In the summer of 1996, Granny's family, J pod, had 21 individuals, K pod had 18 members, and L pod had 58. The offspring of resident orcas stay with their mother and her relatives throughout their lives. They vocalize frequently and use more calls than transients. J, K, and L pods are very chatty and we listen to them on a hydrophone whenever possible.

The residents have fins with a rounded tip. There are many variations in the pattern of their saddle patch, and the patches are set farther back below the dorsal fin than those of the transient. They travel in open water and often set a course in a straight line. Residents are very familiar with our whale-watch boats and rarely try to evade us.

Transient orcas, by contrast, live in smaller pods, from one to seven individuals, and have larger ranges that cover as much as 2,000 miles. Although I used to be on the water at least a hundred days a year, I usually saw transients only once or twice each season. To the untrained eye, they look exactly the same as the residents, but to those of us in the field, the differences are visible. Most transients have a dorsal fin that is more pointed and less curved than a resident's, and their saddle patch is generally solid and begins forward of the midpoint of the dorsal fin. Their sharp, pointed fin looks sharkish, and whenever I saw one it elicited a feeling of danger.

Generally I only saw two or three transients at a time. Pods seem to consist of a mother and her children, although some of her offspring may disperse. Transients have longer dive times than the residents and tend to hug the shoreline. When they are out in open water, they travel erratically, perhaps in an attempt to lose the whale-watch boats.

They prefer marine mammals as their main prey. Scientists believe that resident orcas eat only fish, though they have been observed chasing and tossing seals and porpoises. But transient whales mainly eat seals, porpoises, and even other whales. Hunting warm-blooded prey is a dangerous profession. A seal or a sea lion will fight for its life with its sharp canine teeth. An orca that feeds on marine mammals must know how to take them quickly without being hurt, and transients seem to be experts at it. Also, they rarely vocalize, traveling silently except during or after a kill. These are the guys that earned the name "killer whale."

As for the offshore orcas, little is known about their lifestyle, but they physically resemble residents more than transients. They appear to be somewhat smaller than the other types and have been seen in groups of 25 or more.

In all my hours on the water, I have never seen an offshore orca, but the *Western Prince* did once. On Labor Day in 1993, a group of whales was spotted off Victoria on the southern end of Vancouver Island. The *Western Prince* headed over and when it arrived found about 70 whales. But the whales were evasive and acted very confused. They weren't in the nice orderly travel arrangement we are used to seeing.

The naturalists on all the boats were frantically searching the group for a whale they recognized, but without success. No one could understand what was going on. How could there be 70 whales present and not one they recognized! Finally, an orca researcher arrived and announced that they were offshores.

Amazed, everyone crowded close to get a better look. This didn't sit well with the offshores, who probably rarely encounter boats. They were surrounded by vessels of all shapes and sizes. They continued in the strait for about half an hour and then abruptly made an about-face and headed back out to sea. We've never seen offshores here again. Researchers are still trying to discover more about these whales.

All orcas are beautiful, with their distinctive black-and-white markings, but I always think Granny is particularly gorgeous! She would look great in a toothpaste commercial. At almost 90, her 44 large, conical teeth are still bright and shiny. They curve toward her throat and are very efficient at catching and tearing prey. Each tooth is about three inches long and an inch in diameter. Captive whales often grind their teeth down to stubs out of boredom.

Granny, like all orcas, is a powerful swimmer and can attain speeds of 30 miles per hour in short bursts. Resident orcas travel an average of 75–100 miles per day. By contrast, a boat like the *Western Prince* travels about 12 to 15 miles an hour and has a range of 45–50 miles per four-hour trip, including a few stops. That means if the whales swim 75 miles in one direction, which they often do, we won't see them for a few days.

Orcas have good eyesight both in and out of the water. They are able to adjust the shape of their eye lens to accommodate both mediums. They definitely use their ability to see in air when they breach and spyhop. Breaching is that spectacular behavior when a whale jumps completely out of the water. You see this image on almost every postcard in Friday Harbor.

Spyhopping is the act of rising straight up and coming halfway out of the water to look around. Granny spyhopped right in front of me the first time I met her at Whale Watch Park. Her whole community spyhops so often I assume they are either very visual or quite interested in our world.

The southern residents also have a repertoire of astonishing surface behaviors and are known worldwide for the frequency of

Breech

their acrobatic displays. I can never predict when these displays will occur, but often there is more activity when two or more pods come together. All ages and sexes engage in these activities, but as with most mammals, the youngsters seem to play the most.

Raphaela was treated to a great display during her second trip to the San Juans. It was late September 1996 and she had come for a visit and a whale interview session. I was working on the *Western Prince*, and she came out to enjoy the whales and, if possible, to commune with Granny in person.

It was a little overcast and windy, but we bundled up in warm jackets and set off. Whales had been reported that morning in the Canadian Gulf Islands. It sounded like they were headed for Vancouver, the far end of our four-hour range, so we made a direct run with no stops for seals or eagles. We caught the orcas near East Point, on Saturna Island, just before they were about to round the corner into Georgia Strait.

There were about 25 whales, traveling in a tight group. I scanned the fins to identify some individuals and was disappointed to find that it was L pod. The Js had already gone to Vancouver ahead of them. "We're not going to see Granny today," I said.

"That's too bad," she replied, frowning. "I was really looking forward to seeing her. Who are these whales?"

"It's L pod. I don't think you've ever seen them."

Her frown dissolved into a smile. "Well, I guess I'll just sit back, relax, and enjoy the show."

I hurried back to the wheelhouse as Raphaela settled into her spot on the bow. This group of whales had a good mix of sexes and sizes. They were swimming quickly when suddenly a large male breached, erupting from the water about 80 feet from the boat. A howl went up from the crowd. "Keep watching that same area," I said on the microphone. "Maybe he'll do it again!" Before I could finish my sentence, he was out of the water again.

Within seconds a calf breached. Two females furiously tail-slapped about ten times as they swam through a kelp bed. The calf continued to breach, and then a female and another. A juvenile spyhopped and another slashed its tail back and forth on the surface. The passengers went wild. Some were clapping, others screaming, and the more subdued sounded like spectators at a fireworks display. Raphaela was jumping up and down on the bow screaming at the top of her lungs.

There was nonstop activity for about ten minutes as whales and water flew everywhere. Then, as they rounded the point and headed north, the performance ended. Gasping for breath, Raphaela turned and looked at me in the wheelhouse. She stood shaking her head from side to side, her mouth agape. I gave her the thumbs up and a huge smile. Talk about enjoying the show!

When we returned to Friday Harbor, we hurried home and made dinner. Raphaela was still so excited about the enthusiastic acrobatic display that after dinner I connected with Granny, and we asked her to tell us about breaching.

"Oh, this is great fun," Granny said. *"We love to do that! It is a sensual treat to hit the water. First, we swim a little beneath the*

surface to get some speed. It takes only a few pumps of our power-
ful tails and we explode through the surface, water rushing down
our bodies, feeling the sun again on our skin.

"We travel out of the water with such power. We are free, free
from the limitations that bind us. Then we start to fall, air rushing
by, our bodies twisting, turning. SLAM, we hit the surface and feel
ourselves going back into our home, cold water surrounding us
once again. It is exciting and makes me feel very powerful."

I was struck by Granny's comment about limitations. I'd
always considered the ocean environment a limitless space. Now,
seeing it through Granny's eyes, I realized that there were indeed
limitations. Water limited her vision and exerted drag on her body.
She found it exhilarating to break free from these bonds and sail
through the air.

"This is also an opportunity to look around. It helps us see far
in many directions. It is a treat to our vision—all the colors and
brightness of the above world. We love to play with each other,
jumping completely out of the water, often to see how many times
we can do it or how high we can jump. The children especially love
it."

I thought of the colors I see at every moment and perhaps
take for granted and resolved to appreciate and enjoy them more.
Then Raphaela asked, "Is there an element of communication in
breaching?"

"No, it is exciting and fun, a way of expressing our joy. We get
very worked up when we all come together, or after great feasting.
Breaching is not a form of communication, rather an expression of
our joy, our playful natures."

"Today I saw all kinds of slapping going on. The L pod whales
were using their big front pec fins, their dorsal fins, and their tails.
Why do you slap on the surface so much?"

"That's fun, too. I lift my big fin up and slam it down on the
water. It creates a tingling sensation and makes a beautiful sound.
I love to hear that SMACK. Much of what we do is for enjoyment.
Tail slapping creates wonderful whirlpools of water and forces lit-
tle currents under our bodies that tickle our skin."

"Sometimes you rise vertically, straight up out of the water, and then slide back down again. We call this spyhopping. What is the purpose of this movement?"

"It is to look around. We love to look around. We cannot see much beneath the surface, you know. The light is not good. It is very dull and the colors are not vibrant. Everything is somewhat muted, murky, and hazy. That is why we put our heads above the surface. I am able to see the sights of the land world. I see boats, birds, trees, and rocks. I see the fins of my family in the distance. It is an exciting, sensual treat to break the surface in this way."

Most of the time when I'm communicating with Granny, I get pictures from her or hear words, but tonight I was getting a lot of bodily sensations. "This is so cool," I said. "Granny is letting me feel the water rushing off my body, my nose up in the air breaking the surface, the warm sun contacting my skin. It feels really wonderful. Then BOOM, an explosion of light, color, and activity!"

I was so thrilled to be able to see and feel things from Granny's perspective. I had spent thousands of hours watching whales on the surface, longing to understand how they felt or perceived things. Now here I was inside her skin, experiencing her life directly. Being in Granny's world was the fulfillment of my dream.

Raphaela nodded and went on with her questions. "So spyhopping is a way to look around. Is there anything else you'd like to tell us?"

"Many of our behaviors are games, ways to play with one another. We love to break the surface together, to see one another in the sun, and observe how high we can go. We enjoy this time together, laughing and playing. There is not just one function for this behavior. It depends on the day, the time, and the individual."

"Granny, how does your skin feel?"

"Wonderful. Lots of sensations. It's very sensitive and is able to feel the minutest vibrations in the water. When we're swimming, we get ripples of sensation on our skin as the water passes over it."

While Granny spoke I was inside her body. I could feel the water creating small wrinkles on the surface of her skin. The water pressure in these currents seemed to be physically moving my skin up and down. I also saw Granny's skin billowing back, although I doubt this is something I would have seen with my physical eyes.

"I am showing Mary the underwater sensations of traveling and holding stationary in a current—a wonderful massage. Rubbing on rocks is another delightful sensation."

Now I could feel myself bumping and scraping against rocks, as a cat might rub on a tree. The rocks felt completely different from the water. Water creates a soothing, sometimes tingling sensation on the skin, whereas the rocks scratch an itch. They can also reach deep through the blubber into the muscle layer. It felt wonderful, and I couldn't help moving with the sensations.

Raphaela laughed suddenly. "Do you know you're wiggling all over the place?"

"Yeah, I'm rubbing on rocks."

"Is there anything else you can tell us about your skin?" she asked Granny.

"Beneath the surface we roll and rub with our friends and pod members. This is very, very pleasurable to us, the twisting and turning. Not only do we enjoy the smooth contact of skin to skin, but the rolling, twisting, and turning create little vortices of water that tickle and caress the skin in a very sensual, pleasurable way.

"I am searching to see if there is anything else I can say about skin. Our skin feels wonderful. What would we do without it?"

Raphaela broke into laughter. "Well, you'd leak into the ocean, Granny!"

"Indeed! We would leak. Our skin is our most necessary organ. It keeps us all together and provides us protection as well as pleasure."

"Granny, Mary told me about an area in Canada where the northern residents rub on the rocks. Do you have such a place in your area, or do you go up north to rub sometimes?"

My consciousness followed Granny deep below the surface toward a tight opening to an underwater cave. I described what I saw. "When a whale goes into the cave, it has to scrunch around and wiggle back and forth. Actually, they don't really go into it, but slowly rub at the entrance. There are rocks outside where other whales are rubbing, but the best place is the cave entry where you can slide back and forth on the edge."

"Is this something that you do often, or on a daily basis?"

"You couldn't do it every day or you would get sore. You must be careful not to rub to excess. The place that we go to rub is two weeks away."

"That must be far away. Is there a rubbing place within the area where the whale-watch boats follow you?"

"Yes, there are areas, but they are not nearly as nice, not as encompassing. There are shallow places with pleasant rocks that we use."

"Is rubbing something that the pod may do at any time, or is it part of a special event?"

"Well, when we find a suitable place, we certainly like a good roll. It has health aspects. It sloughs off old skin and parasites and ensures the integrity of the skin."

It is well known that the skin of whales is thin, sensitive, and very fragile. Dolphins and orcas often carry scars and rake marks made by the teeth of other whales. Seabirds have no problem pecking through the skin of a stranded whale, and some will even attack live whales to feed on their skin.

We know that a whale's skin is well supplied with nerves and their sense of touch is highly developed. I often see wild orcas rubbing each other or rubbing on objects they find in the sea. Kelp beds seem to be particularly attractive, offering long soft wisps of leaves that caress and tickle the skin.

Captive whales seek out rubbing and touching by their trainers and delight in being scratched by brushes and sprayed with hoses. Lone captive whales cannot engage in their traditional touching activities with other whales and must look to trainers for this pleasure. Since their environments are usually sterile and devoid of the kelp and rocks that can be used to keep the skin healthy, this activity probably loosens dead skin and maintains its soundness. How much it satisfies their emotional needs is another question.

Raphaela now returned to the subject of sight. "Granny, could you tell me something more about the difference in your sight above and below the water?"

"The difference is clarity. Above the surface things are bright, sharp, and colorful. Beneath the surface, there is a muted quality to our sight. We can see quite well but it's more a matter of contrast, lights, and darks. The focus is not sharp and clear. I know that some people think that we are bumping around in the darkness, but that's not true. The addition of our echolocation faculties makes our sight clear. We see things visually at a short distance and echolocation gives us distance sight and enhances our visual capabilities. It's a merging of sensory information. We really use two organs underwater to see."

"So the areas of the brain concerned with sight and those that handle echolocation communicate with each other. Are they close together?"

"They are so closely aligned and linked that they could not stand on their own."

"And what is the primary use of echolocation?"

"Mapping, travel. Sight is not that useful for long distances, so we constantly use echolocation to see where we are and where we are going."

"Do you ever orient yourself by looking at the shoreline?"

"No, not really. Our travel is mapped underwater. We know exactly where we are and have followed these paths for many, many years. We do not need to look above the surface to know where we are going."

Raphaela now turned from sight to another sense and said, "Granny, please tell us about taste."

I felt Granny shift her focus to address the new subject, but I was totally unprepared for the sudden appearance of a fish in my mouth. Yuk! I'm not fond of fish and really didn't want to know what eating a fish feels like, yet here it was. As it went down my throat it felt slick, yet rough, and there was a slight metallic taste in my mouth rather than a familiar flavor. "It seems that whales do not taste in the way that humans do," I remarked. "I'm getting a chemical reaction instead of a specific taste. Let me see if Granny can explain."

"Yes, you are right in that different fishes produce different reactions in the mouth. It's very subtle. There are things in the water that you may consider we taste, but the differences from one taste to another are so subtle that it's almost on an energy level, as if the vibration is different."

Raphaela paused. "I don't quite understand what you're saying, Granny. Do you have a favorite fish?"

"She's showing me a big red salmon," I said.

"What is it about that fish that makes it a favorite? A human would say it's sweeter, or saltier."

"One thing is the size. Bigger is definitely better. Yes, this salmon does have a sweeter vibration. I get more pleasure with that type. It is quite hard to explain."

I had to agree with Granny. I couldn't begin to explain it. Just as there isn't a lot of vocabulary for human taste, I wasn't finding words or even concepts to describe what I was experiencing. My forehead was wrinkled as I searched for ways to clarify.

"What are you getting?" Raphaela asked.

"Orca taste is very subtle, similar to an aroma. It's not like tasting salt or sweet. As something passes through their mouths there is a minute chemical reaction. I think that if they ate something bad, the reaction would be bigger. It would make them spit it out. Their sense of taste is more like a monitoring system than a pleasuring system. Its function is to ensure that what they eat is food. A piece of rubber would produce a negative alarm and a chemical reaction to get rid of it."

"How about smell? Do you have a sense of smell?"

"My sense of smell is similar to taste. In whales, the two are really combined. When we breathe through our blowholes we can detect things such as a sweetness in the air in the spring, an energy of new things growing. We feel this more than smell it. It would not be characterized as smell in the way that you use your organs. It's also a combined sensing of chemicals and changes in the water. It is functional rather than pleasurable."

Raphaela sighed and paused. "Do you smell the water?"

"I see her running water over her tongue," I said.

"I smell and taste it. Water is not as undifferentiated as you think. To you it all looks dark, maybe green or murky. This is not the case for us. We taste and smell the water, and it gives us a lot of information."

"We have one more sense question. How do you hear?"

"We have internal ears without external openings, although we have remnants of that structure. Most sound reaches our ears by traveling through our jaw bone, but we also receive some sound directly through the skull."

Much of what Granny said during this session corresponded to scientific knowledge. The way they hear and the sensitivity of their skin have been studied and are fairly well understood. Granny's description of the difference in her eyesight beneath the surface and above was more surprising, and the information she gave us about smelling and tasting intrigued me. I was sorry that I couldn't delve deeper into those subjects, but I was unable to explain or describe things further. We humans have our limitations, too. Why couldn't I be free of them?

The discussion of orca taste had turned my mind to food. I had questions I wanted to ask Granny on that subject, but I was feeling rather tired from the active communication session. I guess all that rock rubbing had worn me out!

We decided to stop and make some dinner. It was always wonderful to be connected to Granny, but the experience was draining. Neither Raphaela nor I could maintain our energy for more than about 90 minutes. While in the communicator role, we were totally immersed in Granny's energy field, which is very different from human consciousness. The demands of coping with this foreign environment tired us out quickly. Besides, there was always tomorrow.

FAST FOOD

Morning's light found us well rested and ready for a little walk on the beach. As we picked our way over and around the masses of driftwood and tangled kelp, our eyes searched the horizon for the sight of fins. The sunshine warmed our faces in the brisk morning air and there were only a few wisps of clouds in the azure sky. The sea was totally flat with not a single ripple between us and the Olympic Mountains across the strait.

Fins broke the surface about a half-mile offshore. "Look!" I shouted, pointing to the spot. "Three Dall's porpoises." We watched them travel by in unison, methodically rolling across the surface and disappearing again. Five surfacings and they were gone.

"They are such gorgeous little creatures," Raphaela said with a sigh. "I know transients eat them, but I don't think Granny ever would, do you? It just seems so cruel."

"I don't know for sure, Raphaela. I've never seen a resident eating a porpoise, but I think it's something we should ask her about."

After breakfast, Raphaela began the first session as communicator. It was her last day here and she wanted to spend as much time as she could with Granny. "Let's pick up where we left off last night and ask her about food," I said.

"That would be great," she replied. "Food—one of my favorite subjects!"

I laughed. "Yeah, mine too. I suspect Granny feels the same way."

"Undoubtedly," Raphaela murmured as she settled down and connected.

I began, "We are very curious about your food. What types of fish and—"

Raphaela interrupted, "Before you can finish the question, Granny is showing me long silver fish, salmon."

"These are the best. These are the most enjoyable. We rejoice when they come. We do not limit ourselves to only salmon, but they are delectable."

"Oh, now she's showing me seals!" Raphaela gasped. "Do you really eat those little seals?"

"Yes, sometimes when it's necessary the seals give us their bodies, but not often. There are certain nutrients that our bodies need that we can only get from these creatures. We prefer not to eat them since it is far too dangerous. However, when we are feeling depleted and needing the energy that only the seals can provide, we do occasionally eat them."

There it was again—Granny stating that they sometimes eat seals. I had found this hard to believe the first time she told me, but I accepted it when Raphaela confirmed it back in July. Scientists think that resident orcas like Granny do not eat seals, although they are a very common food of transient orcas.

My mind went back to the first time I had seen transient orcas feeding. It was in the summer of 1995. The *Western Prince* had run across some transient whales from O pod and had been following four females up the west side of Stuart Island. They were zigzagging around, being evasive, and generally not providing a very interesting trip for the passengers. Then one whale abruptly left the group at high speed and headed north.

I strained to see what she was doing, and noticed a small spray shooting up in front of her. "Oh my gosh, one of these females is chasing a Dall's porpoise," I said over the loudspeaker. "Do you see that spray in front of her? We call that a 'rooster tail' and it's being made by a porpoise traveling fast."

"Why is she chasing the porpoise?" someone asked.

"They eat them," I replied, "but I've never seen it before."

The female orca was moving so fast that she was coming halfway out of the water. The porpoise changed direction frequently, trying to throw her off, but she corrected quickly and stayed not far behind. This had continued for about four minutes when another whale approached. As she took up the chase, the first whale dropped off. They were taking turns!

Each female spent four to five minutes pursuing the porpoise while the others watched and rested. One orca swam so fast that she flew completely out of the water and traveled horizontally above the surface. After about 20 minutes of intense swimming, the porpoise was worn out. He just couldn't keep up that pace. Dall's porpoises are gorgeous, playful, and lithe, and passengers love seeing them. They look very much like miniature orcas. Sympathy in the boat was with the porpoise.

Now the orca disappeared and made a run at him from below. She hit him so hard with her rostrum that he flew ten feet into the air—end over end! The passengers gasped and my purser started crying. I was fascinated.

The battering continued for several minutes. The poor porpoise was struck again and again, and then finally an orca surfaced with the porpoise lying crossways in her mouth. She and the others dove down and did not reappear for five minutes. We never saw that porpoise again.

On one trip, in the spring of 1996, we encountered four K pod females chasing Dall's in Haro Strait. The orcas were lined up abreast, screaming down the strait after three porpoises. They flew high out of the water, half exposing their bodies as they drove after the porpoises at high speed. It was as coordinated as those synchronized moves you see at Sea World.

I had assumed that the chasing incident was prompted by play and had been initiated by the porpoises themselves. Now the possibility that K pod had been hunting the porpoises occurred to me. It's one thing for the transients, but . . . my orcas?

"What about porpoises and other cetaceans?" I asked. "I have seen transients eating them. Do the resident whales ever eat porpoises?"

"Yes, they are quick. This is not a staple, not something that we do every day, but it does happen from time to time. We ask them, and they offer."

I was shocked by Granny's words and found myself very uncomfortable with this subject. Perhaps my viewpoint wasn't as objective as I'd like to think. I let the porpoise topic go and asked,

"What do you eat in the winter, Granny, when there are no salmon around?"

"Out at sea, we do find some salmon roaming around. We feed on many things: big flat fish from the bottom, small fish like herring, and octopus. Squid are not very common in these waters now, but we have them occasionally."

Raphaela said, "Now she's showing me little fish darting, quick, turning, traveling in schools. These small fish seem to be the staple diet."

"These are the ones that we herd."

I replied, "They would probably be herring or hake."

"That sounds correct," Raphaela said.

"Granny, you showed Raphaela pictures of herding fish. Could you tell us about your fishing techniques?"

Raphaela replied, "She's showing me an open mouth, a big lunge, and a crunch. Boy, it's pretty visceral. Now a side lunge, and a grasp, bearing down with the jaw. Next I see her cruising through a school of fish with an open mouth, like a shovel or a scoop. The fish just float into her mouth."

"There are many ways to eat. Do you not have many ways to eat?"

"Yes, I do." I replied. "I know what my ways are, and I am very interested in your ways. Do you use sound to stun your food?"

"Yes."

She showed Raphaela a large group of fish that were immobilized.

"This takes more than one whale. It is a group effort."

"Is it a common activity?" I asked.

"It is used when a large group of whales is together. It is hard to feed a large group. Therefore when we are together, we might use this technique to immobilize the fish."

"I have also seen whales tail-slapping in kelp beds, and wondered if you are scaring fish out of the kelp?"

"Yes, yes. This is very entertaining. The youngsters entwine their tails in the kelp and yank, and the fish fly out. Then they

amuse themselves by hunting them. While they are playing, we teach them how to tail-slap to chase out the fish. It's fun."

Raphaela said, "Granny is showing me that two or three whales line up and smack the surface, driving the fish toward the others."

"Do you also sometimes drive fish up against the shoreline?"

"That is exactly what we do."

"Do you eat as much as you can? How does that work?" I asked.

"We eat to satiation, to fullness, but with bodies our size, that requires a lot of fish. It is almost impossible to get full without eating the larger bodies."

"She's showing me whales and porpoises," Raphaela said, wincing. She looked as though her stomach might be upset. I was feeling a bit queasy myself, thinking about eating porpoises and whales. This prompted me to ask, "If a whale gets sick, what do you do?"

"If a whale is sick, in the beginning we ignore it and many times it goes away. If the sickness persists, we may travel more slowly to accommodate her. We may try to fish in the easiest places for her benefit. We send her love, energy, and support, but we do not have medications or medical procedures.

"Whale bodies are vast and most illnesses are external. A whale may have a skin problem, but her internal organs are fine. She may have a deformity, but her digestion and reproductive abilities are sound. There are small illnesses, but they are very external."

This made perfect sense to me and is how I deal with my own occasional minor illness. Pay no attention to it, and it will pass.

I was still bothered by Granny's pronouncement on porpoise eating and couldn't get it out of my mind. I kept thinking about a time, probably in early May, when only J pod was in the area. The *Western Prince* was traveling south with the whales in Haro Strait. Most of the pod was on our left when Ruffles abruptly appeared on our right. I noticed odd little waves around him that I'd never seen before. As I peered intently trying to figure out what they were, a Dall's porpoise exploded from the water just in front of him. Then another leapt over his back.

Ruffles

I couldn't believe it! Porpoises bow-riding on a whale! I gathered all the passengers to watch this unusual spectacle. Every time Ruffles surfaced, the Dall's were there, zipping back and forth in front of him, leaping over his back and generally making a nuisance of themselves. I'd never seen anything like it. One actually slid across his body just in front of his dorsal fin.

It seemed as if Ruffles was trying to get rid of them. He was doing extra-long down times and had increased his speed. Dall's porpoises are the fastest of all the inland cetaceans, so there was no way Ruffles was going to lose them. They seemed to be harassing him mercilessly, like mosquitoes on a hot, muggy night in Minnesota.

"Granny, one time last spring I saw some porpoises harassing the big male, J1, whom we call Ruffles. What was that about?" I inquired.

"That was not harassment. It was play, and Ruffles, what an undignified name, allowed it. Shall I tell you about him?"

"Oh, please!"

"At some time in this project, you should speak directly to him. He is a huge energy and has a gigantic heart. His being is so profound it could fill this entire Sound. You must talk to him. He is a mystical messenger, a prophet, a Buddha, sending out his light to protect us. Yes, Mary, he is my son."

Raphaela's eyes flew open. "Were you just going to ask her that?" she said.

"Yeah, I wanted to know for sure."

Ruffles is considered to be the oldest male in the southern resident community. Scientists estimate that he was born in 1951. The average life span for a male is only about 30 years, so Ruffles is quite elderly, although you'd never know it by looking at him. He is about 27 feet long, weighs around ten tons, and has a dorsal fin close to six feet tall. His impressive fin is wavy and very distinctive, making it easy to identify him from the rear. I think he acquired his name around the time "Ruffles have ridges" was a popular potato chip slogan.

In the genealogical chart of J pod, Ruffles is shown as being possibly related to Granny. I had heard some researchers say he might be her brother; others, her son. Some thought that he was perhaps a nephew. It was exciting to get this information directly from her and to finally know that he was definitely her son.

"How do you feel about connecting to Ruffles?" I asked Raphaela. "I think we should just take Granny's advice and call him in."

Raphaela's left hand clutched her heart. "Oh boy, I don't know. I've only ever talked to Granny." She paused for a moment and then shrieked, "What am I saying? Of course, I'll talk to Ruffles!"

So far, all of our conversations had been with Granny, and we were excited to get another perspective. I showed Raphaela a picture of Ruffles from the ID guide, and she settled back down into the telepathic space. Almost immediately, Ruffles came in.

"I am very pleased to speak with you. What would you like to know?" he asked.

I remembered Granny's comment about what an undignified name "Ruffles" was, so I asked him how he felt about his name and what he preferred.

"Anything you want. We don't have names. You can call me 'Flower' if you like. Ruffles is okay. It's amusing."

"All right, then, Ruffles it is." I had always liked this guy. He had a very friendly, "protective uncle" type of energy and really seemed to enjoy the schoolchildren who came out to see the whales.

Very early in my career as a naturalist, I discovered that the whales were fascinated by the sound frequency emitted by screaming girls. On that day I had a group of second-and third-graders on board. J pod appeared, and Ruffles came within 50 yards of the boat. I gathered all the children on the bow and told them to scream as loud as they could the next time Ruffles surfaced. They enthusiastically agreed and waited impatiently as three long minutes ticked by.

When Ruffles surfaced again, the children cut loose with a shrill scream and Ruffles put on the brakes. He came to a full stop, oriented the front of his head toward the boat and just hung on the surface, listening.

"Keep screaming!" I urged the children. The girls were fabulous, squealing with wild abandon as if hundreds of mice were running through the boat and up their legs.

Ruffles floated motionless on the surface, and it appeared that he enjoyed these peculiar sounds. From that day forward, I encouraged my school and scout groups to scream or chant his name when he appeared. He really seemed to like the chorus "Ruffles, Ruffles, Ruffles," and drew closer to the boat when we started. No wonder he found his name amusing.

"Ruffles, do you like it when young girls scream your name?" I asked.

"I like it. It sends a wave of their energy into my field. They increase my power and I theirs, although they are mere babies. There is a communion between us. I do enjoy the young ones. I

have had human lives, and I understand these little ones very well. I enjoy their growth and visit them in their dreams."

Raphaela said she was getting a vision of the heavens with stars that were getting larger and brighter. Ruffles was showing her a scene reminiscent of a planetarium with constellations wheeling overhead. She didn't understand the significance of the particular stars she saw but was filled with a sense of peace and awe.

I didn't like the way this conversation was going. Frankly it was a bit too creepy for me. What did Ruffles mean "he visits them in their dreams?" Was Raphaela getting this right or had she drifted off somewhere strange and new? And what was all this stuff about stars and the heavens? It was all a little too far out.

I was well aware that the New Age community was smitten with whales and dolphins. Many hold the cetaceans in high esteem and believe they have mystical qualities and extraordinary abilities. Some even claim that cetaceans have extraterrestrial origins and came to earth from stars. This may all be true, but I wasn't quite ready to embrace or investigate that realm.

Raphaela sat quietly, a small smile on her lips. She was still enjoying her celestial show. "Are you aware of this project that we are working on with Granny?" I asked.

"Of course," he replied.

"Would you be willing to talk to us occasionally? It would be wonderful to get your perspective on various aspects of orca life."

"This project is a good thing to do, and I encourage you to be serious and firm in completing it. I will think about my level of participation. I can tell you things, but you may understand more by just feeling my energy."

Raphaela interrupted and said, "He's showing me a picture of us sliding into the water."

"This is a contribution to your project I can make. Come with me now."

Raphaela's smile faded and she opened her eyes. "He wants us to go with him in the water," she said. "I think he wants to show us something."

I could see that she wasn't at all sure about this idea and looked really nervous. "You mean he wants to take us on a journey? That would be fantastic! What are you afraid of?" I asked.

"I don't like being in the water," she admitted. "It's dark and scary and cold."

"Come on, this is an incredible opportunity! We have to do it!"

"Okay. I know you're right. Just give me a minute to get ready," she replied.

"Get quiet. Come with me now," Ruffles instructed.

I closed my eyes and tried to slow my heart, which was beating as fast as a hummingbird's. What was going to happen? A few deep breaths brought a sense of calm, and I felt my consciousness diving deep to meet Ruffles on the telepathic plane.

I floated effortlessly underwater and was surprised that I didn't feel a need to breathe. Everything was dark, but my body felt perfectly normal and comfortable. Out of the blackness, Ruffles appeared on my left. His huge black body loomed next to mine, and I instinctively knew he wanted me to hang on to his pectoral fin. I wrapped my fingers over the thick, smooth edge and let my body float next to his. Although I couldn't see her, I knew Raphaela was holding on to his left flipper.

Ruffles began to pump his huge tail flukes and we glided through the water in an undulating motion. Rocks flashed by on my right so I knew that we couldn't be far from shore. Then he made a slight turn to the left and headed out into deeper water. I didn't see anything now and the water appeared cloudy and murky. Small lighted particles flew by my eyes; otherwise we were in total darkness.

I started feeling a bit bored with no visuals to hold my attention. Ruffles, sensing this, encouraged me to enter his body. I felt his powerful muscles propelling us through the water and sensed that he had complete mastery of his environment.

Suddenly a silvery fish appeared in front of us and we slurped it down. Its cold, hard body slid down my throat without chewing or tasting. It was gone as quickly as it had appeared.

We broke the surface with an explosive exhale, massive lungs contracting and then air rushing to fill the vacuum as they expanded again. My exposed flesh felt cold and prickly in the air compared to the rest of my body, which felt safe and comfortable in the water. Phoooo! Another huge breath and down we went, plunging into the darkness.

Once again I found myself hanging on to his right pectoral fin, my consciousness no longer merged with his. I felt calm, relaxed and very safe with Ruffles. It was pleasant traveling through the water together, very peaceful.

Ruffles began speaking to me telepathically. *"Granny will be leaving this winter. She won't be coming back with the pod next summer. We are preparing for her transition and getting ready for the changes that will occur in our group."*

I felt my heart contract. Granny leaving? How could this be possible? We've only just begun this project. Perhaps this is why Ruffles told us to be "serious and firm" with this project. Her time is short, and we need to get as much information as we can before she leaves her body.

Ruffles faded and my consciousness returned to my living room in Friday Harbor. I was sad about the prospect of losing Granny, but I was also bursting with excitement about the fantastic experience I'd just had with Ruffles. I opened my eyes and found Raphaela staring at me with wild dancing eyes.

"What happened?" she demanded.

"It was incredible," I answered. "Let me get the tape recorder rolling. You first. Tell me what happened."

She took a deep breath. "Well, at first it was very dark, and I was nervous. I didn't like the feeling of being alone underwater, but then Ruffles appeared and had me hold on to his pec fin."

"Me too, me too! I just knew you were on the other side," I exclaimed.

"I was a little reluctant and fearful, but he coaxed me to come. So I hung onto his left fin, and we went cruising through the water. It was so shadowy, and there was nothing to look at. Ruffles noticed and said, *'You think this is boring. Shift into my body.'* Before I could even think about it, I was inside, and a fish came into view. We ate it, but it didn't have much taste, although it was satisfying.

"We cruised a bit more, and then he surfaced to breathe. That was really interesting. I could feel all the air whooshing out and then in again, but it was over immediately and down we went. This time he went out into deeper water. I started feeling anxious so he circled around a small island where there were things I could look at. That made me a little more comfortable."

I couldn't believe what I was hearing. "I had exactly the same journey you did! How is that possible?"

"Seriously? Oh, this is so amazing," she replied.

We were astounded at our parallel experiences. This journey validated that we were telepathically connected to these whales, and we agreed to follow Ruffles' recommendation to be "serious and firm."

"Did he say anything about Granny?" I asked.

"Oh yes," she sighed. "He said she wouldn't be around much longer. I feel so awful. I hardly know her, but she already feels like a grandmother to me. How can she leave now?"

My heart sank. I had hoped that I had gotten it wrong, but if Raphaela had received the same information, maybe it was true. "I just hope we're mistaken," I said. "Things could change, you know. He didn't say she was sick, just that she was leaving. Maybe something will happen to keep her here."

Raphaela nodded. "I guess we have a lot of work to do."

SEX AND THE SINGLE WHALE

The summer of 1996 had not been a spectacular season for sightings in the San Juans—not spectacular, but not disappointing either. As always, I had loved seeing Granny and her pod, but I really didn't mind when we closed down the *Western Prince* at the end of October. The whales and the tourists were gone, and the wind was blowing cold. I was ready for a break. Besides, I was in close contact with the orcas through our telepathic communication and would still be part of their world even though I wasn't out on the water with them every day.

In early November, I headed to Berkeley to continue our conversations with Granny.

"So how was the rest of the season?" Raphaela asked.

"Pretty good, nothing unusual. The whales were around quite a bit. But I didn't see a single sea snake all summer," I whined.

"Oh dear," she said with a worried look. "I'm not familiar with sea snakes. Are they an endangered species?"

I burst out laughing. I sometimes forget that Raphaela doesn't know all the jargon. "You still don't know much about whales, do you?" I teased.

Raphaela pulled herself up two inches taller and looked indignant. "I'm learning," she said. "Give me a break! So what is a sea snake?"

"In the business," I informed her, "a whale's penis is known as a sea snake."

"Oh dear," she said, "and you actually see them?"

"Well, I didn't see any this summer, that's why I'm complaining, but when you do, they're hard to miss. In fact, it's an absolutely awesome sight! A sea snake is about six feet long and six inches across, if you can imagine. They're mostly pink and have mottled dark areas."

Raphaela looked shocked. Her mind whirred trying to process this information. I decided to tell her about a close encounter I'd had in mid-July of 1994.

J and K pods were traveling north in Haro Strait. The fishing had been good, and they'd foraged for several hours. Now they were engrossed in play. The *Western Prince* was in neutral, floating in the current with whales on both sides. Two juveniles on the left were having a breaching contest, jumping out of the water over and over again. All of a sudden mom exploded from the water, only a few feet from the youngsters. She hurled her mighty body skyward as if to say, "This is how you really do it!"

I was on the back deck, enjoying the sun and explaining the various behaviors to the passengers. Suddenly the water behind the boat began to boil. I ran to see what was happening. Black-and-white whale flesh rolled at the surface and I suddenly saw pink! A large erect penis flashed by. Always the voyeur, I peered intently into the depths trying to see. I figured there must be a little inter-pod mingling going on, since that is when mating occurs, but who was down there?

The male broke the surface with a giant leap, coming halfway out of the water. It was one of my favorites, Everett, a teenager from J pod. I had been watching him grow from a juvenile to a sub-adult male for the past three years. "Everett, I thought you were *my* boyfriend," I yelled at him. "Are you after one of the K pod girls?"

He rolled across the water and I could see a female beneath him. His penis flopped around below the surface, its light pink flashing in the dark sea. "Who is it, Everett? Who are you chasing?"

The water churned again and white waves splashed everywhere. A female porpoised out of the water and dove next to the boat with Everett in hot pursuit. "I don't believe it!" I exclaimed. "It's Granny!"

Quite a crowd had gathered to watch the show. When I explained that Everett was 16 years old and Granny was 83, cheers went up from the women on deck. "I'm going to come back as an orca!" one of them called out. "The old girls get to have sex with the teenage boys! What a deal!" As the women laughed uproariously, the men retreated to the wheelhouse to look at the instruments.

Raphaela shook her head and giggled. "That's a great story," she said, "but I don't understand why Everett would try to mate with Granny. She's too old to have calves, isn't she?"

"It might be a teaching situation," I replied. "Resident orcas do not mate within their pod or family group. Instead they breed with individuals from other pods within their community. This preserves genetic diversity and prevents inbreeding. When two pods come together there is a huge party and when it's over, everyone goes home with their mother. But orca researchers have observed mating behavior within a pod between post-reproductive females and subadult males. That's what I observed with Everett and Granny."

Well, "observed" isn't quite the right word. As usual, I really wasn't able to see much, since, like most orca activity, their sex lives take place underwater. It is extremely difficult to determine if two orcas are actually mating. You can see mating behavior such as rolling together or boisterous rubbing, and sometimes if you're lucky you glimpse an erect penis flailing above the water, but that's about it.

I explained that the orcas' sexual development and sex lives are similar to ours in many ways. When young male orcas reach puberty at 12 to 13 years of age, hormones cause their dorsal fins, tail flukes, and pectoral fins to grow. This growth period lasts for six to eight years. They become sexually mature in their mid-teens, but do not reach their full adult size until their late teens or early twenties. At that time they also become socially mature and are able to pursue mates. Everett wouldn't be socially or physically mature for a few more years.

Female orcas in the wild become sexually mature around ten to 14 years of age, but often do not give birth until many years later. They reach their adult size at 18 years. Granny referred to this coming of age as *"an awakening to her potential as a mother."*

The average female produces four to six calves over a 25-year period and then discontinues reproduction. Although she is no longer fertile, she is still sexually active.

Raphaela sighed. "You really didn't see a single sea snake all summer?"

"No. It was so disappointing."

She looked worried. "Maybe we should ask Granny if there's a problem."

"That's a good idea. Do you want to connect with Granny?"

"I'd love to. It's been such a long time since I've spoken to her." She fluffed the pillows around her on the couch and closed her eyes. I took out my notebook and readied the tape recorder.

A smile spread across her face. "Granny is so wonderful," she said. "She's right here whenever I call. Go ahead."

I flipped on the tape recorder and said, "Granny, I didn't see one sea snake this summer, and I am very disappointed. What's going on?"

Raphaela burst into laughter. "Granny's cracking up," she reported through her giggles.

"Hello to you, too," Granny quipped. *"You don't waste any time, do you? No, there's nothing going on, my dear. I am very sorry that you didn't see any of our sexual antics this summer, but it was not for our lack of trying. The usual number of matings occurred. I guess you just missed them."*

I frowned. "It's not fair, Granny. I went out on over a hundred trips this year and never saw any action. I haven't seen much since the time Everett was chasing you behind the *Western Prince*, and that was two years ago!"

"I am pleased that our sexual lives are of such interest to you. They are of great interest to us as well. Would you like to talk about this?"

"You bet," I replied. I was ready with lots of questions. "Do you always mate with members of another pod or is there ever mating within the pod?"

"It would be rare to mate within the immediate family. It has happened, but you could regard it as an accident. It was not a mat-

ing intended to result in pregnancy. The mating or play within our immediate family is educational. We have sexual feelings at all times. Although I am no longer fertile, I still enjoy the attention. Also, it is part of my role to educate the young."

"When Everett was chasing you that day, were you teaching him about sex? Do the older females teach the young males?"

"Yes, we do. When a young male slides up to me with his organ out, this is correct behavior. They need direction and to learn the right way to approach a female. Although their sex organ is prominent and easily seen, it can be floppy when distended. It is difficult to direct such a large organ in a current of water, especially when the water is being churned up by many huge bodies. Therefore, he needs education and focus in how to use his organ, to be firm and able to copulate when the occasion arises.

"Young males also need to be tutored on how to approach delicately but decisively. There is a game, a dance that precedes matings: approach, retreat, approach, and circle. The female must be brought to readiness. She seeks her mate and may have identified him weeks before; nonetheless, the mating dance, the ritual, prepares both partners in even greater detail."

I was overcome by a feeling of tenderness. I pictured two large whales, moving delicately and sweetly together, so graceful and elegant. Their timing was exquisite and unrushed, nothing like the back seat of a car on lover's lane.

"Granny, do you teach just the young males, or is there instruction for females too?"

"I teach them both," she replied. *"It is essential that both partners know and understand their respective roles. Our mating is very complex and requires careful attunement of both male and female energies. This cannot be accomplished quickly or easily. Our couplings are preceded by preparation and song.*

"When we meet our mates in another group, there is much joy, thrashing of the water, uproar, and noise, but we have been tuning up for this encounter perhaps for weeks. This tuning up is preceded by the education of the young."

"How do you teach the females?" I asked.

"First, she must know her body and understand positioning, which is very important. In a body as vast as ours, it is critical to be able to direct the male organ to the female organ efficiently and quickly in the water. This is not easy.

"Then, to develop sexual feelings, her mother strokes her genital area. It focuses and draws her attention and energy to that part of her body. The young female watches her mother mate. In fact, all the young observe and have sexual play during matings."

While the baleen whales have a distinct annual cycle of calving and mating, the toothed whales often do not. Orcas can mate and produce calves at any time of year, although most calves are born in the winter in the Pacific Northwest. Since they have a gestation of close to 17 months, this indicates summer breeding at the time when all three pods meet. I wanted to verify this with Granny, so I asked her if they had a mating season.

"There is not a mating season connected to a particular time of year. When we meet other pods, more than one female mates and often their babies are born together. This is not a true season. We just have more opportunities for mating in the summer.

"We can decide when to prepare and release an egg. Of course, we have to be certain of many things: that there will be an adequate food supply, that our present calf is well on his way to independence, and that a suitable mate will come, although the mate is the least important."

Raphaela found this last comment so surprising and comical that she burst out laughing and then jumped in with a few questions of her own. "What about mates? Are plans laid in advance for coupling with a particular whale, and does that association continue for years, or is it a one-shot deal?"

After chastising Raphaela for asking too many questions at once, Granny said, *"Yes, we may lay plans far in advance for coupling with an attractive male. However, there are also last-minute decisions and spontaneous happenings. One may be overcome with biology, and if the mate you have been yearning for is not present, but your body is primed, you may make another choice."*

I smiled, remembering a song that was popular in my twenties. The chorus went, "If you can't be with the one you love, love the one you're with. Love the one you're with." It seemed the whales agreed with this philosophy.

Granny continued, *"Now, the preparation for whales is long indeed. Sometimes a female may wish to only mate with one male, and he will be the sire of all her children. This is most common between J, K, and L pods, because we meet often and there is plenty of opportunity.*

"Our preparation is sonic. We send and receive songs of love and intention that develop our biological readiness."

"Boy, my body is starting to react to all this sex talk," Raphaela said. "I'm actually getting a throbbing sensation! It's quite erotic."

"Lucky you!" I exclaimed. "Do you want me to take over?"

"Not on your life! Hold on. I'm getting more information now. It looks as if the acts of intercourse are multiple."

"That is correct," Granny stated. *"One act of intercourse is meager, and there is a biological basis to this. Repeated couplings ensure impregnation and may be required for fertility."*

"Granny, tell us about ovulation. Do you have a monthly cycle?" I asked.

"Ovulation does not occur on a regular schedule like you might imagine. It is somewhat voluntary. We have the ability to regulate when we become pregnant. When a female is ready to take on that responsibility, she readies herself for the event so that she can conceive. If necessary, she can also suppress the implantation of a fertilized egg."

The general public believes that orcas mate for life. They've gotten this impression from Hollywood and movies like *Orca*, which made this statement. It is absolutely untrue. The dolphin family as a whole is highly promiscuous and orcas are no exception. Frankly, I was surprised to hear that some orcas might only mate with one male, so I questioned Granny further. "Do some females mate with many males?"

"Yes, I myself have mated with at least eight." Granny also said that a typical female mates as little as every two or three years or as often as every two or three months. She told me that mating between orcas is not only for the purpose of reproduction. There are matings between young and old in teaching situations and some just for pure joy. Mating also strengthens the ties between families.

I asked Granny about J pod's sexual association with other whale communities. She said that although they are aware of the offshore group they do not socialize or mix with them. She didn't know if the offshores associated with the northern resident community but did say that on occasion a southern resident whale will mate with a northern resident.

Then I asked her whether the residents ever mated with the transient whales. Researchers believe that residents and transients have not interbred for a hundred thousand years, so her comments surprised me.

"Yes, but it does not occur often. It is unusual, and let me say that it is different from the way that mating occurs within the community. We spoke about sending out a song to the beloved and preparation for mating. This does not happen with transient matings. It is a brief encounter.

"When we meet transients, there is some fascination with them and fear, yet some titillation. They are exciting, different, and strange. When we are outside our clearly defined home range within the islands, a meeting with the transients can be quite exciting and thrilling. This is not a greeting ceremony, but emotions can get very high. At that time, a spontaneous mating can occur out of sheer excitement that becomes erotic. It is unusual. I would say that it happens maybe once every five years."

Since researchers cannot see who is mating with whom, we could not until recently determine the fathers of the calves that are born each year. However, this question can now be answered by testing a small tissue sample from each whale. In the mid-1990s, Canadian and U.S. researchers worked together to biopsy dart all the whales in the northern and southern resident communities to acquire the tissue samples needed for DNA testing. Soon we will know who fathered each individual. Researchers will also be looking at genetic similarities among the residents, transients, and offshores. Although Granny said that mating with transients could occur, she didn't know if any pregnancies resulted.

There are usually more females than males in any pod. This is normal, since males have a higher death rate and a shorter life span. A male orca, being much bigger, requires two to three times more food than a female needs, three to four hundred pounds of fish per day. Too many males could unnecessarily burden the fish resources available. Granny remarked, *"Males are less important than the females, but one male with his richness has a very special place."*

I asked Granny if there were enough males to keep the gene pool healthy.

"It would be all right if one male, for example, Ruffles, was the sire of many young in one pod because these whales would not mate with one another. This would be a satisfactory situation and would not destroy our diversity.

"A male is capable of breeding more than one female in a day, and in fact may breed more than one female in an encounter. He couples with one, and another is ready. Of course, there is some courtship and waiting. During this period the young males may be flirting with the females who are ready and waiting. These flirtations and play almost never result in impregnation.

"You should also speak to Ruffles about sexual matters."

We decided to wait until the next morning. The hours had flown by and it was far past midnight. But tired as I was, I found it hard to fall asleep. My mind was swirling with all the information we had just received. I wondered how much romance and mystery they had in their encounters. Their love songs sounded very romantic, and I hoped that someday I'd get to hear one. I was trying to imagine what it would sound like as I drifted off to sleep.

Raphaela and I both had wild sexual dreams that night. We laughed about it over breakfast and decided to again approach the subject of sex, but this time from a male perspective. Raphaela was eager to connect telepathically with Ruffles, so I agreed to do the interviewing.

Ruffles and I exchanged a few pleasantries and then dove into the subject at hand. "Ruffles, do you know who your offspring are?"

"No, but I regard all calves as my offspring. Reproduction is very important. We are a species who put a tremendous amount of effort, work, and resources in one baby. We are not like the fish in our environment that have thousands and thousands of eggs. This is not our way. So, the birth of one calf is a great event to be celebrated. The calf will be nurtured and greatly protected. Therefore, I regard all as my offspring."

What a fantastic attitude, I thought. If only we could be more like the whales. What a difference it would make if we too regarded all children as our own.

I inquired about the male coming-of-age process and what it's like when an adolescent reaches puberty and his fin starts to grow.

Ruffles said, *"It is a matter of great pride. We eagerly look forward to seeing how much the young males of the other tribes have grown. The females cast appraising glances at these youngsters and may be quite flirtatious. Males at that age are very eager but a bit shy. They have instruction with older females involving rubbing and playing with the penis. When they reach the age when they are able to impregnate, there are no mysteries about the physical aspects of the process.*

"The young males also have sexual play together. Sex is one of the most pleasurable and interesting aspects of our lives. Of course, it is mainly for biological reproduction, but it also solidifies social relationships. Giving and receiving pleasure in this way creates love and bonding."

I questioned Ruffles at length about an adolescent male's emotional state, wondering if it was the same bewildering, confusing time of surging hormones that human males endure. He assured me that although they have surges of energy, there are always ways to work it off and this was not a frustrating or bewildering time. It is very normal, and the males are well prepared.

Ruffles emphasized that since male bodies are frail, it is extremely important that the males who survive childhood reach breeding age. They must be as fertile and available as possible to preserve the community.

"Ruffles, how do you choose a female to mate with?" I asked.

"She chooses me. My job is to be available. Hers is to choose a mate who can do the job—be fertile and impregnate her. I sing my song telling of my availability, and she responds if she wants. She knows when she is ready and will invite me."

I smiled. She gets to choose. This is truly a female-dominated society—none of the male domination that goes on in so many other species. I remembered a disturbing video I had seen a few years ago taken by dolphin researchers in Australia. It showed very aggressive male dolphins working together to gang-rape females. I wondered if this was aberrant behavior or something that just hadn't been observed in the past. Fortunately, it did not seem to be present in this orca society.

Throughout the years I have observed quite a bit of sex play between male orcas. Ruffles had mentioned that young males engage in this, but I had also seen adult males enjoying each other's company. One incident in particular comes to mind.

It was a calm day in the Strait of Juan de Fuca, and we were bobbing around with about 30 members of L pod. A few weeks earlier Miski, a 45-year-old female, had died, leaving her two sons alone. It is quite unusual for a mother to die before her sons since a female can live twice as long as a male. This was sadly the case for these two. Little four-year-old Mystery looked as if he were glued to Dylan, his 30-year-old brother. We were very touched to see this adult male being so careful and tender, watchful, and vigilant with his little brother. Mystery looked smaller than ever tucked close to Dylan's huge body. There were other small groups in the area feeding and playing, but none of the passengers were watching them. All eyes were on Dylan and Mystery as I relayed their story.

I was in the wheelhouse when I heard a roar go up from the back deck. There were explosive blows and people shrieking, so I ducked down and looked toward the rear deck through the galley. Two black bodies rolled next to the boat, but above the passengers' heads I saw a streak of pink go by. I dropped the microphone and leapt in a single bound to the rear deck.

People were gasping and giggling. I asked a woman standing near the railing, "What happened?"

Her eyes were as big as saucers. "Two whales were rolling around on the surface, rubbing on each other, twisting and turning. They were right next to the boat like we weren't even here! It was so exciting—there was water flying everywhere. Look! My sleeve is all wet."

"Were they both males?" I asked.

She replied, "I don't know; they both had those things."

"That means they're males," I said with a wink.

Red-faced, she laughed nervously and continued, "I thought so. I was shocked to see how long they are, and pink. They were flopping around so much I was afraid I was going to get hit by one. Gosh, that was actually more than I wanted to see."

I would have given anything to be hit by one, but the two whales had gone under the boat, so I ran to the port side. They were just coming up, and now only one of them was trailing a sea snake at his side. The pair continued to roll and rub at the surface and below. They leapt over each other and played like youngsters. Within minutes they disappeared, and I realized I hadn't even identified them. I had been too busy watching their sexual antics.

Now was my chance to ask Ruffles about this behavior. "Ruffles, why do males roll at the surface with their penises extended?" I asked.

"We like the feeling of the sun on them," he replied.

"OK, but what do you get out of it?" I pressed.

"Pleasure."

Raphaela suddenly interrupted. "I'm getting the feeling from him that this pleasure creates a bond between individuals and families."

I asked, "Is there any homosexuality within orca society?"

Raphaela thought that the answer was yes. She said she could see a sexual charge between two males and also between males and females. Then Ruffles chimed in.

"When we engage in sex for pleasure it may be with a female, and it may be with a male. It may or may not involve penetration or intercourse. Pleasure is pleasure."

Well said, Ruffles: simple and straightforward. I like that he doesn't mince words. "Pleasure is pleasure." I could respect this viewpoint.

PILLOW TALK

We were fascinated with the information we had received from Granny and Ruffles about sex, but I was troubled by Granny's earlier reference to their songs. I had read extensively about humpback whale songs and had even heard them live while working on a whale-watch boat in Hawaii, but I had never heard orca sounds referred to as songs. I asked Ruffles to tell us about songs.

"There is a song of loneliness when we have not seen our extended family or tribe for a while. This is a song of sadness. We try to lure them to come home or to come closer."

Raphaela noted, "It seems like there are a lot of vocalizations when they greet somebody. There is a huge uproar and a lot of noise. Ruffles is now showing me the female song or message announcing her readiness for a mate."

Ruffles replied, *"Our vocalizations carry greater meanings in one sound than yours do. You have more variety but fewer layers, less complexity."*

I asked him, "Are you saying that one sound, or what appears to us to be one sound, can have many meanings?"

"Yes, it can have multiple meanings. The meaning of the song is determined by the situation, the context."

Raphaela said, "I think this is also true of some Asian languages. Can't the same sound have different meanings in Chinese? Oh wait, now he's showing me that a male's response to a female's song of availability is something like, "I swoon at your song.""

Ruffles said, *"The 'I swoon at your song' response could also be sung by a mother to a baby without any sexual overtone whatsoever. It would mean, 'I love you, you're safe, you're secure, you're with me,' and it would sound the same as 'I swoon at your song' if the male was singing to a female. Context is all."*

"Raphaela, can we switch back to Granny for a bit? I want to get her perspective on songs."

"Sure, hold on while I thank Ruffles and then get Granny."

I scribbled questions on my pad until Raphaela was ready.

"Granny, you have used the word 'song' several times when talking about verbal communication and mating. I am unfamiliar with that term in orca communication. Could you tell us about songs?"

"All whales sing. It is incorrect to think that some whales have song and others do not."

"Are these songs for specific events or reasons?"

"Yes, and there are many. As I have told you, some prepare for sex. They are courtship songs. A female will send out her readiness to proclaim that she is seeking a male. A male may also communicate his readiness with a shorter song, more like an announcement. There are lullabies that we sing to the calves. This keeps them close to us so that we know where they are at all times."

"Are these songs produced through the vocalizations that we can hear?"

"Yes, you could hear them. There are several ways of producing sounds."

Raphaela held up her hand for me to stop. "I don't know what I'm seeing, but I'll try to describe it. There is some tissue that seems to be really deep in the middle of an immense body. It's red, slick, wet, viscous, and it vibrates. It has air going through it. The opening is changing shape, and when it does, different pitches of various duration are produced."

I almost fell off my chair. I was astounded that Raphaela was describing something that most good naturalists don't know anything about. Even many marine mammalogists are unfamiliar with this part of cetacean anatomy. I had once read about the organ that produces sound, deep within a toothed whale's head, but I knew for a fact that Raphaela hadn't. She was describing what scientists refer to as the monkey lips dorsal bursae complex.

An eerie sense came over me as my flesh broke out in goose bumps. There must have been a small part of me that still wondered if our communication was real or something that we were just making up. But here was Raphaela accurately describing a little-known organ within a whale. Any doubt about the validity of our conversations with Granny was dispelled completely in that moment.

Shaken, I continued. "What are your vocalizations? Is this a language you speak? We know that all the whales in the community use certain calls but each pod has specific calls only they use. Can you tell us about this?"

"These distinct dialects preserve our identities. Orcas can speak to each other telepathically, but we have variations between pods in our vocalizations. In our community we have a common language and speak freely among the three pods. Each pod has individual calls that are specifically for identification. In other geographic areas, the whales' vocal repertoire may be nothing like ours. Of course, we can all understand each other on the universal level, but their calls are different.

"It is similar to a band of indigenous people who have a particular language. They sing a song to the moon or the fish to help them fulfill their needs. The group of people that lives down the shore has a different song. They are all people, but they are different tribes.

"It is the same with us. Our languages fulfill the same purpose: keeping our children close, announcing our presence, changes of direction, rounding up fish, warning each other of danger, announcing 'Here is something good. Come now.' It is fundamental to our native identity to have these distinctions. Of course, we have an affinity with those groups near us. Our languages resemble each other, and we can understand each other very well."

Aristotle and Pliny the Elder first wrote about the clicks and squeals of dolphins nearly 2,000 years ago. Modern scientists only began their research in the 1940s when the first dolphins were captured for aquariums. In the last 50 years, there have been many acoustical studies of cetaceans. John Lilly, M.D., studied dolphin intelligence and communication from 1955 to 1968. In the late 1960s, Roger Payne and his wife, Katy, made the first recordings of humpback whales songs, starting their many years of work in this field.

Research on orca vocalization soon followed. Paul Spong began studying the sensory systems of captive orcas at the Vancouver Aquarium in 1967. He became fascinated with their vocalizations and, by 1970, was researching wild orcas in Johnstone Strait, on the north end of Vancouver Island. The 1970s also brought John Ford to the same area where he studied the orcas' calls. Ford was able to identify distinct dialects in each pod by 1979. Countless other researchers have worked with both captive and wild orcas since then to discover the intricacies of this system, yet they still cannot say whether the orca language is similar to our own in terms of words and concepts.

"Do you share some language with the transients?" I asked.

"Ah, the transients. Their language is less developed, not as complex or evolved as ours. They have a harder life with less leisure. They would like to live in a safe, snug harbor like ours, but they are more oceangoing. We are intrigued by them and would like to hear their tales of life on the outside. They are adventurers, dangerous, strong, and mysterious, but also stimulating."

"Do you use vocal communication with the transients, or is your communication with them telepathic?"

Raphaela said, "I see Granny screaming at them, *'Get out of here!'* She's shrieking and trying to stun them like fish, but their bodies are big, and they don't stun easily. The resident orcas also send out a barrier of sound to keep the transients away. I get the feeling that it's extremely stimulating and arousing to have this interaction with them. The residents get really stirred up. It's rather fun, but it's serious too."

"So there is vocal communication?" I confirmed.

"Yes."

"When you run into the transients, do you say, 'Hey, what's happening on the outer coast?' Do you chitchat with them or ask for news?"

"If an individual whale encountered a transient, there might be some opportunity for conversation of this nature. In a group, it is unlikely that this would happen. The defense and protection instincts are too strong to allow that type of interaction."

I asked, "Which do you use more, vocal or telepathic communication?"

"We speak telepathically to each other and stay in touch that way. This is our main mode of communication—mind-to-mind, telepathic. As you have seen, it is very dark in our world, and I have heard you questioning whether it is your eyes or my eyes. It's not our eyes. It is very dark. Our sight beneath the surface is better than yours, but it is not phenomenal by any means. Since we are unable to see well, we must communicate to know what the others are doing. So as I travel along, I telepathically communicate with other whales in the vicinity.

"Now, there are some situations where vocal communication is better—for example, when we want to announce something quickly to everyone. There may be vocal communication in coordinating foraging and cooperative hunting.

"Sometimes we travel silently for long periods. This does not mean that we are not communicating. Silent or telepathic communication is our primary mode, and vocalizations are used for impact and also for fun. It is very fun to hear these sounds and fun to produce them. Sound lends richness to the environment."

"How would you use sounds in hunting?"

"We often use sound in herding fishes specifically to frighten them. Fish are very vulnerable to loud noises in the environment. If we project loud enough sounds at them, they are momentarily stunned. They are shocked."

Raphaela said, "I am seeing small silvery fish about six inches long traveling in big schools. Then a loud sound makes them stop in shock. Now I'm slurping down fish that are huddled together in fear."

"Sound can shock fish so they stop swimming. This gives us an opportunity to catch and eat them. We also use sound to communicate with other pod members when we are herding fish. When many whales are together, telepathic communication is not as clear. There are so many messages traveling back and forth that the channels can get jammed."

Raphaela said, "I'm seeing a dozen whales in a circle around some fish and lots of telepathic communications zooming around."

"Correct. Yes, you are getting the idea. If we are all communicating with each other telepathically, it can get muddy. When we are feeding cooperatively and herding fish together, it is much easier to vocalize. So if I give a call to move to the left, or cut off that area, everyone can respond, and it's very clear what is needed. There is no interference from other individuals' thought processes."

I thought back to an overcast day in June when I was on the *Western Prince,* traveling north in Haro Strait with J pod. A few of the calves were frolicking in the kelp along the shore, and the adults were foraging lazily. There were about 15 boats with the whales.

I looked out into the strait and noticed a few whales fishing alone. "Let's go out and see who that is," I said to Bob, pointing toward Vancouver Island. "It looks like it might be Everett."

The *Western Prince* slowed down, let the whales and clumps of boats pass us, and then made a sharp left and took off. The whales were about a mile out and milling in a circle. The passengers gathered on the bow as I told them we were changing location to see who was out there alone.

As we approached, I could see that it was indeed Everett with his mother Tahoma. They were foraging together and seemed to be working in concert to herd fish. There were no other boats around so I asked Bob if we could shut down and put the hydrophone into the water. I wanted to see if they were vocalizing.

We dropped the device into the water and plugged it into the boat's loudspeaker system. The air immediately filled with their squeaks and squeals. There was more vocal activity than I had anticipated, and it seemed purposeful, not random. We watched as the two of them broke the surface and swam in a circle then quickly changed direction and went the other way. The entire time they foraged, they made sounds. We stayed for about 20 minutes and then left them alone.

At the time I had wondered how much of what we had heard was communication, or if the sounds were just expressions of emotion. Now, thanks to Granny, I knew that I had listened to these whales communicating about how to capture fish.

"Are there any other uses of direct sound?" I asked Granny.

"We use sound when traveling. You have seen the turn-around."

"Oh yes," Raphaela said. "I was thinking about that."

When the resident whales are in the area they tend to travel together as a group, but they may be spread out over several miles. All the whales will be heading north, and suddenly they all turn around at the same time and go south, no matter how far apart they are. I enjoy it when this happens since it's a great opportunity to explain about the whales' communication system.

"I vocalize to tell everyone to turn around. Sometimes it is easier to use a call because I do not have to consciously think of the individuals I need to contact.

"The situation determines when we communicate telepathically or with sound. We are sound-oriented creatures. There are times we could send a message to our friend saying, 'These are tasty fish. What a wonderful day!' But a shriek of joy says much more. Sound is delightful."

"Thanks, Granny," I said. "How far can you hear each other?"

"It depends upon the obstructions in our environment. We can hear great distances at sea when there are no underwater obstacles to stop the sound waves."

"I'm sorry, I know you hate these quantifying questions, but do great distances mean hundreds of miles?"

"I don't think hundreds of miles, certainly 20, occasionally 50. When we are in big deep channels with long straightaways, we can hear each other very well. When a pod moves around the corner of an island and travels another direction, the sound waves stop. Within the island areas, our hearing is not as acute because of the underwater features, canyons, and mountains, which stop and bounce the sound waves around.

"Of course, other things also influence our hearing, such as boat traffic, large ships, wind. If we are near the surface, wind can muffle our communication and make it difficult to discern, but if we are very deep it does not affect us."

"I assume that there are many different types of communication that you use within your community. You've told us about vocal and telepathic communication. Do you signal with your bodies?"

"Our bodies are capable of great expression. Our features are not as movable as yours, but we can communicate by certain subtle adjustments in our body posture."

Raphaela grinned. "They're leaping out of the water for joy."

"Granny, numerous people have played all kinds of music to whales. There are many documented stories of whales listening for hours and leaving only when the music stopped. Would you comment on this?"

"Oh yes, we love these sounds! There is a common sound in the ocean, a constant buzz or hum of the creatures that are living here and the waves on the surface. As you travel, different areas have different sounds due to the activities in that area.

"Unusual sounds are fun. It's exciting to hear an unfamiliar sound, and we enjoy it very much. Our world is sound-oriented. We map our world, communicate with each other, and travel via sound. To suddenly hear new sounds in the environment is very stimulating and of great interest to us."

"Do whales change their song or their sounds after they have heard a two-hour Frank Sinatra concert? Would that ever happen?"

"Yes," she replied. *"We may attempt to imitate certain sounds that we have heard if those sounds were pleasing. Certainly we do."*

I chuckled as I pictured Granny singing, "Strangers in the Night, exchanging glances. . . ." Oh, those transients! Get a grip, Mary, I thought.

You might assume that the whales make many of their sounds with their blowholes much as we do with our lips, but that is not the case. Most sound is produced inside their heads. Only on occasion have I heard sounds coming from the blowhole and they would most aptly be described as the classic "raspberry." I am thrilled when I get to hear these rare sounds above the surface and wish they would make them more often.

During the late 1980s, when I was a volunteer at The Marine Mammal Center in California, I had the opportunity to spend many nights monitoring cetaceans that had beached themselves. These animals were rehabilitated at Marine World Africa USA in Vallejo, and our staff and volunteers shared the responsibility with their personnel.

One foggy, cold February night, I was sitting at a pool with a coworker, watching a Dall's porpoise that had beached about four days earlier. It was suffering from an infection, and we were hoping that with antibiotics and nutritious meals it would recover and be released.

I was feeling stiff from sitting in the damp air and needed to stretch. I wandered over to the tank adjacent to our rehab area that housed four bottlenose dolphins in training for the shows. I had always loved dolphins and being this close to them was a delight. A large male circling the tank lifted one eye out of the water and looked at me as he passed by. A flood of warmth filled my heart.

I had just taken my first animal communication class about a month earlier, and it suddenly occurred to me that I could try talking to this dolphin. As he came by again, I mentally called out to him, "Hello, my name is Mary. Would you be so kind as to show me how your blowhole works?" I don't know why I asked this. It just popped into my head!

The dolphin stopped and lay motionless on the surface in front of me. He opened his blowhole and exhaled with a loud "Phoo." Then he inhaled and closed it again. My heart was beating furiously. Was this really happening? On the next exhale, he held the blowhole open and I leaned over the tank to peer inside. In the dim light, I couldn't see much. He inhaled again and remained on the surface, just two feet from me. He continued to breathe and allowed me to observe the movement of this unusual aperture until I felt I had absorbed all I could in that moment. I thanked him for his demonstration, and with a quick pump of his flukes he resumed his circular swimming.

While at Marine World, I had observed the dolphins swimming slowly in one direction going around and around their tanks. The pace was very measured and hypnotic, and I found that they always had one eye closed. If I checked on them later, often they would still be circling, but now the other eye was closed.

When I researched this perplexing habit, I found that captive dolphins rest or sleep one half of their brain at a time. Since cetaceans are conscious breathers, they cannot go to sleep as we do. They need to be alert enough to open their blowhole and breathe. If they slipped into the unconscious state we enjoy at night, they would suffocate and die. The closed eye corresponded to the part of the brain that was resting.

I had always wondered how the orcas slept. Since they are dolphins, I assumed that they would be alternating the sides of the brain, but in the wild it is very difficult to determine exactly what the whales are doing. The northern residents tend to log on the surface or just float when they are resting, but Granny's family is always on the move. There are times, though, when a southern resident pod gathers together almost touching. Their movements become highly synchronized, and they travel as one unit. Researchers believe this is when they are sleeping.

Now was my chance to ask Granny about it. "Could you address the subject of sleep?" I asked.

"Ah, sleep," she replied.

Raphaela said, "She's giving me a feeling of basking in the sun. I feel warm, and one side of my body is humming."

"Humming?" I asked.

"Yes. That's the only way I can describe it. I feel very relaxed, like I'm floating effortlessly."

I asked Granny, "How much sleep time do you require a day?"

"Less than two hours."

"Wow, that seems amazing," I replied. "We see you resting at the surface and traveling slowly together as a group. Is this when you are sleeping?"

We are resting at those times and not traveling. Our motion is just to keep our bodies on the surface, but we are not actually going anywhere. At least one pod member stays fully alert to warn us of any approaching dangers. This rest period can last up to six hours, but it's not the same as sleep.

Raphaela opened her eyes. "I just had a period where for a while my whole body was humming and now it's just the left side. I wish you could feel this; it's hard to describe."

I thought about the dolphins in the tank with one eye open and one closed. "So it switched from one side to the other?" I asked.

"Yes, it's like her consciousness goes from side to side in her body. It's fun!"

"Granny, when you are in this rest state, are you still conscious?" I inquired.

There is a distinction between this rest state that Raphaela is experiencing and true sleep. We rest one side of the body at a time. True sleep is a deeper state and we require less of it. In fact, we can go for many days without this deep sleep. It depends on our needs.

Only one or two individuals in the pod are in this deep sleep state at a time. They would be in the center of the group, and everyone else would be resting. If we rest long enough they may change places. Not all whales require the deep sleep every day.

"So, this sleep state is required to do what?"

It is a restorative and repairing time. Adults do not require it every day unless they are ill. It is cleansing for them, but calves need a few hours of sleep for their growth.

Raphaela opened her eyes. "I think it's time to quit," she murmured. "All this humming has made me very tired."

"No doubt, and you've been communicating for hours. Let's call it a day," I said.

Granny's comments about the deep sleep were intriguing. I couldn't recall any research that even hinted at such a state. Most rest or sleep research has been done with dolphins in captivity, and these animals are often alone or in very small groups. Perhaps living without pod members makes them unable to create a safe environment in which to sleep. So in a captive situation, particularly in a research environment, they might not get to experience this deep sleep. This could certainly contribute to some of their seeming madness in captivity. Sleep deprivation causes serious problems in humans. Could it be the same with cetaceans?

ALL IN THE FAMILY

The world of telepathic communication is quite small. There were few people in Friday Harbor with whom I could share this passion, so it was always stimulating and fun to be with Raphaela. We share many spiritual beliefs and practices, and when we were together she reminded me of all the tools and methods I'd learned for growth that had slipped into the background. Life seemed to take over, and I'd get so busy with the boat and stranded harbor seals that I'd forget to meditate or focus on the positive. I just didn't have time! Together, we recalled how far we'd come and how far we still had to go on the road to enlightenment. It was great to be back in Berkeley.

Raphaela was in the kitchen putting the finishing touches on the birds' breakfasts. I had banished myself to the living room because Sancho, that two ounces of feathered fury, was patrolling around the kitchen counters. I didn't want to start my day off with blood spurting from a limb.

Tootsie and I were idly looking through the TV guide. I called from the living room, "Hey, did you ever see the movie *Andre*?

"No, I don't think so. Is it good?" she shouted.

"It makes me totally nuts. It's about a harbor seal, but they used a California sea lion to play the part. That's like having Morris the cat play Lassie! No wonder people don't know the difference."

Raphaela headed upstairs with her trays of bird food. I started thinking about the vast amount of bad information about animals floating around. For instance, I remembered an incident last summer on the *Western Prince* when I heard a mom explaining what they were seeing to her youngest child.

"Look, Suzie, there's the daddy, the mommy, and their two children—just like our family."

Suzie nodded and repeated what she'd heard, "Daddy, mommy, and babies!"

I leaned over and quietly told the mom, "Actually, this is a female and her three children. One just happens to be an adult male. The two calves are her younger children."

Further down the railing was a dreamy-eyed woman wearing a T-shirt depicting humpback whales floating through a galaxy. She turned to her friend and pointed to the same large male. "Isn't he beautiful?" she sighed. "You know orcas mate for life. Isn't that romantic?"

I headed to the wheelhouse, took a deep breath, and picked up the microphone.

"The group of whales we are watching on the right is a typical family. The large female with the open saddle is Grace. She's traveling with Splash, her adult daughter; Orcan, her adult son; and Wave Walker, her young son. She has another sub-adult calf named Gaia, but I don't see her right now. She must be off somewhere with her cousins."

Many people on my trips come with their own preconceived ideas about orcas. It's natural for people to project human society onto animals, but most of the time they are so far from the truth. And the truth about orcas is so much more interesting than anything you could make up.

Resident orcas have a unique society that is very different from ours. Their pods do not consist of a nuclear family as ours ideally do, with a mother, father, and children. Instead they live in extended family groups of maternal subpods—mothers and their calves. All pod members are closely related. They are brothers, sisters, aunts, uncles, cousins, mothers, and grandmothers. However, the fathers of these individuals live in other pods.

In most species, including our own, when the children mature they leave their mothers, find mates, and start their own families. In many mammalian societies the grown males leave, while the daughters remain. However, in orca society all calves stay with their mothers throughout their entire lives. Even the adult males remain close to her side forever. In fact, the adult males are most often seen swimming and foraging right next to their moms, much more often than their sisters.

I often heard women on the boat commenting on how sweet it is that orcas stay together for life. Although they found it endearing, I wondered if they could personally engage in it for long. A complete shift in thinking and attitude would be needed to adopt this lifestyle. As a society, we would have to relinquish our reverence for individual freedom and become more group-minded. If I were going to try life as a whale, I would have to be a baleen whale. They are generally solitary but gather together on feeding grounds and for mating. I doubt I could embrace the continual day-to-day togetherness of the orcas.

I was still thinking about family when Raphaela entered the living room. "Are you ready to get started with Granny?" she asked.

"Yeah, I was just thinking about how tightly knit orca families are. Let's ask her about that aspect of her life."

"Good idea. Can I connect with her first?"

"Sure, go ahead."

"Hi, Granny. We believe that the resident orcas have very close family ties, bonds that last a lifetime. Is this true? Please elaborate as long as you'd like."

"Yes, that is true. We are very devoted to our family. We move as a unit. The group and its energy are the most important things in our system. Individuality is secondary. When we are traveling, we may be close or we may be far apart, but it is the unity of the pod that makes us one.

"Although there is space between us, we are connected energetically. As we flow up the strait, our family is encompassed in a huge energy field. We bask in the warmth of this field, and it contains us. There is hardly any separation between the members of a pod, so closely are our hearts and energies aligned."

I couldn't even imagine that level of closeness. My immediate family lives in Minnesota, Washington, Oregon, and Alaska—thousands of miles apart. Granny continued.

"There are qualities that each individual provides, certain energies they bring to the group to balance and harmonize it. However, we do not see each other in the separate way that humans

do. I see my children as an extension of myself, not merely as separate individuals.

"I mentioned before that my son, Ruffles, has a huge energy and balances the pod. He has taken on the role of what you might call an oversoul. He holds much of the pod's energy and keeps things flowing. I see him and my other children, and my children's children, all as an extension of myself. We are all one."

This is certainly different, I thought. In our society, seeing our children as an extension of ourselves would be considered a psychological problem perhaps requiring counseling. We are encouraged to let our children go in order to create their own lives.

"How do you feel about your family?" I asked.

"We have nothing but love for one another, as we love ourselves. There is no competition, and everything is done for the good of the family. We stay together forever, joined through energy, love, and harmony. We play together; we sleep together; we even have adventures together. The primary goal is for the pod to live together as one. Everything is done for the good of the group, not the individual."

This sounded like the ultimate experience of socialism. Insect colonies are known to live within a "group mind" and are not concerned with individuals. The colony is more important than any individual, but I was surprised to hear this view from such a small colony and such a large species. There are only 22 members in J pod.

I wondered how the closeness that Granny described influenced them. I had understood her to say that there were hardly any boundaries between them, so I asked, "How do you recognize one another?"

Granny explained, *"We recognize each other through the unique vibration and pattern of energy that each individual emits. Sight is not primary. There is some recognition through sound, but the majority is through that individual's vibration and energy pattern."*

"How is their vibration or pattern sensed?" I asked. "How does that information come to you?"

"It is a knowing. I feel each individual in the pod around me. I can scan the energy and see if everyone is here. Our group as a whole has an energy tone, a vibration, and if someone is missing, the vibration is off. We feel that 'Ralph's energy is not present.' Everyone's energy must be present for the pod to feel whole and complete."

I've experienced knowing that someone walked into a room without seeing them, by picking up their energy. This I could understand, but needing everyone to be present to feel whole was a concept beyond my comprehension. I have lived alone for many years and feel uncomfortable if forced to be with others for days at a time. I could never make it as an orca.

"Granny, we often see you and other adults in the company of juveniles. Can you tell us about that? Do you baby-sit only for your own grandchildren or do you baby-sit for others? What do you do when you baby-sit? How did it get started? What is . . ."

Raphaela started chuckling and waving her hands in front of her face. "Granny is cracking up," she said.

"Way too many questions, Mary. Please, just one at a time."

I laughed. "I'm sorry, Granny. This is so exciting. Please, go ahead."

She paused and took a deep breath. I could feel Granny collecting her thoughts.

"Baby-sitting. OK. I am a very good baby-sitter. I love the little ones, so I am called upon often to watch over the calves. It is beneficial for everyone. A mother obviously needs a break from the constant antics and attention that is required, making sure that her calf is safe and does not wander or get into trouble. She takes this break for her own peace of mind and to relax, as well as to forage.

"There are many advantages for everyone involved. It is very good for the calves to spend time with other pod members. It is important that the calves understand their place in the family. If we're with other pods, they also get to know their cousins. When a calf spends too much time alone with its mother, it does not get the opportunity to fully investigate other family members. So the mother passes the responsibility of the calf to someone else and the youngster

has an opportunity to get to know and spend time with another individual.

"Now, the same is also true of the baby-sitter. It is important that everyone in the pod be bonded and intimately know every pod member. How can the adults understand the youngsters without spending time with them? So, it benefits everyone. Everyone gains from the baby-sitting experience."

"Granny, when you are baby-sitting, do you teach a youngster, or do you just have fun and interact socially?"

"It depends. There is no agenda. We see what is happening. It may be that we are foraging or playing, and suddenly we meet K pod. There is great joy. I must stay with my responsibility for the calf. In such a situation there might be great teachings, great learnings that come about through our interactions. Whatever occurs determines our activities. My granddaughter Samish would not say, 'Can you baby-sit today and teach Riptide about octopus?' It's not like that. We experience whatever happens."

I had heard this theme before. "Is this another example of how whales live in the moment?"

"Yes, this is correct."

"You mentioned that calves need to learn about their place in the pod and go through an important socialization process in their first few years. Could you please tell us about social roles within the pod?"

"This is a very interesting subject. First, the young are vulnerable, so we take great care of them. We are extremely tolerant and do not discipline them; however, they must be respectful of their elders.

"We do not have private property or possessions, so this eliminates many conflicts. Of course, we have our territory and feeding grounds, but if we are not here it is acceptable for others to come in.

"Both males and females must learn their social roles, who they are and their sexuality, but overall their lives are much the same. Feeding behavior and herding of fish are all-important, and lessons begin early."

Raphaela commented, "Now she's showing me something about positioning, some precise instructions. I see the whales in a circle, and boy, this is a very large circle. Most of them are facing the middle where they have herded some fish. Calves go into the circle but hover directly beneath their mothers.

"Now the circle is changing. It's not a perfect geometrical shape and at one end fish are streaming out. One whale is trying to use its bulk to block them. It's convenient to feed this way because it takes less energy than chasing after schools of fish. I also see that it's near the shore."

"This is a very important skill for the young to learn."

Feeding is probably the most important, I thought. The calves learn through observation before they are physically able to participate in herding and foraging. I asked Granny to tell us more about social roles.

"We have a simple society, and because we are not hierarchical, we live in equality. The young must learn to be deferential to their elders, although we are very tolerant and encourage and enjoy play. We never reject the youngsters, no matter how bumptious their play is. As you have seen, I enjoy the male youngsters."

Granny was referring to several incidents over the past six years where she was observed baby-sitting for young males. Often these calves proudly displayed their penises and engaged in sex play in her company. Several naturalists and whale-watch captains have remarked about this activity to me.

"Now, it is important for children to learn who their family is. They need to distinguish the pods and must know their playmates and cousins. They need to learn the language and the songs, and they begin doing this in a very natural way at an early age. Their mothers sing to them over and over and listen to their answers."

It's a little like humans singing the alphabet, I thought.

"By the age of three, an orca calf is very proficient in many songs. The songs can mean: Where are you? I am lost. What direction are we going? Where is my playmate? Where is my mother? These objects are interesting.

"It is at this age that they also become very proficient with echolocation. All whales are born with this capacity, but interpreting the data, the feedback, takes incredible refinement and discrimination. If a sound wave comes back to you and you think it's a certain distance, but then it turns out to be more or less, you constantly refine your sense. This is the process the calves go through. They are their own school."

"She is giving me the feeling that rather than getting instruction, the calves instruct themselves through experience."

"So they have an experience and analyze it?" I asked.

"Right, and make adjustments."

"Granny, human children often ask questions like 'What makes waves? What is the moon?' Do calves ask questions about the physical universe and how it came into being? If so, how are those questions addressed?"

"Yes, the youngsters are brimming with questions. I love that they are so curious and full of wonder and light. In my experience our calves want to know how things work, not where they came from. They are very concerned with things they see in the water. They are extremely playful and much of their energy goes into finding things to investigate and play with or amuse themselves. Most things are very entertaining, and they spend considerable energy understanding how things work and how to take care of themselves.

"In our society, the youngsters need to care for themselves at a much earlier age than in yours. Our calves are nursed for only one year or two, and by then must know how to feed themselves. They must keep up with the pod and develop their abilities to echolocate and navigate. Calves are not as dependent upon their families as human children are, so there is much for them to learn in a very short period of time.

"They do not wonder where the sea came from, but learning how to be in the sea and how to catch fish engrosses them. There is also much they need to comprehend about living within the family and our social interactions with other pods.

"So the calves do not ask questions like 'How deep is the sea? How high is the sky?' They are curious about the sky and things

they see above the surface; however, they are much more concerned in the early years with learning how to survive and how to understand their world more completely.

"Questions of grand significance and pondering greater things come later in life. Once we are established within our lives, things are working well, and we know our place in society, then thoughts of this nature may arise. We can give them some time and energy because we have mastered the skills required to live our lives successfully."

I began to think about the bigger picture, how each individual fits into its pod and also into the larger community. J, K, and L pods are so tightly intertwined. There appears to be great joy when they come together, expressed by aerial displays and excited play. This reminded me of something that I had always wanted to know more about. I said, "Granny, tell us about the greeting ceremony."

I watched Raphaela's face change. Her eyes were still closed but her face tensed up, as if she were struggling to see something in the distance or to understand what she was seeing. Then she spoke.

"It looks like a football field with whales lined up on each side, rather regimented looking. There are some babies in the background who are not taking part. It has a certain dignity and solemnity, but also an element of danger."

"This is a formal way of acknowledging other whales who have a right to be in our waters. This formality is necessary to disarm the natural tendency to defend."

"I don't understand this. Their actions seem like part of a ritual. There is an element of confrontation that they have transformed into this greeting ceremony. This allows them to mingle.

"After they line up, I see uproar. I see mayhem! Well, not mayhem, but enthusiastic shouts and rushing into the middle ground and across each other. Then they come tearing back. It's uproarious, quite exciting and exuberant with a little element of danger, which makes it really spicy."

Wow! Goose bumps crawled over my body. Once more I was in awe of the accuracy of Raphaela's communication. I knew she had never seen a greeting ceremony and perhaps had never even heard of this ritual. But I didn't understand one of her comments, and I found it odd. "Danger?" I asked. "I always thought that this was a wonderful, joyous greeting. What is the danger?"

Granny replied, *"There is an element of danger here. We have to be sure they are our friends, that they have a right to be here and are not intruders. Of course, we are enthusiastic! Of course, we are joyous! But we are also vigilant. The greeting ceremony comes from the same place that a protection action would spring from if it were necessary. So in our greeting ceremony, if they were strangers, we would be prepared for an attack, and we would attack with the same vigor."*

I was confused. "I thought that you can hear the vocalizations and chatter of whales quite some distance as they travel. Don't you know who these whales are long before you encounter them?"

"Well, yes, but there is still a lot of drama involved with the visual contact. Also, the tone that a pod makes can change over time. If we have not encountered them for a period, there may be subtle shifts that would be of great interest to us and may tell us something about their wanderings and doings. Also, if they have new family members their tone will change. Yes, when we meet them the anticipation is 'It's our beloved cousins,' but we could be wrong!"

"She's laughing," Raphaela said. "I think it's a bit of a game."

My thoughts exactly. It seemed like the remnants of an ancient ritual that is no longer necessary, but is still part of the play.

Granny added, *"It is so much more exciting if there is this little element of danger and spiciness. It makes the joy even more forceful, strong, and vigorous. Contrast, contrast is all, my daughters."*

Sara and James Heimlich-Boran mention the greeting ceremony in their book, which, like Mike Bigg's book, is also called *Killer Whales*. "Greeting ceremonies are unique to southern [resident] killer whales. When reunited after a separation of a day or more, each pod forms a row, and hovers at the surface facing the other pod. They then swarm into each other, each individual rubbing and rolling against the others . . . like social ceremonies in wild dogs and elephants, [it] appears to reaffirm social bonds."

I asked Granny if the Heimlich-Boran view was right—that this ceremony was peculiar to her community. *"The greeting ceremony is not unique to our pods, although we have refined it to a high state. Other whales do it in a more diffuse way with less drama. This is a ceremony of whales."*

Raphaela remarked that greeting ceremonies and attacks seemed to have almost the same biological charge and are very explosive.

"That's very interesting," I said. "I've never seen an attack and have only been privileged to see a greeting ceremony once. It is electrifying and doesn't happen very often. I am amazed at the detail you gave me. You described it perfectly! Let me tell you about the one that I saw."

The greeting ceremony that I witnessed occurred at Turn Point on Stuart Island. It was the summer of 1994, and I was traveling north in the *Western Prince* with K pod. A few whales had slowed to play in the kelp beds near the Turn Point lighthouse. Lea and her calf, Lobo, were tail-slapping and causing quite a commotion. Another female cartwheeled in the kelp, splashing water onto the rocks. There was an air of joviality in the water and onboard.

As we rounded the point with a few females and calves, a young male suddenly bounded in front of us. "Who was that?" I asked Captain Bob.

"Beats me," he said. "I didn't get a good look at him." I knew there weren't any subadult males in K pod, so I scanned the surface, hoping the stranger would reappear. Within seconds, he burst from the water practically leaping over one of the females.

"It's Everett," I shouted. "What's he doing here? I haven't seen any J pod whales today."

My attention was drawn to the shoreline just below the lighthouse, and I could not believe what I saw. J pod was around the corner, tucked in along the cliff in a straight line as if they were waiting in ambush for the Ks. You could almost hear the whales chuckling to themselves as their unsuspecting relatives approached, but now the surprise was over. Everett's teenage enthusiasm had overcome him, and he had darted out to greet them.

J pod stayed in tight formation along the shore while K pod gathered and milled around. Then every K pod whale dove and stayed beneath the surface for about five minutes. When they reappeared they were lined up facing J pod.

Although I had never seen a greeting ceremony, I had read about them and heard many stories from researchers, captains, and other naturalists. It was a very special event.

I whispered into the microphone like an announcer at a golf tournament just before the putt. "We are about to see a greeting ceremony. This is the first one I have ever witnessed." Everyone onboard held his or her breath.

The whales faced each other for a few minutes floating on the surface. The air was filled with a sense of anticipation, as close to 40 whales lay silently, unmoving. Then suddenly they swam forward at high speed. The lines met; whales twisted and turned, rolling across each other. Black and white flashed in every direction, water flying. Whales leapt and rubbed in a mass of confusion. It was impossible to identify anyone in the white water. Later, I wished we'd had a hydrophone in the water to capture their underwater squeaks and squeals. The sounds must have been magnificent.

The whales played intensely for about ten minutes and then slowly started to travel north again. The two pods were now intermingled and small groups had formed. A few were still playing, but most had resumed their journey to Vancouver. We didn't follow them, but watched as their fins grew smaller in the distance.

I knew that I had just observed something that few people ever experience. I thanked the whales and the gods, and we headed back to port.

As I finished my story, I could see Raphaela's brown eyes were wide with excitement. "Wow, that's exactly what I saw earlier," she said. "I'd sure like to see a greeting ceremony in person someday."

"It was one of the most spectacular things I've ever seen. Hey, I'm starving. Why don't we break for lunch?" I said.

Over lunch we discussed the information we'd gotten in the morning. Most of what Granny had said about their lives was in line with what scientists believed, although we had acquired information about subjects that researchers can't explore. Moreover, Granny had refuted the idea that greeting ceremonies were unique to her community. We had also been able to discover the kinds of questions the calves ask and how individuals are viewed within the pod—subjects that cannot be examined within the context of current scientific investigation.

Raphaela was touched by the whales' devotion to their families, but I couldn't fathom their profound family bond. I was more astounded at her description of a greeting ceremony. As we cleaned up our lunch dishes, we decided to continue interviewing Granny about social relationships, but I would take over as communicator.

FRIEND OR FOE

I settled myself into the large beige chair in Raphaela's living room and quietly tuned in to Granny. Her immediate, hearty welcome was calming and reassuring. I was enveloped by her warm presence and felt my consciousness sink into the watery depths of her world. My breathing deepened, and my heart rate slowed.

Raphaela began, "Granny, we would like to ask you some more questions about social relationships within the pod and the community. Could you tell us about friendships?"

"Yes, certain whales have an affinity with each other. They enjoy each other's company, much like you and Mary. They are on the same wavelength and have the same concerns. Among my contemporaries, I have two such friends."

I wanted to know who these friends were. "Give me a minute," I said. "Let me see if I can get names." I immediately got a picture of Lummi, the leader of K pod. Scientists think that she is one year older than Granny and the oldest whale in the whole community. That made perfect sense to me. J and K pods travel together frequently.

I tried to see who the other whale was, but the picture wasn't clear. "I am seeing a whale who has an A name that is in her seventies. Granny is telling me that she is the leader of L pod, but I'm not sure who this is."

"Granny, what is your relationship with her?" Raphaela asked.

"We are on the same wavelength. We have the same duties. We share the same concerns. She has the same role in her tribe that I have with J pod."

I opened my eyes. "I'm getting that this whale's number is 3 or 4, but I don't know L pod that well. Let me stop a minute and see if I can find her in the ID book."

Raphaela dug around through the books on the coffee table and found the latest edition of *Killer Whales*, by Ford, Ellis, and

Balcomb. I scanned the photographs, looking for the whale I had seen.

L3, Oriana, is a female estimated to have been born in 1946. L4, Sonar, is also a female thought to have been born in 1949, but neither of them seemed quite right when I looked at their pictures. L pod has 49 members, so it took a while to find the oldest whale. It's L25, Ocean Sun, born in 1928, but when I looked at L12, born in 1933, I knew it was her. L12's name is Alexis.

"This is her," I said to Raphaela. "According to this book she's not the oldest, but these birth dates are estimates and could be wrong."

I could feel Granny tugging gently at my consciousness. I tuned back in to her. *"She is the oldest member of L pod. I knew other older whales in that group who are now departed. You could consider her a spiritual sister. I call her Anileeta."*

I got a strong sense of wisdom and grace about this whale.

"Although we do not see each other all that frequently, we stay in touch and share our concerns. She is aware of the work I am doing with you and supports it. She is very interested and you might want to talk to her. She is a member of the council."

Raphaela gasped a bit and her reaction made me open my eyes. She looked at me as if to say, "Now what?" I shrugged and went back to Granny.

"What is the council?" Raphaela asked.

"The council is a group of decision makers and information sharers. There are six in our present council. Anileeta, Lummi, myself and three more northerly whales."

I received an image of three very distinct circles moving outward. I interpreted this as the southern resident community, the northern resident community, and the Alaskan resident community.

"We share information about the environment and other things of importance within our areas. Our alliance has been in place for more than 50 years."

"Can you tell me more about your friendships?"

"My primary social contacts or friends are within my pod, even though I have close relationships with council members."

I got the feeling that establishing friendships in orca society is very different from what we experience. They may even be unnecessary. The bond among pod members surpasses our definition of friendship. Orcas are friendly and familiar with other whales and may even have close associations, but are mainly focused on their immediate family and pod.

Raphaela asked, "Are you most often friends with animals of your own gender?"

"Yes, there are simply more females. This is a matriarchal society. The males bring something very special and unique, but even their relationships are primarily with females. Males do enjoy playing with each other."

"Is there a custom of reverence for the older whales in a community, and are they given special treatment?"

"No and no. Although it is a pleasure for me to be recognized by you."

I smiled. I do have reverence for Granny. Each spring I worry that when the *Western Prince* goes out and for the first time encounters J pod, Granny will not be there. I really didn't want to think about Granny dying. I would miss her so much, and I doubt that Ruffles would stick around for long. He is very bonded to his mother. J pod just wouldn't be the same without them.

"What happens when a leader dies?" Raphaela asked.

"It is a loss when a leader with age and experience goes, but she has had many years to impart her wisdom and her ways to her daughters. My leaving will not imperil my pod."

"Please don't leave anytime soon."

"I will see what I can do."

This conversation about leadership reminded me of a day back in September when Raphaela was visiting. We were out on the *Western Prince*, and both J and K pods were spread out over about a two-mile area, heading east in the Strait of Juan de Fuca off the south end of San Juan Island. She had come out to communicate with Granny while I was working, and the dear old girl had come right over to the boat to say "Hi" to her. She swam alongside for about three minutes, then dove down. The next time Granny surfaced, she was back with her family.

High-speed travel

The whales continued east for about ten minutes when suddenly they all turned and headed west. I carefully searched out whales in every direction and sure enough, they had all turned as well.

"What we have just seen is a turnaround," I said on the microphone. "This is a great example of how orca communication works. The pod leader has decided that it is time to go back the other way, and when she puts that call out, everyone obeys."

It's quite dramatic to see 40 whales turn at once and Raphaela was really excited. "I want to ask Granny about this," she said, jumping up and down a bit.

"Go for it," I replied.

She sat down and quieted herself, holding a little dictation recorder to her mouth. "Granny, how is the decision to turn around made?" she said into the device. There was a pause, and then Granny spoke.

"Ninety percent of the time I make the decision, but other whales can have input. A female might tell me that her calf is tired or wants to float in the current, so I will decide to make the going

easier. That is what just happened. Sometimes, of course, it's dictated by where the fish are."

I couldn't stand it. I had to ask a question too. "What about when two pods are present?"

"We defer to one another. If the leader of K pod had decided to turn, we would have honored that, as they honored our turnaround."

As we were speaking to Granny, I noticed that the whales had slowed down so I asked her why.

"We have had plenty of fish to eat today, so we can afford to travel more leisurely and accommodate our tired calf."

This was one of the few times we interviewed Granny on the water. I wish that it had been possible for us to engage this way more often, but the simple truth was that when I was on the water, I was busy with the passengers. There was little time for me to speak to Granny in this way, although I always greeted her telepathically as well as verbally. Once in a while I did sneak in a question or two, but that was unusual.

Raphaela's voice pulled me back to her living room. "Do whales have particular jobs within the pod?"

"When we are encircling fish, each whale has a temporary job to maintain its position in the line."

"Right. But there are not whales that fish, and whales that teach the young?"

"No. We all do everything."

Something was nagging at me. So far, Granny had painted a picture of a peaceful and loving existence, yet I knew from experience that life is rarely so idyllic. Problems and concerns always arise. Maybe we weren't asking the right questions. Was there a darker side that we were missing? "Can I ask a question here?"

"Sure, go ahead."

"Are there ever disagreements or arguments within the pod?" I asked.

"Of course, there are. Where there is life there is conflict. We are very good at minimizing discontents and disagreements. However, just as in your society, we are not always on the same

wavelength. Whales have personalities, and where there are person-
alities, conflicts can exist."

"She's showing me something about mating behavior," I said.

"For example, two females in a pod may desire the attentions
of one male in another pod. Because meetings and matings are not
all that frequent, there may be disagreement about who will enjoy
his favors. There may also be competition and vying for his atten-
tion. The female who is left out might be angry, jealous, and bitter.
As she matures, she will become more philosophical, but in such a
situation these two females may avoid each other. Disagreements
are a part of life, but only a small part."

"Are disagreements usually settled between the parties or do
they have to go to someone like you or the council to settle their
differences?" Raphaela questioned.

"A disagreement of this nature would be worked out between
them or by simple distance. This does not require the attention of
the council."

"Granny, is there ever violence within your community?"

"Yes, there can be. There have been some notable examples.
When this occurs, it is almost irreconcilable. Fortunately it is
extremely rare. I will tell you of an episode that occurred, although
not in my lifetime."

I was surprised by the image that appeared. It didn't make
sense to me from the experience that I've had with these animals.
"I don't understand this. I am seeing two male whales fighting, and
it's bloody."

"Granny, were these whales pod members or from different
pods?" she asked.

"They were in the same pod. This is why it is rare to have
many breeding bulls in a pod. This kind of aggression is a great dan-
ger."

"Did this scene that you are showing Mary happen at a time
when there were too many males in a pod and disagreements
broke out?"

"I'm getting pictures," I said. "I am trying to see the origin of
this fight, but I can't get it. There was some significant damage,

but no one died. Afterward, one of these whales was always, always on the periphery. He was never really completely integrated into the pod again and was always trailing in the background. I'm sorry, that's all I can get."

"That's okay," Raphaela said. "So, Granny, in your lifetime you have not experienced this level of violence within your own pod?"

"*That is correct.*"

"And what about violence between your pod and K or L pod?"

"*No, this would not occur. This would be extremely rare, especially not at our present numbers. Just as in human society, as our numbers rise, the danger of conflict increases. This is not a problem at the present time.*"

"Granny, in the course of our talks, you have mentioned boundaries several times. I know it is difficult to explain in my terms, but is there any way you can tell us where your boundaries are?"

"Oh boy," I said with a sigh. "I don't have a clue what I'm seeing. She shows me water, and then a mile-wide swath of water that looks as if it were a different color."

"Water coming out of a river maybe?" she speculated.

"Something like that. I cannot tell you why it's different there, but it is a boundary of some sort."

"*Our element is water. Water flows; it comes and goes. We cannot own the water. We go into this area that I am showing you, and we go even farther. Other whales may also come in. Boundary is defined more by where we are.*

"*We have our home waters, which you, Mary, are very well aware of; however, it is less formalized than you might imagine. An analogy might be air. How can you own the air? You cannot. What you breathe in and out this minute may be breathed in and out by another very soon. Our boundaries are more flexible than you believe, a lot less rigid.*"

"Now I am seeing this wide swath of water again. She is showing me that if there are whales on the other side, then J pod may move back and not choose to encounter the whales that are there. I think she is revealing a flexible boundary. I'm starting to get it."

"How are these boundaries determined?" Raphaela asked.

"Occupation. Occupying."

"Oh, I see. So if it becomes known in the community that certain whales travel these waters, then there is respect for that territory from the others?"

"The answer to your question is very simple. We are born here! We are born here! If our population ever reached such numbers that we would need more room, we would expand. This will probably never happen. It is so unlikely. This is a very ample homeland."

"So these are traditional areas that have been established for a very long time."

"Exactly. We stay where we are born and learn the landmarks of our family."

I exhaled loudly. "Wow. Now she's showing me a scale of landmarks that is inconceivably huge. I think these landmarks are not for orcas, but for baleen whales that are much more solitary. They seem so big that the continents would be landmarks to them. Wow. I cannot really describe what I am seeing. I see a vast body that does not appear to have a territory. It seems like it could travel anywhere. I think this is another type of whale. Granny, why are you showing me this?"

"Because you are interested in territory. This is another concept or way of territory. These whales are singular and rarely meet, but know vast spaces."

"These are baleen whales?" I confirmed.

"Yes."

"Thanks, Granny," Raphaela said. "I'd like to explore the topic of celebrations with you. In human society, we have celebrations at various landmarks in life or at certain times of the year. For example, in the fall when our gardens are harvested we celebrate Thanksgiving. At this feast we thank nature for her bounty and for the food that we are going to eat this winter. We also celebrate each passing year of our life with a birthday celebration.

These are two examples of human celebrations. Do whales have such festivities?"

"Yes, we do. We celebrate the coming of the salmon. The season when the salmon arrive and head to the rivers is a time of great celebration for us. This is a meeting time when we gather in the islands and greet each other after our long separation. It is a time of great bounty and abundance when we feed together. The children get acquainted with their cousins and play with others outside their immediate family. It is a time for mating. This is a time of great joy when we come together to celebrate the great bounty of the fish. It is our favorite time of the year."

The feeling I got from Granny reminded me of Christmas. It's a celebration and gathering of friends and family, feasting and parties—a time of great joy.

"We do not celebrate birthdays. Our personal celebrations signify passage into a new phase. First, there is passing from a juvenile into independence, being more grown up. Then a progression into sexual maturity. Later, there are celebrations as you shift into older years, such as for females when they become post-reproductive. So our celebrations revolve around passages from one phase of life into the next. It is a celebration of the completion or successes of the last phase and looking forward to a new part of your life."

"What happens in these celebrations?"

"If we are celebrating the passage of a female into maturity, there will be much joy and play within the pod. That individual is given recognition. We express our appreciation for her and everything that she has learned and contributed to the family."

"It's recognition," I added. "They show honor or respect to this individual for having attained this level and for now moving on to the next phase."

"What a lovely custom," Raphaela noted. "Are there rules of conduct within the pod?"

"Mary, you will understand this better than Raphaela. You are more conversant with whale society. Rules of conduct are biologically based. They are for the purpose of survival, prolonging our

existence, and keeping us safe. They are based on biological imperatives.

"For example, when herding fish, we do not all rush in and scatter them. This is not how things are done. Forbearance, tolerance, and patience are required. One whale, sometimes two at the most, goes in and eats and then returns to the circle. Then one or two more go in. Calves are taught that these are the rules. You cannot indulge in greediness."

"So greediness is a rule of conduct?" Raphaela asked.

I broke into laughter. Granny said, *"The avoidance of greediness!"*

"Oh, of course. I'm sorry, Granny. It's getting late. I think we'd better call it day. Thank you so much for talking to us today."

"You are most welcome, my dear. I enjoy answering your questions and will be available whenever you call."

TRANSIENTS, OH MY!

I stepped out of the ferry terminal onto the dock just as the walk-on passengers disembarked the ferry *Elwha*. The cold January wind whipped through my hair. There had been a bit of snow last week, but it was gone now, and I was thankful the sun was shining today.

I spotted Raphaela trudging up the gangplank with a large bag in each hand, her head bent against the wind. How glad I was to see her again! We hadn't been together since my last trip to Berkeley, although we had talked frequently over the holidays. I ran to help her.

"Mary! It's great to see you!" She set her bags down and gave me a hug.

"It's wonderful to see you too!" I replied. "How was your trip?"

She rolled her eyes. "Oh God, you know. It takes *forever* to get here. I don't know why you insist on living out here in the boonies."

I laughed. "The whales don't range very far inland, you know."

"Oh, all right. If it's for the *whales*, I'll just have to deal with it." Her brown eyes twinkled. "Let's go," she said. "I'm freezing!"

My house was warm and toasty when we arrived. My cats, Lester and Franny, were sound asleep, stretched their full lengths next to the wood stove. Raphaela sat down on the floor and began rubbing their long bellies. "Miss Fran and Mr. Lester, it's so good to see you again," she murmured. They both stretched out even further to make it easier for her to stroke every bit of them.

I made some tea, and we settled down at the table with a plate of chocolate chip cookies. There were so many things to catch up on: Raphaela's animals, new books, movies, tapes, workshops, friends. Before we knew it, it was dark.

I pulled the last of the pesto I had made during the summer out of the freezer and threw together a nice salad. We spent the evening talking, laughing, and eating—about the only things to do in Friday Harbor in January. We talked far into the night, even after the lights were out and we were tucked into our beds.

The next morning it was overcast and cold. After meditation and breakfast, we cleared the table and brought out the tape recorder. "Can I communicate with Granny first?" Raphaela asked.

"Sure, go ahead," I replied. "Is there anything special you want me to ask her?"

"No, ask what you like. I just want to be in her presence." She closed her eyes to center herself. After a minute she said, "God, I love this whale. She's right here, so eager to talk to us."

"Good morning, Granny," I said. "Thank you for speaking to us again."

"You are so very welcome. I enjoy our conversations and look forward to them."

"How are you doing?" I asked.

"I am fine, very good, in fact."

"I'm glad to hear that. Where are you right now?"

"We are out in the Pacific and are ready for some sociability."

"Where are the Ks and Ls?" I asked.

"I don't know," she replied, *"but I would not mind meeting up with a group of what you call transients."*

That got my full attention. I had assumed she wanted to socialize with residents, not transients! This was very strange. Current research indicates that residents and transients rarely interact. Certainly there is no scientific evidence that these two groups mingle. "Why would you want to meet some transients?" I asked.

"We do not know them well and find it very stimulating to be around less familiar whales."

"Raphaela, what are you getting here? I'm confused. Is Granny saying that they hang out with the transients?"

She sighed. "Yes, to some extent. Granny is showing me an interaction with them. I see some huffing and puffing going on, and it looks really tentative. The transients are a little threatening and are bullying and nudging the resident whales, but then the scene becomes more peaceful. All the whales are swimming together. The transients can be aggressive to resident calves, so protecting the calves is their big concern, but Granny is definitely saying that they like the excitement and the interaction. I'm getting that this interaction is sexually provocative. It stirs them up and gets them ready for . . ."

I interrupted her. "Do you see them mating with the transients?"

"I don't see that, but it does seem stimulating."

I remembered that Granny once said that on occasion mating could occur between a resident and transient. I was totally surprised at the time because scientists don't think that the two groups interbreed. Now she was also saying that they actually enjoy encounters with the transients. It seemed very odd. I questioned whether we were getting the information correctly. I felt that Granny's statements were in conflict with each other, and coping with inconsistencies is not one of my strong points. I hoped that further probing would clarify her position.

I had once heard about a violent event that occurred between J pod and some transients, and I decided to ask Granny about it. "There was an incident about three years ago near Nanaimo on Vancouver Island that was observed by Canadian researcher Graeme Ellis. He got the impression that J pod was beating up on some members of O pod, a transient group. The Js were trying to ram the transients onto shore. It looked like a very aggressive encounter. A ferry pulling out broke it up, and all the whales scattered. Do you remember this incident? What was that about?"

"*I do remember. The transients were in our territory. They are not allowed in this area and needed to be disciplined. We would have killed them if we could, but it rarely comes to that. They would have fled.*"

Raphaela gasped and opened her eyes. "She's serious. I think they would have killed them. It's so hard to hear this. Peace and love just flew out the window."

I, too, was shocked. This was a very different Granny from the one we knew. "Let's stay with this for a few minutes." I was curious about their territories and how they were enforced. She nodded and closed her eyes again.

"So are there certain areas where the transients have agreed not to be?"

"Well, it's not that clear-cut. We know that other whales come and go in our area. If we are not here, it does not matter. But that time in Nanaimo, the transients knew we were coming. They had plenty of opportunity to leave, but chose not to. They provoked the situation by not leaving. They can hear our noises just as clearly as our pod can hear theirs, yet they chose not to leave.

"However, it should be said in their defense that they are less inured to people noises than we are and may have been confused about our location. Still, they should have known. We have told them, 'Do not come farther than here, and do not eat more than 10 percent.' Do you understand?"

"Not really," I replied. "We believe that you and the transients eat different things. Transients eat harbor seals and porpoises in this area and you residents mainly eat fish. Why do you need an agreement from them to eat only 10 percent?"

"It is true that the major ingredients in our respective diets are different. That is a function of scarcity and the changing times. This is an agreement that was made to preserve resources. Transients do eat fish, but there is not too much danger that they could take more than 10 percent, as we keep them out of this area.

"In the open ocean it is more difficult to collect or herd fish than it is in our more enclosed area. The transients have to work harder to catch them than we do. You might say that their lives are harder, and they are wilder."

Granny's defense of the transients sounded more like the peaceful, loving whale we knew. I was fascinated to learn that transients do eat fish, and about the uncannily precise agreement that they were restricted to ten percent of the catch in the residents' area. I wanted to know more about J pod's interactions with them. "Granny, do you recall any other incidents of violence with transients?"

"Well, we are always exercising vigilance to keep them out of our area. There are always skirmishes."

Skirmishes. I had heard the word in my mind before Raphaela said it. "There are always skirmishes, but do they ever result in bloodshed?" I asked.

This time Raphaela answered directly, instead of speaking for Granny. "Yes, she is showing me a picture of one whale ramming another. I do not see blood in the water, but she may be referring to internal bleeding."

"Is there any reason resident orcas would be violent toward other species, other than pursuing them as food? Are there perhaps disagreements with octopus or porpoises?"

Again Raphaela answered, "Granny is showing me a group of orcas chasing dolphins. They have a high-spirited way of tossing these dolphins around that reminds me of a cat with a mouse. There is a bloodthirsty quality here as well."

"I have seen transients do that," I commented, "but not residents. Granny, do the residents really fling dolphins into the air?"

"Yes, we do, but it is rare. I know this looks quite heartless to you. It's not even necessarily for feeding. There may be a recklessness, a hunger for pursuit, that comes over us."

"I feel as if they take leave of their senses. It seems like they are out of control," I said.

Raphaela looked distressed. "I'm getting that, too. I keep looking for an analogy in human life about what happens to us during battles. All I can think of is bloodlust, but that's so judgmental. I don't want to pursue this any further, okay?"

I was very interested in learning about the predatory aspect of orcas and didn't really want to stop. I was often struck by the different reactions Raphaela and I had to certain situations and information. She had become upset by the image of whales tossing dolphins around, feeling compassion for the prey and not wanting to see their demise. I, on the other hand, tend to understand the predator's point of view. I'm more apt to marvel at their precision in the kill than worry about the prey. My analytical, scientific way of looking at things often shields me from the emotional responses that tear her heart open.

I deferred to Raphaela's request and suggested we take a break.

A cup of tea and some soothing kitty energy from Franny restored her peace. We decided to go on, and I asked if she wanted me to take over as communicator.

"No, I'll continue until lunch, and then you can take over this afternoon. Okay?"

"Perfect," I said. "I'm ready to go when you are."

She closed her eyes and went inside. A small smile began to form at the corners of her mouth and her facial muscles relaxed. I knew she had linked up with Granny. "Go ahead," she said.

I decided to broach a less threatening topic. "Granny, in the past few months, have you visited the northern residents?"

"Yes."

"What interactions did you have with them?"

Raphaela said, "She is showing me that they met a pod that has 20-some whales in it. They are all participating in a greeting ceremony. It is not the 'football field lineup' that I saw before, but there is a lot of uproar, tail-slapping, and excitement. The water is just boiling with bodies. It looks as if some mating might have happened."

I, too, was getting the impression that they were mating.

"It was very exciting. Very exciting. Mary wants to know what pod this was," Granny said.

"That's right, Granny, I do. Do you know?"

Raphaela's closed eyes were squinting. "Is there an R pod?" she asked.

"Yes, R pod is a northern resident group. Let me check the book and see how many are in that family." I pulled out the "bible"—*Killer Whales* by Ford, Ellis, and Balcomb. As of 1994, R pod had a total of 23 individuals. They could easily be the group she described.

"How many days did you spend up there with these whales?"

Raphaela commented, "It looks as if they were together for three or four days."

"How is the northern community faring? What news do you bring from the north?" I asked.

"They have had a birth."

"It looks like a boy," she said. "I'm not sure how I'm getting this information—not visually. It seems like he is a few months old."

"The whole uproar between the pods when we met almost took the new calf's breath away. His mom had to shelter him and keep him to the side. When things settled down, he was properly introduced to everyone. We are very, very glad to have this new member. That is their biggest news."

Ten years ago scientists thought that the northern and southern residents had a dividing line around the middle of Vancouver Island that they rarely crossed. Observations in recent years have proven this wrong, yet we don't know how much the two groups socialize with each other. Maybe Granny could give us some insight.

"Granny, how many times per year do you visit the northern residents?"

"Well, we like to travel there mostly in the winter. It varies. I would say four, possibly six times each year our travels take us there."

I also decided to ask Granny what she knew about the offshores. "Do you know the orcas that live offshore and rarely come into our waters?"

"There are numerous families of orcas offshore. Do we know them? As individuals, no, but of course we know of their existence. We know that they live there, just as you know that there are people in New York. When we are in these cold, deep waters far offshore, we still have a consciousness of the landmasses and their distance from us. In the same way, we are aware of the offshore

whales. We do not interfere with them, but they are not always around."

I wanted to be sure I understood what Granny was saying. "So you do not interact with the offshore orcas?"

"We try to avoid them as the transients here try to avoid us. We would not want to be caught in their waters. That could be very dangerous."

"There was a time about four years ago when a group of about 70 of these whales were in your territory. They came in the Strait of Juan de Fuca to Victoria. You weren't around that day, but I was wondering if you knew they had come into this area."

"I do not recall this event."

I paused for a minute and thought about the other creatures in the ocean, wondering if Granny interacted with them. "Granny, do you communicate with other species? How do you relate to them?"

"We are aware of their movements, their purposes, their intentions, and their activities, and they are aware of ours. It is much the same as you on the land. Do you not talk to and have relations with birds? Of course, you do. You observe their activities, and they observe yours. This is a form of communication. This is similar to our relationship with all the denizens of our world, the sea."

"Granny, what are your relations with the porpoises of this area?"

"We regard the porpoises as our brothers and sisters. They are whales like us. We understand their ways, and they understand ours. We are sometimes required to dine on them, although they can avoid us if they do not wish to offer their bodies. They are our neighbors. That is our relationship."

"Speaking of porpoises, I want to ask you about an unusual animal that's been seen in the islands. It's been suggested by scientists that it is a cross between a Dall's and a harbor porpoise. Do you have any information or knowledge about this?"

"Yes, I know exactly what you are talking about. It is a cross between those two types. There are perhaps six that travel within

your area. They are quite beautiful little creatures. It is very inter-esting to see something different appear."

"Why are they interbreeding?"

"I do not believe that it happens often. Perhaps it may be a very small number, a few individuals who are engaging in this cross sex. I do not think that it is widespread within their community."

When Granny gave me this answer, it was the first confirmation that the unusual animals we had observed from the *Western Prince* were indeed hybrids of Dall's and harbor porpoises. Since this conversation, DNA testing has confirmed it as well. I am always relieved when Granny's statements correspond with science. It reduces the conflict I feel between my naturalist self and my animal communicator persona.

"Granny, do resident orcas have any interactions with baleen whales? I am curious in particular about the minkes that come here in the summer, and the humpbacks, grays, and other species that pass through your waters."

"I have answered this question before," Granny replied. *"We are aware of their presence, as you are aware of the presence of other people on other boats. Is this not clear? We do not share a language. We swim in the same waters. We breathe the air.*

"Perhaps the simple answer is no. No, we do not interact with them. We do not have a social relationship with them. On the other hand, we regard them as fellow citizens, just as you regard others of your species as fellow citizens. Is this not clear? What other question can you have about this subject?"

I thought Granny sounded exasperated. "She's getting a little testy," Raphaela said. I was mildly chagrined. I had not listened closely enough to Granny's answers and was asking the same question over and over about different animals. I hadn't understood the universality of her response.

"I'm sorry, Granny. There are many different land species that interact with each other. In my own house I have cats, and other people have dogs and birds. We all do interact, but in very different ways, and that's why I'm curious."

Granny seemed to accept my apology and replied profoundly, *"We interact to the extent that we attempt to avoid infringing on each other's rights. All are welcome to the bounty, and none should go hungry. Yes, the sea and the land are very different places. We cannot really understand each other. The seals have their flippers in both worlds. They are not firmly rooted in either. Perhaps they are the lucky ones. They get to experience both sides.*

"I am the master of the sea. You are the master of the land. Neither of us can ever fully know the delights of each other's world. We can visit it briefly and get a glimpse, perhaps, but we will never know the depth of understanding that the seals and the sea lions possess."

"Granny, what is your relationship to the seals and the sea lions?" As soon as the words were out I thought, 'Oh, no, I've done it again!' I braced myself for an impatient reply, but instead Granny responded graciously.

"They are part of our home and share this world with us. Sometimes we play with them, and sometimes we eat them, but most of the time we do not interact. I think you have creatures that share your world in the same way."

Raphaela said, "I am getting a picture of a deer."

I understood Granny's analogy and answered, "Yes, these creatures share our land. Sometimes we eat them; sometimes we play with them. Most of the time we ignore them or, at most, curiously observe each other. There is little interaction between most humans and deer. So you are comparing your relationship with seals and sea lions to our relationship with deer?"

"Yes, that's it, dear."

"Granny's chuckling and says she made a little joke."

Laughing, I replied, "Yes, you did, Granny. You certainly did."

On this cheerful note we decided to break for lunch. Whenever I was in Berkeley, I took Raphaela out to lunch and when she was here, she reciprocated. This was our lunch-out day, so we bundled up and headed into town, bound for Katrina's, her favorite place.

WATCHING THE GRAYS

The sun was peeking through the clouds as we left the restaurant and we hoped that the skies would clear shortly. "Let's drive out to the west side and see if the whales are around," I said to Raphaela.

Her eyes flew open wide. "Is there a chance they might be?" she asked.

"Well, it's not too likely, but it could happen. They only come through a few times each January, but it could just as easily be today as any other day."

We drove out to Lime Kiln Lighthouse. The wind was whipping the waves into whitecaps, and the madrone trees swayed rhythmically. We stood on the bluff, scanning the water. Tears filled our eyes as the cold wind seared them, and we could see nothing but waves. We hunkered down in a large crevice in the rocks that sheltered us from the wind, and we gazed out into Haro Strait. The sun had retreated into the overcast.

"I wonder where they are," Raphaela said after a few minutes.

"We should have asked them before we came out here," I replied. "They're probably way out at sea, or even up north."

She nodded. "Oh, remember that time we asked Ruffles where they were and he said, 'We're out watching the grays.' That was so unbelievable!"

I will never forget that conversation. It seemed like yesterday, although it had taken place the previous November. We were in Berkeley interviewing Granny and she had suggested we communicate with Ruffles. Raphaela tuned in to him and said, "I have Ruffles, and he is greeting us with such warmth. He's like a big, cheerful bear. Gentle, expansive, welcoming the questions."

"Ask away!" Ruffles said enthusiastically.

"Ruffles, where are you geographically, physically, right now?" I asked.

"We are far from you. Very far from you. You are not in your island home, Mary. Although our communication is excellent, I can tell that you are quite a distance. This is different. I am used to talking to you and having your communication come to me from your boat or your island home. We are quite a ways out. There are no landmarks around me to tell you my bearing at the moment."

I wanted to figure out just how far their range was and where they spent their time in the winter. Since there were no visual landmarks, I would have to use distance. "Ruffles, how long would it take to get back to the islands? How many days?"

"Seven to nine days."

Raphaela asked me how many miles orcas could travel in a day.

"Seventy-five to a hundred," I answered. "That means they could be as much as 900 miles away. That's a lot farther than I would expect them to go. They probably travel more slowly in the stormy winter seas. Ruffles, what are you doing out there?"

"We are watching the migration of other whales."

I was astonished. I had never entertained the idea that orcas would go whale-watching. "Who are you seeing?"

"The large ones that you call grays. Large groups are coming by. We cheer them on!"

A scene appeared in my mind. Orcas were lined up side by side, their noses pointing to sea, watching a freight train of gray whales heading south. It was reminiscent of a Fourth of July parade, but the spectators were only on one side. The orcas were urging them on.

I was without words except, "Oh, wow, wow, wow." This was the most bizarre yet exciting image they had ever shown me. I was astonished and delighted that they would go out and root for the migrating whales.

"How long will you be out there?" I asked.

"We could stay out here quite a while, but it is not our usual routine to be gone for long. You might call us homebodies. We love our home, but we do come out here in the winter. We like to observe the migrations.

"At a point in our long distant history we did some of this our-selves. Now our migrations are much more confined since our biology adapted and we no longer require warmer waters for the birth of our young."

"Ruffles, where are the other pods right now?" I inquired.

"K pod is the closest to us, but they are probably a day or two away. L pod is north of them. They let us know that the gray whales were coming. There is much excitement around this activity, which is an annual event. We thought it must be time to go and see where the grays are, and a friend in L pod sent us a message. 'They are coming. They are coming. We are seeing them. They are coming your way!' At this distance we do not engage in long conversations, but we do get messages about what is happening in different areas. Do you understand?"

"Yes, I think I do."

Raphaela broke in excitedly. "OK, wait. He is showing me a picture of the grays going by. I love this. Oh, I love this!" She was laughing and chuckling and nearly jumping off the couch with joy.

"Yes, we are wishing them Godspeed."

A gust of cold wind made its way into our crevice on the cliff. With a start I returned to the present time and place. I turned to Raphaela. "There shouldn't be any gray whales going by this time of year. It's too early for them to be on their way back to Alaska."

"I'll never forget those images as long as I live," she replied.

"Hey, let's go gray whale-watching this year," I suggested.

Raphaela smiled. "That sounds great, but right now I'd like to go home. I don't think the whales are within a hundred miles of here."

On the drive home, we discussed the problems that were wor-rying us about the whales' environment. Widespread pollution of the oceans is a major threat to all cetaceans. Throughout history, the ocean has been used as the ultimate dumping ground for garbage, nuclear waste, agricultural runoff, sewage, industrial by-products, and other chemicals. With our vastly increased population we are producing much more of everything. We have reached a critical point where the buffering action of the seas can no longer sufficiently dilute these materials.

Cetaceans and other marine mammals are paying the price for our pollution. We know that some chemicals, pesticides, and heavy metals accumulate in organisms. Low-level contamination in small prey species becomes concentrated in the tissues of larger predators at the top of the food chain. In marine mammals, these contaminants are carried in their blubber.

Coastal populations of seals, sea lions, and resident orcas are particularly vulnerable to toxic chemical pollution. These chemicals produce stress in an animal's body that may weaken its defenses against other disease-causing organisms such as bacteria and viruses.

One of the greatest threats to wildlife worldwide is loss of habitat. The marine environment is no exception. Coastal development has eliminated much of the pristine habitat necessary for young fish to grow. Logging causes silting of salmon-spawning rivers, which kills the eggs. In the past 50 years, Washington's salmon production has dropped sharply due to dams and destruction of their spawning habitat. In addition, the degradation of water quality through pollution and coastal industries affects the species that cetaceans prey on, thus reducing their food resources.

Overfishing is another grave threat. Human exploitation of marine resources has immensely altered the food chain and put severe stress on many populations. The Steller sea lion community in the Bering Sea has dropped off by 80 percent in the past 40 years—a decline that is being blamed on overfishing in that area. The salmon of Washington and British Columbia, which Granny's family depends heavily upon for their survival, are quickly disappearing.

Add to these factors sound pollution from coastal industries, shipping, and government experiments, oil spills, and an increase in the temperature of the sea, and it's obvious that the entire marine environment is under siege. I worried about Granny and her family and wondered how they were dealing with all these changes. Would they be able to survive? We decided that this would be the next topic to take up with Granny.

Back in my living room, we settled down and I chose to be the communicator this afternoon. With Franny and Lester asleep next to the wood stove, I quieted and calmed myself. My consciousness began diving deep, going down, down into the depths until it reached "orca level"—the place where I can communicate with Granny.

"Granny, are you there?" I called out.

"Yes, I'm here," she replied.

I nodded to Raphaela and she began. "Hi, Granny. We want to ask you a few questions about your environment. Is the pollution in the ocean affecting you and, if so, how?"

"The major effect today is that there are fewer salmon. This is not due to pollution, but from overfishing. We are not in danger of starving, but there is no comparison between the number of salmon today and the numbers even 30 years ago. This is the biggest effect that the presence of humans has caused in our environment and the most important one from our current point of view.

"There is also more debris in the water, but this does not have a great effect on us. There is certainly much more sound, which can complicate our signals to one another. This is also not a critical problem.

"There is pollution; we are feeling its effects, but not critically. The decrease in fish is having the largest effect."

This was more or less what I had suspected. Raphaela continued. "Have you seen any changes in water quality in Puget Sound since you were a calf?"

"There have been many differences. Things have gotten better, and things have gotten worse, and things have gotten better again. It has been an up-and-down cycle. When I was very young, the water here was quite clear and vibrant; it was full of life."

I found myself in the water looking through Granny's eyes. The water was clean, sparkly, and healthy-looking. The plant life was green with masses of microscopic plants and animals. It was totally filled with life. The water was absolutely packed with fish that streamed by me constantly. I remembered that Granny had given this image to Raphaela once. It was remarkable to see the sheer mass of this dense school.

Then the scene changed. I told Raphaela, "There's a period around 1940, when the water became quite dark and silty. There was an industry that came in and started discharging chemicals into Puget Sound. Granny is showing me that period now."

"In the days of my youth, the water was pretty good. Sometimes it got cloudy when the runoff came from the rivers, and the silt would repress some of the life. In the 1940s, there were lots of chemicals in the water that cut back on the abundance of life. Certain species were lost. Certain things that inhabited these waters are no more."

"Could you describe these species?" Raphaela asked. "Can you tell us about a couple of these that were lost?"

A scene appeared that I described. "I have a picture of a sea anemone that grows in the intertidal zone—not the typical green kind you always see, but one that is white and pinkish. I've never seen one in real life. It grew in a lower zone, about three feet below the green ones commonly seen on the shoreline.

"I also see shrimplike creatures jumping up and down in the mid-water column. They were smaller than the big shrimp that walk on the bottom and are still harvested today, maybe about two inches long. I see hundreds of these things bouncing around."

"Harbor seals used to eat them. We did not."

Raphaela paused for a minute. I continued to watch the shrimp jumping around. They were such busy little critters.

"Mary tells me that the harbor porpoises are disappearing from this area, and I'd like to know if you have any knowledge of why that's happening?"

"Many species are disappearing. The harbor porpoises will disappear entirely. They are sensitive; they are ancient and have difficulty tolerating the change in circumstances. They are not as vigorous and hardy as they could be, but they have chosen to leave."

Nothing could have prepared me for the image I received. I saw harbor porpoises traveling through outer space! "Oh God, this is so weird. I'm seeing porpoises swimming through the galaxies. What does this mean? I have lots more questions, and yet I am getting the feeling that Granny is done with the subject and won't tell us any more. I would like to ask why they are leaving. Is it a physical thing? Are there too many people on the planet? What conditions are making them want to leave?"

Before Raphaela could say anything, I heard Granny chime in.

"I will give you some information on this. They are choosing to leave. They are not originally from this planet. They have fulfilled their time here. More species are coming to the earth, species that we cannot even imagine right now, and at the same time many species are leaving."

"She's showing me bears," I said.

"Many species will leave. Even your species, the humans, are changing dramatically. Remarkable innovations in bodies and in senses are on their way. This form of communication which we are experimenting with now is a forerunner of the changes that will come."

As always, when the conversation took a turn to the far-out fringe, I began to feel uncomfortable. I'm not ready for all this cosmic information, I thought to myself. I guess Raphaela felt the same way, because she quickly changed the subject back to the environment.

"Granny, a few times you've mentioned the environmental crisis. What is that in your view?"

"The environmental crisis is known to every species of the earth. Human numbers are out of control and your destructive capabilities are well known. Our waters are filled with silt. There are toxins, oil spills, and poisons. These are all affecting our reproductive abilities and the ability of our calves to survive. We perceive that the water is actually changing its temperature. This is a crisis."

"How is it changing?" she asked.

"It's getting warmer. We are aware that humans are becoming more conscious of this crisis. As we feel the love, respect, and admiration of the people on the whale-watch boats, we hope that their consciousness will lift humankind into a new state, or back to an old one. You are living in the middle period, a very difficult time indeed."

I explained what I thought Granny meant. "The old consciousness that she's referring to is that of indigenous peoples who had respect for the land and for all creatures. There may also be a new consciousness coming that could be quite different from anything we've known. We are waiting to see if humans return to an old way of relating or move forward into a completely new way."

"This project will help in this effort."

I fervently hoped so. It was heartening to hear that Granny thought it would.

"Granny, what is the greatest threat to your family right now?"

"The warming of the waters. The warming of the waters is changing the survival of the fish that are here."

Raphaela let out a little humming sound. "What about the effects of logging? In areas where most of the trees have been cut down, soil is washing into the streams and rivers. Is this having an effect on you?"

"It certainly affects the water quality. The silt coming in changes the oxygen composition of the water and kills the salmon eggs. As soil washes down, there are alterations in the tributaries that lead into the bays. Some entrances are now blocked and the salmon can't get back to their spawning areas. So we are affected."

"Are you aware of the sewage outfall at the city of Victoria as you come in the strait? Is that affecting you in any way, or have you seen any effects of all that sewage?"

The picture Granny gave me in reply looked pretty bad. I saw a huge proliferation of algae that was green and really, really dense. The ecology of the whole area seemed out of balance, as if the algae were choking out other life forms. I reported that it appeared to be detrimentally affecting the whole environment.

"That's awful," Raphaela said. "Granny, what other things along the shoreline affect you? Are coastal industries, discharges, or noise particularly troublesome?"

"The most troublesome thing is the shrinking salmon."

"Okay, so it's still the food. Do earthquakes have any effect on you?"

"When a huge mass of land moves, shifts, and adjusts, it causes swellings, ripples, currents, and tides that of course we feel."

"Did the eruption of Mount St. Helens affect the water quality?"

Granny's laughter filled my head. I was always amazed at her ability to be so lighthearted in the midst of what I perceived as weighty or depressing discussions.

"Well, it stirred things up a bit. Any major movement of the earth gives the water a cloudy appearance for some time.

"Occasionally, gases are released through the seafloor. We feel movements of the earth from thousands of miles away, especially from that very active area to the north."

"I'm getting a picture of the Aleutian Islands in Alaska," I said.

"We feel waves coming from that area quite frequently."

"Sound waves?" Raphaela asked.

"That's right, sound waves caused by underwater movements. This is very common in our experience. Our sensitivity to these sound waves is very acute, and so we are aware of things that many other creatures are not."

When Granny mentioned sound waves it made me think about the whale-watching industry. I knew how sensitive their hearing is, and I wondered if we were causing them problems with all our high-tech sonic equipment. "Ask her about the depth sounders on the boats," I requested.

"Granny, are orcas affected by depth sounders?"

"I know what you are speaking about. Mary is showing me the sound coming from the bottom of the boat. We have become accustomed to this sound. Distance makes a big difference. These sounds are projected at the bottom so their horizontal range in the water is not extremely disturbing. If we swim through it . . ."

My face contorted as I saw an odd picture of Granny being hit in the head with sound waves. It was like an explosion—Bam!

Raphaela noticed and asked, "You're getting a sensation in your head?"

"No, I'm actually seeing the effect. You don't want to get hit by this sound beam, that's for sure," I said.

"So they try to avoid it?"

"Correct. We avoid that area. When I swim alongside the boat, it does not disturb me much. At times 100 boats surround us, and half of them may have these devices. There is a lot of sound in our environment, more and more each year. We are adjusting to that sound, even though we don't care for it. There is nothing we can do."

I could hear the concern in Raphaela's voice as she asked, "Granny, would it be helpful if the whale-watch boats turned their depth sounders off when they are around you?"

"Of course, this would be helpful. Any decrease in the amount of sound would bring some relief."

I should talk to Captain Bob about this, I thought. Maybe we could get all the whale-watch boats to turn them off when they're with the whales. Generally we were in fairly deep water, and they weren't really necessary.

Raphaela moved to the couch. She was getting tired, I thought. We should probably have wrapped up this session and gotten dinner started, but she continued with another question.

"Granny, I've always wondered if the weather above the surface affects you. It has a large influence on us. Is it the same with orcas?"

"Not really. It does not matter to us whether it is sunny or cloudy. Even rain does not affect us. As we exhale, we blast everything out of our blowholes. We do not get rain in our blowholes except in an extreme downpour or very windy conditions.

"Windy conditions affect us more than anything, causing big waves and surface disturbance. Sometimes that makes it a little more difficult to navigate because it increases the sound in our environment and causes some distortion in our hearing.

"It also makes it more difficult for the youngsters to breathe. They have to be much more careful about how they surface. We notice wind because of the increased sound and turbulence in the water."

I remembered a passage from Roger Payne's book, *Among Whales*, where he describes humpbacks trying to breathe in 30-foot seas created by fierce winds. They were forced to launch themselves out of the water through the steepest face of a wave to keep from inhaling the spray at the surface. Although they appeared to have excellent timing and were able to breathe in this way, he doubted that a young calf or weakened individual could survive.

"Do general trends in the weather affect you at all? Land animals tend to get thicker fur than usual if it's going to be a very cold and hard winter. Do you see any effects like that in the sea?"

"No, our home is not influenced by the weather. The water is vast, and the temperature does not fluctuate much with the change of seasons. There are some seasonal differences, of course, due mainly to river runoff bringing warm water into our area. That decreases during the winter months, but all in all, one winter is pretty much the same as the next in our experience."

"Do you know what type of winter we will have this year?"

"No, we do not concern ourselves with the future, nor with things that do not directly affect us."

That's right, I thought. They are very present-oriented. In all our conversations with Granny we hadn't discovered a single thing that they plan for, other than mating, and that's only a week or two in advance. I wished that I could stay that focused on the present and not waste my energy worrying about things that might never happen. I doubted there were any wild orcas with ulcers or emotional stress disorders.

Raphaela interrupted my thoughts. "Other than food, is there anything that we can do to improve your environment in the wild?"

"Limit your numbers.
The less you do for us the better.
We don't need to be managed."

ORCAS AND HUMANS

At our very first session in Berkeley, August 1996, I realized that Granny knew an incredible amount about people. For example, she told us that the military once used dolphins to locate enemy ships but that they are not used much anymore. This caught me off guard. I asked her how she knew about the military.

Granny said that wild whales speak telepathically with captives and that the navy dolphins had informed them about the military. They also hear about world events from cetaceans passing through their waters.

Now I could believe that she talked with other whales, but how did *they* know? Granny's depth of information and knowledge seemed more than what she could learn just from passing cetaceans, so I asked her how she knew so much about our world.

"We get information in many ways. Do you know how many thousands of ships have plied these waters in my lifetime? Do you know how many conversations we have listened to with eager interest? Do you know how many radio broadcasts I have heard? Besides, as you well know, we are very capable of telepathic communication."

Raphaela said, "She is showing me a picture of men on a ship who are telling stories and she is below the boat, listening."

I pictured Granny and a few other whales hovering silently beneath a boat, eavesdropping. They could learn a lot that way. Suddenly the image changed, and I received other information from Granny.

"I'm getting something from her right now," I said. "Some animals share information and tell stories about what is happening on land—creatures like river otters, ones that split their time between land and sea, bring news back and forth."

"That's correct," Granny said. *"Your stories, myths, legends, and news are sources of great interest and entertainment to us."*

I had the distinct impression that "entertainment" was the key word in that sentence. I felt a little embarrassed to be a human, knowing that these peaceful beings were aware of our activities. How much do they really know? I probed a bit more.

"We get many of our perceptions from the people who see us from shore or on whale-watch boats. Raphaela, don't you teach that animals understand the thought pictures of people?"

"Absolutely," she replied.

"We receive thought pictures from many people, and this helps us learn about your world. People are not very focused with their thoughts. They see us and become excited and send messages of love or ask us to do things—always they want us to do things. Then images of a movie they watched last night, or images of a friend, pop into their minds, and we continue to get those pictures. They do not stay focused with their intent, so we are constantly picking up information about their world."

I realized they must be bombarded with information constantly. Boy, I wonder what I've been thinking about on the water. I have a difficult time holding a single thought, and my mind is all over the place. The idea that Granny might have "heard" or "seen" my thoughts about my romantic evening last week made me squirm.

I began to think about orcas and their interactions with humans. Until recently, Granny would not have considered these encounters "entertaining." What did they do for laughs before we arrived 120,000 years ago? The first cetaceans had already appeared 50 million years earlier. It must have been pretty boring for them without our human antics. Even the whales we know today have changed little in the past ten or 12 million years, but their interactions with people have only occurred in recent history.

Stone Age peoples weren't much fun. They didn't have the technology to venture into the ocean, so their interactions were restricted to whales that were beached or trapped in shallow water. Those encounters usually ended with the cetacean being served for dinner and were chronicled in cave paintings more than 4,000 years ago.

Things got more interesting around 1200 B.C., when the ancient Greeks and Romans fell in love with dolphins and incorporated them into their culture through art and legend. They recognized dolphins as messengers from God, and it was unthinkable to harm one. However, I don't think they realized that orcas are members of the dolphin family, judging from the first written accounts by Pliny the Elder. He called orcas "the enemy of other whales" and described them as savage killers.

For centuries humans have feared orcas. Our marine lore is filled with tales of orcas as ferocious predators that are extremely dangerous to people. The mere sight of them evoked terror and loathing, and they were often depicted leaping from the water, searching for boats to sink.

Until very recently they have been hated and feared and referred to as "killer whales." This term was derived from their reputation as "whale killers," a name they were given by eighteenth century Spanish whalers who were often harassed by orcas that followed their boats and fed on harvested whales. These whalers would sometimes kill the orcas but would leave them behind due to their small size and lack of commercial value.

Later, as the large baleen whale stocks became severely depleted, the Soviet Union and Norway began hunting orcas in the North Atlantic and the Southern Hemisphere. Close to 8,000 orcas were killed between 1938 and 1980. Fortunately for Granny, this whaling didn't occur within the United States or British Columbia.

Orcas have also been hated and shot by fishermen throughout the twentieth century because of competition for fish. The Norwegian and Canadian governments waged campaigns to eliminate "this threat" to herring and salmon stocks as recently as 1980. Many orcas today carry the scars of bullet wounds from these encounters.

For example, in the July–August 1957 issue of *Water World: The Aquatic Sports Magazine*, there appears an article entitled "Meanest Thing in the Sea," by Dewey Linze. Linze wrote, "The boxcar build of the orca and its speed in the water make it one of the most feared of mammals, but this coupled with its savageness should put it in the lone category of being the most terrible thing in the sea." The entire article was filled with similar fear-inspiring statements.

Fortunately, an exception to this hatred and fear was found in native peoples from coastal regions around the world. Many of them, particularly the northwest-coast tribes of North America, revered and respected the killer whale. They were an important part of native culture, featured in their art and legends, and remain a significant part of native traditions today.

Our perception of orcas as savage beasts persisted until the mid-1960s, when the first orcas were captured and displayed to the public. The Vancouver Aquarium harpooned Moby Doll, a southern resident whale, in 1964, to serve as a model for a sculpture. When he failed to die, he was exhibited to the public until his death, three months later.

The following year in June, an adult male orca and a calf were caught in a fishing net at the town of Namu, not far from the north end of Vancouver Island. Within a few days the calf had escaped, but the large male remained.

The fishermen offered him for sale, and Ted Griffin, owner of the Seattle Aquarium, quickly purchased him. He was named Namu and swam more than 300 miles to Seattle in a specially constructed cage. Namu's journey brought him through the heart of Granny's territory. What a strange sight it must have been! A large steel-and-net pen being towed by a tug with a large orca swimming inside, small escort boats running alongside and behind. I wondered if Granny knew about him.

"Granny, I'd like to ask you about a whale named Namu. Did you or any of your pod members see Namu swimming in a cage?"

"We did see a conveyance with a whale in it. We kept our distance although we were interested and curious. Namu was hungry and tired when we saw him. His family stopped following him when he got into our waters, and we kept our distance."

"What else do you know about him?" I asked.

"Although he was tired, he was curious about the men and interested in what his new life would be like. He could have chosen to die if he had not wanted to participate in this experiment. I understand that he did not live long. He told his family telepathically that he was enjoying the people, but that his conditions were abysmal. He was the first saint."

Raphaela's face became contorted. "What's going on?" I asked.

"I'm in his pen in Seattle," she replied. "The water's murky, and it hurt his eyes. There seems to be a lot of urine or nitrogen in this water; stuff growing everywhere. It feels very unhealthy."

"There may have been a pipe nearby discharging untreated sewage or other things into Puget Sound at that time. The water quality was definitely worse than it is today. Namu's pen was right in downtown Seattle," I told her.

Raphaela was feeling emotionally distressed from her encounter with Namu and his conditions and requested a break. I had wanted to talk further with Granny about her reference to Namu as a "saint," but decided it could wait.

Over a cup of tea, we discussed how Ted Griffin fed him by hand and swam and played with him. He loved that whale and proved that orcas were gentle creatures and not the vicious killers of popular belief. Namu only lived for 11 months, but he was such a sensation with the general public that aquariums and marine parks around the world wanted an orca in their collection.

Up to that point, Granny and her family had been subjected to hatred from humans and had been shot at on occasion. They were well aware that humans were uncomfortable in their presence. Little did they know that Namu would start a whole new chapter in their history.

Namu's popularity created a surge of interest in orcas. Captures in Washington and British Columbia began in earnest in 1965 and continued until 1976. Entire pods were captured repeatedly. Each time, the captors removed specific individuals, and then the rest were released.

The Marine Mammal Protection Act of 1972, and protest from American and Canadian citizens, put a halt to the captures in northwest waters by late 1976, but this did not end the industry. Instead it moved to the coastal waters of Iceland and Japan, where another 100 or more orcas were removed and sent to aquariums.

The captures in the Pacific Northwest prompted the scientific studies by Dr. Mike Bigg and others that gave us the more complete picture of orcas that we have today. At the same time that research on wild orcas was giving us this new understanding, research on captive whales was also broadening our knowledge and changing our perception. Trainers found them to be intelligent and sociable, gentle and cooperative. People saw firsthand that they were not ferocious creatures. The captives gave a huge number of people the opportunity to see them up close and marvel at their magnificence.

As attitudes changed, humans became fascinated with orcas instead of fearful. People sought to encounter wild whales, and commercial whale-watching began in the Johnstone Strait area of British Columbia. Soon it spread to the San Juan Islands. My boat, the *Western Prince,* was the first whale-watch boat in Granny's territory. In a very short period of time, animals that had been feared, hated, and shot on sight were now respected and loved.

"I had no idea that things changed so rapidly for the orcas," Raphaela said. "I wonder how this unexpected transformation in attitude affected them?"

"Certainly the decrease in whaling and captures allowed them to live a more peaceful existence, but I wonder how it changed their perceptions of us," I replied.

"Right!" she exclaimed. "Do they know that things have shifted? Do they understand why? I want to ask some questions about this. Are you ready to take over as communicator for a while?"

"Sure, let's do it."

While I settled into my meditative state, Raphaela stuck a new tape into the recorder and wrote down a few questions she wanted to ask. She started with, "Granny, how do you feel about people?"

"When I was young, I thought people were all the same. Now I have experienced many. I feel the vibrations and energies of those who come to see and admire us. I am aware of the steady affectionate attention of the researchers. I experience the unsteady attention of the whale-watchers, their peaks and valleys of excitement, love, worries, and fears. How do we feel about people? I cannot speak for all whales, except that we would like you to limit your numbers."

The *Western Prince* started its whale and wildlife tours in 1986. Slowly new boats appeared and the whales had more company, but most tours ran for only four hours each afternoon. The whales were left alone the rest of the time, except for the occasional private boater or researcher.

However, by 1995, the whale-watch industry had exploded. More and more boats appeared, and some ran as many trips each day as they could. Whale-watch tours began at eight in the morning and didn't finish until dark. By 1997, there were 85 known commercial vessels taking people out to see the whales. For at least 12 hours a day, boats and people now surrounded the orcas.

In my years on the water, I never observed the whales acting aggressively toward the boats. It seemed that they were tolerating our presence, but I was worried about how this attention might affect them. Were they able to fish and carry on with their lives? With so many boats crowding around them, it was hard to imagine that they could accomplish more than not being hit. That in itself seemed a feat. Perhaps we were creating a problem that we couldn't even imagine. Raphaela and I had discussed this many times, and in fact it was among the first questions she had ever asked Granny. Although I felt that the whales were coping, we wanted to know for sure.

"Granny, how do you feel about the whale-watching boats?" Raphaela asked.

"This is a complex question. I know that many humans, and you two in particular, are very concerned about it. The number of boats has increased enormously over the last few years, and they are sometimes a nuisance.

"We acknowledge and appreciate humankind's concern for our well-being and understand that this concern is enhanced by seeing us. The love and reverence that come to us from the people on the whale-watch boats are a joy to receive. We like this very much and send our greetings back to them.

"Now, that said, I must tell you that we do not like the noise, but we have become accustomed to it. As the seasons change, there are fewer boats, and we get some relief. We actually look forward to seeing you again in the spring."

I had worried about the noise level. Orcas, like all toothed whales, are highly acoustic creatures. They rely on sound to navigate and fish through the use of echolocation. An intricate and finely developed system of calls or vocalizations is used to coordinate travel and fishing activities. The resident orcas are extremely vocal and communicate much of the time. The engines and depth sounders of 50 to a 100 boats in their immediate vicinity must be nearly deafening.

"Is it stressful to have boats around you so much?"

"Yes, we do receive a tremendous amount of stimulation from all the boats and the depth sounders. Although we have adapted to these things, it is a relief to have a period without them. Of course, it is quieter at night and this gives us some relaxation and a chance to be more our natural selves."

It occurred to me that the orcas of the southern resident community had become urban whales. During the day they were surrounded by noise and commotion, but at night, things calmed down; this was similar to the life of a city dweller. They have adapted in the same way that someone from the country does when he moves to a city.

"What about kayaks? Do they bother you?"

"They are small and silent but sometimes come too close for comfort. When a large group moves in front of us, it is very annoying. We have to deviate from our path and that requires extra energy."

"Granny, when I go to an animal shelter, a large number of animals in cages all want my attention, and the cacophony of sound is unbearable. I close down because I don't want to experience their suffering. What is it like for whales when you hear our cries, 'Jump, jump, jump'? Do you shut down?"

"I understand perfectly what you are saying. It is the same experience, but it depends on the situation and our frame of mind. If we encounter hordes of people with wishes and desires when we are fishing, we tune them out. We are busy—it's eating time. However, if we have fed well, are traveling, enjoying the day, and the people arrive, we may engage with them. We may listen to them. The uproar of sounds coming from many people at once is far too confusing to relate to, so we focus on one individual."

"Then it's exactly the same," Raphaela noted.

"Exactly the same. We find a channel and say, 'That is an interesting sound. Let's see what it is saying.' Sometimes a particular energy coming from an individual draws our attention.

"In the case of my friend Mary, I hear her calling me mentally, I hear her shouting out the window, and then I hear many people saying, 'Oh, that is Granny. I must see Granny.' I feel the attention and energy from many individuals. I can feel that as a group or I can choose to focus on one. There are often intense emotions coming from many people, joy and sharing. I feel that as well as hearing their sounds."

As Granny spoke, I experienced her basking in the good wishes sent by the whale-watchers. I felt peaceful, warm, and embraced by their love.

"Granny, you are no doubt aware that the presence of orcas evokes reverence, respect, and love. Right now you are considered a 'glamour species.'"

"We are happy that attitudes have changed. Until recently we were feared and hated. Most of our encounters with humans were hostile. We are glad that human perception has changed."

Raphaela sighed. "Granny, the love and admiration humans now have for orcas open them to respect for all creatures on the planet. We are very grateful for your effect on people. It's really wonderful. Thank you."

"Whatever it takes," she replied.

Everything that Granny had said about being able to hear people's thoughts rang true to me. That is exactly how my telepathic communication with animals works during a consultation. It was only logical that whales could tune in to us. They interact with all other living creatures telepathically. It is only humans who do not usually communicate on that level.

There are many anecdotes documenting human-whale interactions. Almost everyone who has had a close encounter with a whale can tell you a story about the experience. Very often people

Granny and Ruffles

tell me about the time they sat on the shore and asked a whale to come over and it did. Peter Fromm's book *Whale Tales* is a collection of stories about human interactions with whales, and the following two excerpts show how orcas "hear" our thoughts.

In *Communication,* Michael Baker tells of his encounter with a male orca in the San Juan Islands. He was traveling in a small 14-foot dory when a huge male surfaced next to him and then went under his boat. Could it have been Ruffles? Michael writes,

> I immediately was awash with this feeling of fear because the whale was right there, under the dory. I was practically surrounded by him.
>
> An instant after fear washed over me, a much more compelling consciousness washed over that

[was] this very, very simple, basic thought-feeling: "Don't be afraid. Be observant. Watch my family."

Then it went away. They were emotions: don't fear, observe, family. It was so clearly communication that not only was I not afraid, at that moment I was in awe. Here I was, talking with my mind to this whale.

I remember that I was crying. . . .

There was no doubt in my mind that we had communicated. I felt he was holding back because he figured he would probably burn my brain cells out if we had more than fleeting images or concepts. I had this sense there was a really tremendous awareness there which had taken a moment to communicate to me to make sure I didn't get upset because of his presence. . . .

In the question of whale consciousness and their vast intelligence, I don't need faith anymore.

I know for sure.

We have spoken.

In the following excerpt from *I'm a Boy!* Tom Faue tells of his experience with an orca in the same area who heard his thoughts and responded.

The whale had a fairly small dorsal fin, so we all agreed, "This must be a female." No sooner [had we] said it must be a female than the whale came alongside the boat, five feet away again.

He turned over on his side and exposed himself to us, flashing us! Here is this great big "red sea snake" hanging there. We all cracked up laughing. It was as if he had heard our words or thoughts and wanted to make sure we knew that he was a male, not a female.

It was now January 1997 and Raphaela was still in Friday Harbor, continuing our conversations with Granny. Although it was a typical winter day, blustery and misty, we were warm, snuggled up next to the wood stove. Our morning sessions went smoothly except for the interruption caused by my cat Franny who presented us with a dead mouse.

We were plowing through our list of questions, making great headway, when Raphaela decided to turn the tables. I was surprised when she asked Granny if there was anything the whale would like to ask us.

I could feel a rush of excitement from Granny running through my body. *"I thought you'd never ask!"* she replied, laughing. Then her tone became serious.

"Long ago, humans were more like whales, and whales were more like humans. Humanity chose a route of complexity with objects. Whales chose a route of depth in our feelings. Your technology has had some wonderful results and some ghastly ones. What are humans doing to limit their numbers and to repair their excesses?"

How interesting, I thought, that when given the opportunity to ask us a question, Granny asked about overpopulation. She had mentioned this before. It seemed to be a big concern of hers.

Raphaela explained that this was a complex question and that many people are limiting reproduction while others are not. "I don't think it will change much without a great event that wakes people up," she said.

"Then a great event may be necessary for the sake of all."

"Granny, do whales make judgments? People make lots of judgments. It's part of our critical or intellectual faculties."

"That is one of your biggest problems!" she boomed.

Raphaela was overcome with laughter. "Do you mean me in particular, Granny?"

"No, my dear. I do not mean you specifically. I mean 'you' as humans. Critical, analytical thinking is one of your biggest problems. Whales are not judgmental. We live in the moment and deal with things as they come. Certainly there are unacceptable things

occurring. Dumping pollutants and nuclear explosions underwater cause great pain and damage to our home.

"It is useless to judge those humans who create these difficulties. Our judging you does not stop or fix the problem. It only wastes our energy, and we are excellent conservationists. We use our energy in effective ways."

Raphaela shifted in her chair. I could tell she was getting ready to head into other territory. "I'm glad you brought up the idea of energy, because Sam, a friend of ours, wanted to ask you a question. He wants to know how he can have more time in his life."

My head was filled with the peals of Granny's laughter. Then I could feel her settling down, organizing her thoughts.

"Time—your eternal preoccupation. Whales have plenty of time. We never think about time. Humans are so busy. You cannot get more time, but you can relax and let go of your busyness. The world will continue even if you do not get everything done. Time is endless! You cannot get more of something that is infinite.

"Perhaps 'How can I get more time?' is not the right question. Your Sam needs to examine what he really wants and look at his priorities. We all have the same amount of time."

I was totally enjoying being in that Granny "space." As we headed into philosophical areas instead of the day-to-day lives of whales, I felt my awareness expanding with hers. I loved it when Granny waxed on and on about a subject. Her views were practical and full of wisdom.

Raphaela went with the mood and asked, "Granny, what do you think is the most valuable thing that a creature of the earth can do with its life?"

"Participate in the circle with contentment and awareness. The circle of death, birth, and regeneration."

"That's a difficult order for most people. How can we accomplish that goal? Why are people so discontented?"

"Live simply. Discontent rises with your numbers. Before, lives were simpler, contentment was greater, and people lived closer to

nature. The natural universe is the source of contentment and awareness."

"I think there are many people who are eager to reconnect with nature. That's why they come to see you," Raphaela explained.

Granny paused a moment and replied, *"I am not your experience of nature. I am an individual. I am my own experience. People are themselves natural animals. They can experience nature by being natural themselves. They don't need to observe an animal."*

Raphaela let out a sigh. "But, Granny, it does bring us much closer when we see you. People are awestruck by the whales. Many people live in the city and are not even close to a woods or a lake. They have so lost their connection with nature that they are starving for it."

"Yes, they are starving for it. This is one of the functions of your pets."

There was a question that I just had to ask. "What do you think of our evolution? Are we approaching the level of whales?"

Her reply was quick and light. *"You may get there!"*

Wistfully, Raphaela asked, "Is there hope, Granny? Sometimes we get so discouraged about ourselves. No matter how hard we try, peace and contentment seem to elude us. So many people are thoughtless and destructive."

"Yes, of course there is hope. Humans are intelligent, vivacious, endlessly inventive, complex creatures. Their love affair with their inventions and technology has had some destructive effects, but certainly there is a new planetary consciousness. For example, 30 years ago this conversation would not have been possible."

"I guess not. Granny, is there something that humans can do to help the whales?"

"There are two things that people can do to help the whales. One is to leave us alone. We existed for millennia before humans appeared and will continue to exist. The other is to love, admire, and respect whales as fellow inhabitants of our beautiful earth, and we will extend that courtesy of love and respect to you."

"When you say 'leave whales alone,' do you mean limit whale-watching and research, or are you talking about catching and killing?"

"*Catching, killing, and displaying, although there has been some benefit from the captives. I've heard scientists say that they want to understand this or that process, in order to 'manage' us. We do not need to be managed! We are entirely capable of managing ourselves and did so quite beautifully long before the creation and evolution of human beings. This is what I meant by 'Leave us alone.' You do not need to do anything to manipulate us or our environment. The less done the better.*"

OUT OF THEIR ELEMENT

My interest in stranded marine mammals began in 1986, when I became a volunteer at the Marine Mammal Center. While most of the animals I worked with were seals and sea lions, there were those rare occasions when a cetacean stranded in the Bay Area. These unfortunate creatures were taken to Marine World Africa USA, where we attempted to rehabilitate them, although most cetaceans died within a week.

Cetacean strandings are not a new phenomenon. Ancient cave paintings depict beached whales, indicating that these strandings have occurred for a very long time, perhaps since cetaceans returned to the sea 50 to 60 million years ago. Coastal people undoubtedly looked forward to these events since they could harvest vast quantities of meat with little effort.

Strandings occur throughout the world in all oceans. While baleen whales strand occasionally, it's the toothed whales that find themselves ashore most often. Orcas rarely strand, yet their close relatives the pilot whales are well known for their mass strandings. Similar events have been recorded with sperm whales, but why?

Some whales find themselves stranded when they venture too close to shore, or into a small inlet in areas of large tides. As the tide goes out, the water level lowers quickly, leaving the whales high and dry. Five orcas were stuck on a beach in Turnagain Arm near Anchorage in 1993, when the tide changed quickly. Several belugas were also beached further down the shoreline. A young male orca was closest to shore and had been feeding on a beluga whale. He was in great distress lying on his full stomach. When the tide rose 12 hours later, this male was dead, but the three females and large adult male who were nearby all managed to swim away.

In cases of single strandings, the individual is usually sick or injured. When a cetacean becomes too weak to swim or stay afloat, coming ashore is the only way to avoid drowning. Necropsies of these animals show infections, parasites, old age, disease, or organ failure. Injuries are often incurred through accidents such as net entanglement, collisions with boats, and encounters with sharks.

Mass strandings are more puzzling, yet there are several plausible theories to explain them. In some cases the animals were found to have heavy infestations of parasites in their sinuses, inner ear, or brain. Scientists think that these worms affect their ability to echolocate, resulting in disorientation.

Strandings also occur in areas where there are fluctuations in the magnetic field. It is possible that some cetaceans navigate by following magnetic lines. In areas where these are disturbed, whales might continue to follow the magnetic force, even if it continues onto land.

In a common mass-stranding scenario, one or two of the beached individuals are sick. It appears that the entire pod comes ashore, responding to their distress calls or to support these whales. The strong social ties that are so beneficial to whales at sea are devastating on land. Generally, when the ill individuals are removed, the rest of the pod can be coaxed back to sea.

Today many people believe that stranded whales are trying to tell us something. Are they letting us know that the ocean is sick and dying? Are they pointing the finger at the human race for the degradation of their home?

I had wanted to ask Granny about this subject for quite some time. Since Raphaela would be going back to Berkeley tomorrow, she wanted to communicate with Granny today. As she settled into her space, I readied my questions.

"Granny, we are curious about whale strandings. There seem to be certain areas where whales strand a lot, particularly in the Atlantic. I've heard theories that it has to do with magnetic disturbance. Do whales navigate by following magnetic forces or energy waves?"

Granny replied, *"The answer is yes. Of course, we do."*

Raphaela said, "Granny is showing me a tiny silvery glandlike organ deep in her brain. Do you have any idea what this might be?"

I told her that some research states that the cetacean brain has a material named "magnetite" that helps whales navigate. As we were discussing this, Granny volunteered, *"The big, oceangoing whales rely less on landmarks than we do, and more on this magnetic sense."*

I found that interesting since the whales that were suspected of following the magnetic forces to land were generally pilot or other toothed whales, not the big baleen whales. "Granny," I asked, "are these strandings caused by a geological anomaly that confuses the whales' sonar, or by a physical malfunctioning in their echolocation ability?"

"The whales' sonar can be misled by a disturbance in the magnetic field. It's not that there is something wrong with their echolocation equipment, but one's sonar can be disrupted or confused by intense or continuous sound waves so that it becomes impossible to pinpoint a physical object or location. That could cause a stranding."

I had always wondered about a time in 1991, when J pod had entered Sechelt Inlet, near North Vancouver, and stayed there for about ten days. Onlookers noticed that the whales seemed afraid to leave the inlet. Finally, just before a rescue operation was mounted, the whales swam out.

"What happened at Sechelt Inlet, Granny? Were you stranded there?"

"We went into Sechelt Inlet after a youngster who was playing. After we got in we found many fish and stayed and fed. The tide went out, and the water level fell, but we were not stranded."

"Several observers said that you and the other whales repeatedly swam to the entrance of the Inlet, but then didn't go out. Why?"

"We felt the presence of a bar, an energy barrier. This is hard for you to understand. There was an energy field that contained us. We felt it as a repelling force."

Raphaela said that she had the sensation of trying to force the positive ends of two magnets together. She got an image of the whales approaching the exit and being pushed back, approaching and being pushed back. Granny commented, *"Yes, that's right. I can't explain this in any greater detail."*

I was reminded of our country's most publicized stranding—Humphrey the humpback. In 1985, Humphrey entered San Francisco Bay and continued swimming up into the Sacramento River delta. The waters of the delta travel through prime Sacramento Valley agricultural land, through rice fields and inland marshes. Imagine a 45-ton whale serenely swimming past hay-fields, acres of corn, and fields of grazing cattle, accompanied by a flotilla of marine mammal experts, scientists, and assorted whale lovers in boats of all descriptions.

This procession continued for 26 days and was filmed and broadcast daily by the local television stations. How I wish I had been into whales at the time! What a sight I missed. Eventually Humphrey returned to the bay and swam out to sea, to the relief of his fans and escorts.

Five years later, in October 1990, I spent the night at Marine World Africa USA, tending a sick porpoise. As soon as the sun rose, the phone began ringing. There was a humpback whale stranded near Candlestick Park in San Francisco Bay right next to the freeway! I contacted the Marine Mammal Center and the Coast Guard, and an investigation team was assembled. As I was leaving the park a few hours later, I ran into Dr. Laurie Gage, Marine World's vet. She invited me to accompany her in a helicopter to the stranding site. I jumped at the chance.

The helicopter dropped us in the parking lot of Candlestick Park, where Laurie was whisked off to a Coast Guard cutter, and I was left standing alone. I knew I was in trouble, or was it an adventure? I had left everything in my car back at Marine World, 40 miles away. I wasn't carrying a dime.

I hurried over to a crowd of people gathered on shore and hooked up with friends from the Marine Mammal Center. A small Coast Guard boat was trying to coax the whale out of the mud. Within a few hours he had swum a little offshore and around a corner, but then turned into a small cove and promptly beached himself again on a rock pile.

By now the scene was a madhouse. Hundreds of volunteers and curious citizens were present, and a huge rescue effort was underway. There were Coast Guard vessels and boats of all shapes and sizes standing by. Volunteers tried pushing him and attempted to pry his enormous body out of the mud and rocks using huge pieces of lumber. Laurie took blood samples and administered dextrose solution to give him energy. As the tide went out, more and more of the humpback's massive body was exposed. Volunteers covered his skin with towels and poured water over him to keep his delicate skin moist.

Late that afternoon Ken Balcomb of the Center for Whale Research on San Juan Island arrived. He had come to the Bay Area to see the whale and hopefully identify him. Humpbacks have distinct and unique markings on the underside of their tail flukes. As he approached the humpback's tail flukes, looking for these markings, the whale obligingly lifted his tail for inspection. It was Humphrey! His unusual markings were well known by the whale researchers who had spent nearly a month with him on his journey up the delta.

As the tide receded, it became more and more difficult for Humphrey to breathe. Each breath was a long shuddering gasp that echoed through the cove. It was obvious that his enormous weight, unsupported by water, was crushing his internal organs and literally squeezing the air out of him. Close to a hundred Humphrey fans lined the shore through the night, many sobbing.

It was extremely hard to watch Humphrey struggle for each breath. I felt hopeless and sad and exhausted from my all-night shift at Marine World. By nine o'clock that evening I'd had it. A friend from the Mammal Center drove me back to Marine World to get my car. I arrived home around midnight.

Humphrey lived through the night, so I hurried back in the morning to see if I could help. Now there were close to a thousand people gathered on the shore: news teams, photographers, school children, scientists, and housewives stood side by side, watching and praying.

At high tide around two o'clock that afternoon, an all-out effort was mounted to free Humphrey. The Coast Guard placed a net around his rostrum and ran lines back to the boat. Volunteers armed with two-by-fours tried to pry his massive body out of the mud while others forced compressed air under him. As the Coast Guard boat attempted to tow him off the rocks, the boat engine strained against Humphrey's weight. His massive body lurched and gradually moved backward off the shore, but then the rope shifted, swung across his back and tore a piece of his dorsal fin off. The crowd gasped. Humphrey actually swam a bit, but then turned back to the shore and beached himself again.

Once more the net was put in place, and the Coast Guard boat towed him, this time a little farther out. Finally Humphrey began swimming. The flotilla of boats in the area followed him with people banging on metal pipes, trying to herd him out to the safety of deep water. This time he seemed to get his bearings and left the cove.

Humphrey was last seen passing under the Golden Gate Bridge headed out to the Pacific Ocean. We didn't know if he had sustained internal injuries. I prayed that he would survive his ordeal, but he has never been seen again.

I wanted to ask Granny what she knew about Humphrey and why he stranded. Raphaela took a break and I tuned in to Granny.

"Are you aware of the humpback whale called Humphrey who beached himself in the delta and San Francisco Bay? Do you have any idea why he stranded and if he is still alive?"

Granny replied, *"The one you call Humphrey was a great adventurer. He had a very curious nature. We have heard stories of him from humpbacks traveling through our area."*

With a little pause Granny went on, *"Yes, there are more humpbacks coming into this area. We're seeing them more and more often on the outer edge."*

I laughed and commented that Granny was responding to an internal question I had about whether more humpbacks were coming into the San Juan Islands.

"Tell us more about Humphrey," Raphaela said.

"There was not a physical problem with Humphrey. He wasn't disoriented. He was just an adventurous guy, and that last time he came ashore in San Francisco was too much for him. He hurt himself so badly he was unable to survive."

"Granny, when you say Humphrey was adventurous, do you think he beached himself to draw attention to the predicament of whales, or was he acting purely on his own for an adventure?"

"Well, I can't speak to his individual motives since I didn't know him. I've just heard stories of him in the sea, of that adventurous one, traveling into places where the rest of the whales would not go.

"He was just a bit of an oddball and would go into places most whales considered dangerous or uninteresting. And he wanted to see everything, so he went into the bay and swam all the way up the delta—out of curiosity more than stupidity."

"Granny, we'd like to know why large groups of whales beach together."

"Sometimes whales become stranded because of illness and disorientation. They misjudge the depth of the water, the tide goes out, and they are stranded.

"It may be a deliberate strategy in cases of illness to hasten death. This has happened, and scientists can examine the bodies and tell whether there were parasites or perhaps a virus. Some whales may become stranded in youth because of disorientation, an inability to discern direction and use their echolocation equipment. So that can be a problem.

"Now, as to large groups, this does not happen frequently. When it does it is a very significant event. It may be that a large group of whales chooses to accompany a 'saint' who is dying in a public way to raise awareness of how humans are affecting the natural balance."

Raphaela asked if this was similar to the Buddhist monks and nuns in Vietnam and Cambodia who set themselves on fire to protest and draw attention to the Vietnam War.

"Yes, that is correct. But there were group strandings before the need to draw attention to the environmental crisis. Some whales

chose to give their bodies to the native People. They were called by the People to help them with a donation of their meat, blubber, and bones. This was a religious time, and other whales sometimes accompanied the whale that was donating her body."

We silently considered this for a few minutes. Traditionally, Native American hunters fasted and prayed before a hunt, purifying themselves and respectfully requesting the help and cooperation of the bison, deer, or whatever animal was being hunted. Were animals really so accommodating? It was hard to imagine.

"I don't quite understand or believe that animals would give themselves freely to us, but this discussion is reminding me of the captives. I wonder if this is similar," I said.

"Good point. Let's ask her. Granny, please tell us why some orcas choose to be captured."

"This is one lifetime out of hundreds, out of thousands. We can afford to sacrifice a few of our number who personally choose to do this for the sake of the planet. Your numbers, human numbers, have increased at a staggering rate. Your use of the seas is making a dramatic impact on the natural balance. These few will sacrifice one life to increase awareness of what you are doing to the seas. They have a mission, and yes, they suffer, but we do not abandon them. We stay in touch with them. We bring them our songs, and we tell their stories to our youngsters—stories about these heroic ones."

Raphaela began to cry. "Granny, I feel miserable to be part of the human race, hurting whales and damaging their world. It's unconscionable what we've done."

Granny boomed out, *"Dry those tears! You must be made of sterner stuff to communicate with me. Your feelings do you credit, but remember that the whales of the world support the captive ones. We are all involved. We do not forget. We watch over our captive brothers and sisters.*"

Granny's words hit Raphaela like a slap in the face. She stopped sobbing. Granny was not interested in our human emotions. She had something to show us.

"Granny is showing me pictures of captive whales surrounded by golden light," I said. "They have a holy quality to them, and I keep getting the word deity. They feel sacred, like they've come from another world. I don't know how to put it exactly, maybe like a saint."

"Yes, you may think of them that way," she replied. *"This doesn't mean that they are superior in intellect; in fact they may be considered fools, but there is definitely sacredness about them, and we revere them and support them in this ordeal."*

I remembered that Granny once referred to Namu as the first saint. Her comment had puzzled me at the time, but now it made sense. Namu, and many other whales, have given up their freedom, their families, and their normal lives to be of service to mankind. Whether or not they consciously chose to be captured, they made a choice to live or die. Those that live sacrifice their lives so that humans may experience and understand our brothers, the whales.

We took a break. I knew that it was time to talk to Granny about the captures. We had been dreading it and putting it off, knowing that it would be emotional for everyone. When you are in telepathic contact with an animal, you merge with their consciousness and experience their sights, sounds, and feelings. While this is often an enjoyable and thrilling experience, being captured would not be.

Raphaela felt that she would be too emotional to communicate with Granny. I wasn't keen on experiencing the horror she must have felt either, but I knew we had to do it. What was it like for these gentle whales to be surrounded by boats and nets? To see their calves being pulled from the water, never to return? What did they think?

I settled into my chair uneasily, asking the universe for guidance and protection. A few deep breaths and I felt my consciousness reconnecting with Granny. It felt safe and familiar, and my body relaxed.

Raphaela began, "Granny, would you tell us about a capture? Would you be willing to describe what that was like?"

There was a long pause before Granny responded. I was flooded with sadness, and my heart beat quickly. *"Yes, I will tell you the story of the first capture I experienced. I was already mature and had given birth to three calves by that time. Here are the events as best I can give them."*

I sank into the cold water and merged completely with Granny. I could feel the water slapping on my skin, the warm sun on my back, the cooler water rushing over my pectoral fins. Oh my gosh, I thought. She's not going to tell us a story. She's going to take me there and let me experience it myself. I fought back at the anxiety and struggled to stay in the moment.

I am in Granny's body, traveling with the rest of J pod. It's a sunny day, and we are lazily heading south after a good bout of fishing. Two calves are having a great time harassing Ruffles, who is growing into a fine young male. I enjoy watching their play and listening to their squeals of delight as Ruffles pretends he is going to "get" them. It's like so many other days that have come before. My heart is full, and we swim contentedly enjoying the day and each other.

In the distance I hear boats approaching, but I pay no attention. We hear boats all the time and they rarely come close or stay long. The hypnotic waves rock me gently as I move along, and I close my eyes for a short nap. Warm sun on my back; family nearby; all is well.

The boat noise is getting very loud and wakes me from my sleep. There are now many boats, and they are surrounding the family. This is most annoying. Can't they see that we are resting?

I pick up the pace and start swimming faster, but the boats are zooming around us now, in a circle. They are throwing something into the water. I can't see what it is, but I hear it hitting the surface. I'm starting to feel very uneasy, and my heart rate is increasing. Where are the children? My calls to the pod tell them to group together.

My eyes break the surface to take a better look. Boats filled with men who are all motioning and yelling at each other surround us. I feel the intensity of their emotions. Something is wrong. What are they so excited about?

Diving down I tell the pod to follow me, but we immediately run into a net. What is this? I have seen nets behind fishing boats but always managed to avoid them. I make a sharp turn to the right, but the net continues that way. Turning to the left, there is nothing but net. Fear grips me.

The whole pod is being squeezed together now. We are all bumping into each other and panicking. I must stay calm, but what is happening? I do not understand.

The water is filled with the screams of my family. We are being forced into a very small area, and there is not enough room for everyone to breathe. I am beneath the surface looking for a way out, but there is none. There are nets everywhere. Can I charge the net and get out? I've never tried such a thing, and I'm not sure what to do.

I need air. I need to breathe, but the water above me is churning, bodies rolling over one another. There is no room to surface without pushing someone else below. Tails are slapping, bodies twisting and turning, trying to find a way out. I cannot see with all the bubbles. Have to get some air. Have to get some air. I burst through the mass of flesh, gasping.

Above the surface I see the men lowering something into the water. They are trying to get something into a sling. Oh my God! It's one of the calves! They are taking our baby! The calf is thrashing around, squealing and squealing. Its terror-stricken mother below is doing the same. The roar of the whales is deafening. Clicks, moans, squeaks, and squeals. I am overwhelmed by the sounds and emotions. I feel the distress of my family, and for once I don't know what to do. Why are they taking our children? What can we do?

There is confusion and panic. No one is thinking clearly. We rush back and forth, back and forth. The men continue to pull whales out of the water. We continue to wail and shriek. My heart feels as if it will burst at any moment. The adrenaline pumping through me is impairing my thoughts. I can't think. I can only react. We have to save ourselves. I need to breathe. Where is the air? Where are Ruffles and Sissy?

We are suspended in this nightmare for an eternity. Time no longer exists. We are attacked again and again. No way out. No way to stop them. Will they take us all? Take us where? This is our home! Why are they taking our family from our home? We will die out of the water!

I am completely exhausted. My family lies gasping on the surface in total shock. Fear is replaced by despair and hopelessness. I see no way to stop this. I feel so utterly helpless and try to understand, but there is no understanding, only anguish.

The boats are leaving now, but I am unable to move. We float in a state of numbness, unable to comprehend what has transpired. I call out and scan the water, checking to see who is here and who is not. The energy is disturbed. Our pod is no longer whole. Ruffles and Sissy return my calls, but we are missing two calves and a juvenile. It is hard to gather our senses, so we stay huddled together, breathing heavily, our hearts breaking.

The whales and the water faded away, and I came back to myself. I could not shake the anguish of the pod. My heart overflowed with sadness at the loss of these children. I knew that this scene was repeated again and again for more than a decade. The pain these whales endured was incomprehensible.

"These events are over now, thank God. We know that humans have stopped capturing orcas here. Those were dreadful times. Babies were ripped from their mothers. The whole family felt assaulted, and we thought humans were barbarians.

"Imagine how you would feel if a civilization from another part of the world, or perhaps another part of the cosmos, decided to take your babies away? Imagine the mothers' hearts. Imagine the mind-numbing fear and grief we suffered at this time. I do not wish to recall it again."

I said, "Granny, I understand how terrifying it must have been to have these captures start, and I know that they went on for about ten years. I heard that the whales never fought back or tried to get away. Why is that?"

Granny replied, *"If it had continued, it is possible that we would have tried to defend ourselves. We may even have been forced to leave our territory. We felt confused, just confused and grief-stricken.*

"This was not a threat that we knew how to deal with. We know how to defend our boundaries. We know how to manage our relations with other whales and, indeed, all the creatures of the sea. But we did not know how to resist such a foreign threat.

"We whales do not devise strategies such as those the dolphins have been taught by the military. This is not part of our nature. It was only beginning to occur to me that we could attack humans, but I did not wish to do it. And I didn't know how to do it. That is not how we are made."

Again, I felt their intense confusion and that the whales' only defense against madness was to shut down during a capture. It was impossible for them to comprehend what was happening or why.

"My daughters, do not question me more about this period. I have recalled the first capture and told you that it happened many more times. You feel our confusion, and I see that Mary has received the pictures clearly of the boats and the humans in the wet suits. She hears the screams of the terrified juveniles and feels the heartbreak of the mothers. What more can I tell you?"

I felt nauseated as I sat with Granny's despair and grief. This was her family and now the pod was no longer whole. They mourned the loss of each individual. Of the approximately 60 orcas taken from Granny's community during the capture era, only one, Lolita, is still alive.

How could Granny extend her friendship and knowledge to us after the cruelty humans have inflicted on the whales? Meet us without bitterness, opening her heart and her world? Call us her daughters? It brought tears to my eyes.

Saints in Tanks

Raphaela called me one morning, very upset. She had just heard that the previous week, on February 9, 1997, ten orcas had been captured in the waters off Taiji, Japan, by the Japanese marine park industry. An entire pod had been driven against the shore and the area netted off to prevent them from escaping. Five of the captured whales were taken to a holding facility, and the rest were released.

"Aren't captures illegal?" she wailed. "I thought they ended in the 1970s."

It was hard for me to tell her that captures are illegal in only a few countries and that whaling is actually increasing. The Marine Mammal Protection Act of the United States ensures that orcas in our waters will not be hunted. Canada has similar legislation that forbids the capture of orcas, but they are still capturing beluga whales for aquariums.

People throughout the world were shocked by the Taiji capture. It was the first time in nine years that orcas had been seized. Animal rights groups and concerned citizens worldwide protested and picketed Japanese embassies. They wrote letters and organized demonstrations, but to no avail.

The five captive orcas were taken from the holding facility and transported to three separate marine parks in Japan. One of them, a pregnant female, refused to eat and her health deteriorated. She miscarried in April and died in mid-June. A young male also died, possibly due to a bacterial infection. The three remaining whales, which were most likely family members, were held in separate parks and housed with whales they didn't know. It was a shocking setback for orcas and those who care about them.

It's hard for me to remember that the history of orcas in captivity is so brief. They are such a big part of American life. Every child grows up wanting a trip to Sea World to see Shamu, yet this industry only began just over 30 years ago with the captures of

Moby Doll and Namu. The first Shamu was captured late in 1965 to be Namu's companion, but because she was difficult to handle, she was soon sold to Marineland in California. Marineland became Sea World and there has been a Shamu there ever since. The name has been given to many orcas. As one Shamu dies, another immediately takes her place.

Ashley Anderson

After the success of Namu and Shamu, captures of orcas began in earnest in Washington and British Columbia and continued from 1965 until mid-1976. No one knows for certain how many whales were taken to captive facilities or died in the captures during that 11-year period, but we estimate that it is more than 65. At least 45 whales were taken from the southern resident community, decreasing their population to about 70 percent of its peak size. It has not yet recovered to its pre-capture numbers.

For a decade, captive orcas charmed people and transformed their perception of them. Yet many people no longer wanted orcas to be captured and held captive. In response to huge public outcry, the United States and Canada established a moratorium on capturing orcas in 1976.

Ashley Anderson

Iceland then entered the business. Approximately 300 orcas had been killed around Iceland in the previous 20 years because of conflicts with fishing interests. The Icelandic fishing industry now saw that capturing orcas for marine parks would both decrease their numbers and provide an excellent source of income. More than 60 whales were captured for marine parks in Icelandic waters in the subsequent year. Japan also entered the orca capture business in 1978. The 50 orcas in captivity today came from the waters of the United States, Canada, Iceland, Japan, and Argentina.

In March, a month after the Taiji captures, I traveled to Berkeley to continue our interviews with Granny. The captive whales were still in the news, but hope was fading that enough pressure would be applied to convince Japan to release them. Pleas to the United States government to impose economic sanctions went unanswered. Profit was more important than five whales.

I was distressed about this new development and saddened that Japan had not reacted to the protest. We decided to talk to Granny about it.

Raphaela sat down on the couch and arranged a few cushions behind her back, prompting her dog, Tootsie, to jump up and settle in next to her. I unwrapped a new tape and inserted it in the tape recorder. When she was ready, I began.

"Granny, are you aware that a few weeks ago the Japanese captured a group of orcas who will be kept in marine parks?"

"Yes, a call went out through the oceans to let everyone know that this has happened. We are aware of this most distressing development. The activity of capturing orcas appeared to be over. It has been quite some time since we have had captures.

"We see this as a step backward. This is something we had not anticipated, and we are reevaluating the direction that we thought humanity was heading. It is a great shame that this is continuing, and we feel saddened for our brothers who have been taken. There is no need to capture more whales for display. There are plenty that can be shared.

"We feel great alarm from people in your area about this."

"Yes, Granny, we are alarmed. There are many people who are fighting to get these whales released," I answered. "Things do not look promising, though. I am sorry."

"It is not your fault, my dear. This is a terrible thing that has happened."

Granny's sadness filled the room like fog on a December morning. The air was thick with emotion, and I was at a loss for words. I was sickened that the world would allow these captures without sanctioning Japan. Three more whales would have to endure the pain of captivity.

I decided to press on with this issue. "Granny, you once said that you keep track of your captive brothers and sisters. Are you familiar with the whales that are in captivity around the world at this time?"

"Yes, there are many captive whales and dolphins. We know where they are. We know about their lives and their experiences. We talk to them."

"Have you spoken to these new captives in Japan?"

"I have not, but others have. The whales of the world will support them."

"How do you support captive cetaceans?"

"These animals are deprived of their natural culture and therefore have a slave mentality. They do not have a clear understanding

of their place in the world or their natural abilities. This is sad, but we work with them. We will not abandon them."

Tears were rolling down Raphaela's cheeks.

Granny continued. *"I see you are moved by this, but would you not do the same for your brothers? Of course, you would never abandon them. We communicate telepathically with these beings. We try to give them a sense of their heritage, abilities, and options.*

"These beings are heroic. Some came into captive bodies with the intent of working with scientists and researchers. Unfortunately, they didn't entirely understand what that meant. The biggest problem is that they are sensorily deprived and without their native culture. This is a tragedy."

Granny spoke about how small the tanks are and how painful it is for an orca to be confined in such a small space. She also said that the enclosures are dangerous. She showed Raphaela an image of a tank and said, *"To you it looks large, but to us it is excruciatingly small. You have no idea how painful it is for a whale that travels thousands of miles to be in this small enclosure. We feel so passionately about this. You must make people understand that even though some whales choose to do this service, you must provide a more livable habitat for them."*

Raphaela commented, "I see whales bumping into walls. There seems to be a disorientation or numbing, a sensory loss."

I wanted to hear more about this. "Granny, do captive whales lose some of their ability to hear and echolocate? Can they use their communication skills in a round tank?"

"What happens is that they shut down. There is nothing fresh. Why use your senses if there is nothing to sense? This is mind-numbing boredom, and they go a little crazy. The shows are the greatest excitement and activity they have. Their interactions with the trainers can be pleasurable, even respectful, but it is such a meager use of our abilities. However, some have chosen this way."

"There are many people who would like to bring Corky back home from San Diego to A pod on the north end of Vancouver Island. How do you feel about that?"

"The most important issue is how Corky feels about it. That would depend on what contribution she feels she can still make to the San Diegans. You would have to ask her. I do not know her feelings on this matter. She accepted this burden as a youngster."

"How do you and the resident whales feel about captive whales coming home?"

"If the conditions that required their captivity were erased, we would be joyous. If their mission were complete, and your mission were complete, what a homecoming it would be."

I was unsure what Granny meant by "their mission" and "your mission," so I asked her to explain.

Raphaela interjected, "She's saying that the mission of the captive whales and the mission that you and I and Granny have with this project are the same—to raise the consciousness of humanity."

"If that mission were accomplished, we would welcome them home, and it would be an indescribably joyous homecoming.

"Now, this is not to say that there would not be fights and scrapes. There would! Although we keep in touch and embrace them to the extent that we are able, these brothers will be different and feel foreign. It would take a while."

"Granny, if these whales were released, could they be integrated into their pods?"

"Much would depend upon which members of the pod remember them. Even though we would remember that there was a whale that was taken from us, he or she would feel foreign. They might be an outcast and exist on the periphery. They would have freedom from these tanks, but would have to keep their distance from us.

"It might be years before they could be intimately integrated into the family structure. It might be never. I don't know if this would be good for them or not. In any event, it doesn't matter because the job is not entirely done. However, the fact that you can ask the question and that there are people who contemplate their release tells us much and fills us with rejoicing."

"Granny is giving me a picture of these whales trailing a long way behind the pod," Raphaela clarified. "I think they are within vocal range, but it's not clear to me if they would benefit from pod activities and cooperation at such a great distance."

"Granny, I do not understand why this animal would have trouble integrating. Why would it not be welcomed into the pod and wholeheartedly embraced?" I asked.

"It is a complex issue and requires a greater understanding of us than you currently have. Your comprehension will increase as we continue this process, but I will try to help you understand.

"Although we keep in touch with these brothers, know about their lives, and thank them for their choice, they are in a way no longer part of us. You might think of them as foreigners, as aliens, or deities. What if your Jesus came to earth? Would you welcome him with open arms? Would you be able to sit down and have dinner with him? Would you feel entirely comfortable having sex with him?

This was a striking image indeed! I had to admit that I could not treat Jesus like any other man. I wouldn't be comfortable. Our worlds are too far apart.

"You must realize that a story, a myth, a body of legends has grown up around them. They are different from us now. They are just different. Besides, through no fault of their own, they lack many of the required skills to live as members of an orca family."

Raphaela said, "Now she's showing me an enormous bay with a net across it."

"Maybe they could live inside the net, and we could cruise by and talk to them. This area should be large enough to have fish, rocks, islands, natural objects, variety, and places for them to wake up their senses and learn how to act. If this could happen, it would be a vast improvement in their quality of life.

"If many captives were together having this experience, they could perhaps be released together and form their own pod. I do not know if this is possible."

"Granny, there is only one whale left in captivity today who came from your community—a female we call Lolita, who is at the Miami Seaquarium. We believe that she came from L pod. Are you still in touch with Lolita?

"Not really. Lolita has adapted to her life. She has some pleasure and enjoyment in entertaining the crowds, and she knows that she is doing a valuable service. There are whales on that side that talk to her more frequently than we do. Lolita is cut off from us in many ways."

Raphaela interrupted. "She's showing me orcas in the Atlantic. I think that's what she means by 'whales on that side.' Again I get the feeling that these orcas hold Lolita in very high esteem, almost as though she is a saint or a deity. It's very interesting.

"Now Granny is showing me pictures of Lolita doing leaps and various maneuvers, and she's saying that Lolita gets pleasure in performing in part because it's the most exercise she gets."

I wasn't surprised she enjoyed the exercise. Lolita has been in the smallest whale enclosure in the United States since her capture in 1970. Her pool is only twice as long as she is and 20 feet deep. Also, Lolita has been without an orca companion since 1980 when her pool mate, Hugo, died.

"It would be humane to find a much, much larger place. Since humans are so good with nets, could you not give her a much larger natural enclosure where she could have a better environment?"

I sighed. "Well, that's exactly what has been proposed for her. There are people at home who are trying to get Lolita and bring her back to your waters. She would live in a netted-off area, just as you suggested, until her release."

"This would be highly desirable. This would be excellent. It would be a demonstration of your evolution. If this could be arranged, we would approve."

"Do you think that she would survive?" I asked. "We worry that after 25 years in a small tank she will not be able to keep up with the pod and travel long distances. How will she dive deeply and catch her food?"

"Lolita will learn. She has native capabilities that have never been tapped. Placing her in a safe spot is very desirable. It will allow her a period of adjustment. The netted-off area would have

to be large enough for fish to come and go so that she can learn natural feeding. She could still reproduce and have children."

A smile came over Raphaela's face. "Oh, I see shimmering. I think it's schools of fish, coming and going, darting, and Lolita is going after them. I see her jerking and tossing her mouth. She would have a lot to learn."

"It's never too late to learn to eat! However, the social aspects are less clear. I do not know what might happen. She may join the transients, or she may come back to L pod. I do not know how this will work. This is unprecedented, but it would be a great development."

We had actually spoken to Lolita about six months earlier. Raphaela had connected with her and found her depressed and not engaged with life. She wasn't interested in being released and was so shut down that she seemed barely alive.

I had wanted to speak with her because she was the only survivor of the 45 or more whales captured from the southern resident community. Lolita was born into L pod around 1964, before the days of orca research. In August 1970, at the tender age of six or seven, she was taken during a capture in Penn Cove, Washington, along with six other whales. Two of these youngsters were shipped to a marine park in Japan, and the rest were sent alone to Texas, the United Kingdom, Australia, and France. Lolita was bought by the Miami Seaquarium as a companion for their young male, Hugo, who had been captured in Puget Sound the previous year. She was originally named Tokitae, which means "beautiful day" in the Chinook language.

Somehow, the tape of that first conversation with Lolita was lost. Now that we were discussing captivity with Granny, I wanted to talk to Lolita again. If we were to get a complete picture of orca life, then captive whales were part of that picture. However, Raphaela was reluctant. Her earlier conversation had been heartbreaking. She compared Lolita to a shell, an empty container, and experienced her energy as "dim."

"I'll talk to her," I said. "I'd like to see what she's like."

Shaking her head, she replied, "You won't like it. It's awful, but go ahead. I'll ask her some questions."

Pushing the tape recorder across the table, I moved back deeper into my chair and closed my eyes. I was a little nervous. After several deep breaths I imagined myself connected to the center of the earth. My consciousness traveled down, deeper and deeper as my breathing slowed. I pictured Lolita in her tiny tank in Miami and called out to her, "Lolita, are you there?" When there was no answer I tried again. "Lolita, where are you?"

This time I heard a faint voice. *"I am here."*

I nodded, indicating that I was ready.

"Hello, Lolita," she started. "This is Raphaela. Mary and I spoke to you before. Do you remember?"

"Vaguely."

"Would you be willing to talk to us again?" she asked.

"Yes."

"Could you tell us about your life in Miami?"

As if in reply to the question, I felt the physical sensation of heat. "Both the ambient air and the water temperature seem hot to her," I said.

"Lolita, do you feel uncomfortable in the heat? Is the water temperature too warm for you?"

"Yes, very much. I would feel so much more alive and vigorous if I were cooler."

I searched for a way to explain what I was feeling. "It's as if she is operating at half-mast. I have a feeling of being shut down."

"Lolita, are you happy with your life?" asked Raphaela.

"I can't say that I am happy. I made a choice, a decision to live, in spite of the capture. I stick by that choice. It is a great sacrifice. This is not who I really am. You notice the dimming of my senses, perceptions, and speed. This is necessary to sustain myself here, but I do not feel that I will last long."

I was filled with a strong sense that she would only live another five years at the most. There was sadness mixed with this feeling.

Raphaela continued, "Lolita, what would happen if you did not shut down to this half-awareness state?"

"I would go mad."

"She's just trying to protect herself," I said. "If she didn't shut down, she would die of grief in a matter of hours."

"I see. Lolita, do you wish there were another orca with you?"

"That would make such a difference, an inconceivable difference."

"So you miss your old friends?"

"Yes, but don't capture someone for me."

"Are you aware that Japan just captured five orcas? How do you feel about that?"

"It is inexcusable. There is absolutely no need for it. This should have stopped with my generation."

I could feel Lolita's grief and her compassion for these orcas. She knew what they would now have to endure. Lolita has experienced the loss of her family and her freedom. She has watched her natural abilities diminish. It was a life that she would not wish on anyone.

"Lolita, did you make a conscious choice to dedicate your life to captivity?" Raphaela inquired.

"During the capture when I was taken, which was not the first time my family and I had been captured, I had to decide right then and there what I would do. Should I leave my body and die, or should I try to sustain this?"

Lolita began giving me pictures. I saw her trapped in a net. Her frantic mother was calling to her. There were many whales encircled and the confusion was overwhelming. Whales thrashed and the water churned. The air was filled with their squeaks and squeals. Lolita was crying and screaming for help. Her eyes were locked on her mother who pleaded with her to survive no matter what.

"So I chose to live."

"Has it been worthwhile to stay alive?" Raphaela asked her.

"Well, I am not exactly alive." There was a hint of humor in her response. *"It has been worthwhile for the possible harmony and well-being of other whales."*

"Are you aware of the great contribution that you and other captive whales have made to wake up humans?"

"Yes, I am aware of my contribution," she replied softly.

"On behalf of the humans and the whales of the planet, I would like to personally thank you for your sacrifice. The publicity about the Japan captures would not be happening if it were not for you and the other whales who have so enlightened humans. In the span of 30 years, you have totally changed people's view of who you are as a species. That is an incredible contribution."

I could feel a shift in Lolita's consciousness, a slight swelling of pride in her accomplishments and a sense of reconnecting with her purpose.

"It's very good to hear this acknowledgment. Thank you."

"You are welcome," Raphaela said. "Do you remember your life in Puget Sound, and if so, can you tell me a memory from then?"

"It was cold."

Lolita's feelings and pictures came flooding in and I relayed them. "She liked it cold. The next words that come are 'clean' and 'space.' She was only about six when she was captured. Oh, now she's showing me a memory. She and another calf are swimming circles around a very big whale's tail, nipping at each other and doing flips."

"She does remember it there," Raphaela marveled. "Lolita, there are a lot of people who would like to bring you back to Puget Sound. How do you feel about that?"

"It would be wonderful."

"Do you think that you would be able to feed yourself and keep up with the pod?" she asked.

"Even if I couldn't, it would be so wonderful to be there. Even if I died in a matter of months, I would want to go."

Uh-oh, I thought. This is different from what she said six months ago. Am I getting this right?

Raphaela inquired, "What is your favorite activity in the Seaquarium?"

"The shows. It's not that they are highly desirable, but they are the least boring part of my day. I do have a heart connection with the children and the people at the shows. It reminds me of why I made the choice to live."

"What about the trainers? Do you have good associations with them?"

"Some are more clever, able, and perceptive than others. Some have been arrogant know-it-alls and braggarts."

I felt that she really didn't have a close relationship with anyone. Lolita showed me many people coming and going from her life. It seemed as if there had been quite a procession of trainers.

"Lolita, I understand that there is a dolphin friend that lives with you. Could you tell me a little bit about him?"

"Yes, he is good and lively. Without him life would be unbearable."

"Do you like your food?" she inquired.

"Not enough. There is never enough food."

"Lolita, what could be done to improve your life there? What would you like?"

"A bigger tank. If I have to stay here, make it bigger, much bigger. And more fish, bigger fish."

"Are you still in touch with the whales from your pod?"

"No, but I do hear local orcas. They are very interesting and different. Just knowing they are there is a comfort."

"Do these orcas contact you when they are in the area? Do they find you a bit odd perhaps?"

"We don't have the same dialect, but we communicate telepathically. They tell me the news of the world. They're from Cuba."

Cuban orcas? This was strange. There are orcas throughout the world, but I'd never heard about any in that area. I wondered if she was perhaps speaking to pilot whales, since there are many off Florida and they're closely related to orcas. I decided to let it go since Lolita was captured as a calf. She might not have had any experience with other types of whales and just assumed that they were orcas.

"Lolita, how do you feel about people? What do you think of them?"

There was a long pause. *"You ask me a difficult question,"* she answered.

Quietly Raphaela said, "I realize that."

"In the long-term scheme of life on the planet, this life, this choice, will have been worthwhile. I do not harbor hate, but my life has been misery. How can I hate the children and the people who come to see me, who open their hearts and love me? Yet the physical conditions of my life here are so terrible that it is difficult to keep a perspective. I realize that it may be ignorance and not sadism, but the physical effects are the same. Humans are the rulers and the planet groans under your feet."

After such an indictment, what could we say? Raphaela just said, "Thank you, Lolita. We appreciate you talking to us."

"Oh please, let's do it again."

I thanked Lolita quietly, surrounding her with light, love, and healing energy, then I opened my eyes. "She has a lot of bitterness that she's keeping in check," I remarked. "She is a great soul, but quite miserable."

I thought back to her statement that she would like to be released. When we'd asked her that six months earlier, she had said no. This time, when she said yes, I was initially alarmed at the inconsistency and worried that I had misunderstood. Now I realized that inconsistency was probably characteristic of a depressed state. One day you don't care about life and would just as soon die, and the next day something piques your interest and you want to stick around. I hoped that our conversation would lift her spirits as she remembered her mission.

Although I hadn't found Lolita as depressed as Raphaela had, she was a far cry from Granny or Ruffles. She had no spark or vitality and spoke slowly, taking a long time to think and answer. Lolita, unlike Granny, seemed quite disconnected from her body. How could a whale like this ever survive in the wild?

YAKA, VIGGA, AND KEIKO

The next day we drove to Marine World Africa USA in Vallejo, California, to meet their resident orcas, Yaka and Vigga. Marine World is similar to a zoo and has a wonderful collection of animals, including elephants, giraffes, tigers, exotic birds, seals and sea lions, dolphins, and these two orcas. In addition to the exhibits, there are at least four different shows daily.

I was excited to be going to Marine World again. I hadn't been there for seven years. During the late 1980s, when I was a volunteer at the Marine Mammal Center, I had spent many nights at Marine World tending to small cetaceans that had stranded and were being rehabilitated. These animals required around-the-clock care and monitoring, and I felt privileged to be part of the rehabilitation crew.

I loved the night shifts poolside. Lions roared in the distance and mysterious noises from other jungle creatures kept me company. Once in a while I heard the sea lions barking from their pool less than a block away.

Now I was returning to interview the stars of the show, the orcas. When we arrived, the parking lot was nearly empty. Marine World is quiet in the winter, and we practically had the park to ourselves. Raphaela scanned the program that we were given at the front gate. It was almost time for the whale show, so we hurried over to the stadium and found good seats in the center about a third of the way up. I knew better than to sit in the front rows, which is the splash zone.

We could see the whales circling in their pool behind the stage. Raphaela and I giggled like schoolgirls. This was her first encounter with Yaka and Vigga, though I had seen them many times before. No matter how often I see orcas, each encounter is thrilling. Even in a captive situation when I know how difficult their lives are, I still get caught up in the excitement of the show. Today my anticipation was high.

The music swelled, and the show began. The whales came into the main pool and began swimming laps, following the trainer's signals. I found myself wishing that I too could control them—that they would obey my every command. I felt ashamed that I was not exempt from the universal human desire to dominate animals. Surely I was more evolved than this. I love these animals and have enormous respect for them. Why am I so enamored with control, I wondered?

The whales breached and splashed everyone in the front row. They did somersaults and synchronized movements. They were gorgeous. Because the trainers told you where to watch, it was possible to see them with crystal clarity.

Tears trickled down my face. Raphaela looked over and put her arm around me. "You're sad because they're stuck in this little tank," she said sympathetically.

"No, I'm not," I said. "I'm crying because they are so beautiful. I never get to see them this clearly in the wild. How can those huge bodies stay suspended in the air that long? They are so magnificent."

Near the end of the show, the whales hauled themselves out onto a platform. "This is where some lucky kid gets an orca tongue smashed to the side of his face," I announced. I wanted to be that kid, but we were up too high, and I was way too big to get picked anyway. My eyes were riveted on the orcas, attempting to drink in every detail and preserve it for all time. I barely saw the lucky kid.

Despite all my years on the water, I still responded to their charismatic charm like a ten-year-old. Their allure was compelling. Could I touch them and hold them? In a flash it was over, and they slid back into the water. Now sadness enveloped me. I wanted more—lots more.

As everyone left the stadium, we went down to the pool and introduced ourselves to Paul Povey, a trainer who was working with the whales. We watched as Yaka and Vigga dove down and picked up leaves and bits of paper off the bottom of their pool. They brought these items to Paul, who rewarded them with a few fish.

Paul and I swapped stories about the whale researchers we both knew, and then he told us a little history about the two females in his charge. Yaka was captured in British Columbia in December 1969 and has lived at Marine World ever since. I had forgotten that Yaka was from the northern resident community. She and Corky at Sea World are the last captives from northern Vancouver Island that are still alive. Vigga was captured in Iceland in November 1980 and was brought to Marine World after a short stop at a facility in Iceland and the Vancouver Aquarium in British Columbia.

Paul took the whales to a pool behind the stage, so we walked down to the underwater viewing windows, hoping to get a better look. Yaka and Vigga were being fed and had their heads above the surface. We could only see the lower part of their bodies suspended in the tank.

We telepathically spoke to the whales, introducing ourselves and telling them that we wanted to interview them. After a few minutes, Yaka turned and swam toward the bottom. She came over to the window where we stood and looked long and hard at me. Then she turned and looked Raphaela over thoroughly. What happened next surprised both of us. Still looking at us, Yaka opened and closed her mouth a few times as if to say something and then floated back to the surface. We both felt she had clearly acknowledged our presence.

We were very excited to have made this contact with her and wanted to sit right down on the concrete and begin talking. But they were feeding and we knew from Granny that this important event was not to be interrupted. We decided to put off our interview until tomorrow, when we would be back at Raphaela's, in a quiet space when the whales weren't so busy.

The next morning, we sat down in the kitchen and decided that we would each interview one of the whales. Raphaela chose to communicate with Yaka, so as she settled down I thought about the questions I would like to ask. When she was ready I began.

"Yaka, I really enjoyed seeing you in person yesterday. Your show was great! You can do such wonderful things. Do you enjoy the shows?"

"First, I want to tell you that I am aware of your project. I have been waiting to see you. I did look you both over carefully yesterday and am glad to make your acquaintance. I am happy you are here, and I know that I can make a great contribution to this project and to the literature on captive whales. Now, your first question was 'Do I enjoy the shows?'"

Holy smokes! Where did this whale come from? I was flabbergasted by her directness and knowledge. How did she know about our project? What did she mean she'd been waiting to see us? Before I could say anything she continued.

"Yes, of course I enjoy the shows and the acrobatics."

Raphaela said, "She's showing me the big breaches that get everyone wet. She thinks that's hilarious."

"What I do not enjoy, and what I wish to change with this project, is that people see only my physical capabilities and not my real essence. They are dazzled, and rightfully so, by our physical prowess. It seems quite amazing to them, especially the children, that we could learn these tricks. But because the tricks are clever and the repertoire of behaviors is beautiful and fascinating, the children and the adults do not look further.

"My expectation is that this project will go a long way toward reversing that."

"Wonderful," I replied. Yaka was blowing my mind. "We hope so, too! Who told you about this project?"

"You are asking if I heard about it from Granny or from one of the other whales that you have spoken to. I did not hear it from them directly, although I am aware that you have been speaking to them.

"I heard it from you! In your discussions, when you told Raphaela about me, my capture, my situation, and my home, you pulled my focus and I. . . ."

Raphaela explained, "She hears us and tunes in."

"Yes, it's like overhearing someone saying your name. Even in a crowded room you are going to turn around, 'Oh, are they calling me?'"

"Wow!" I exclaimed. "Is it really that easy to get your attention?"

"Well, as you have seen, we lack stimulation. Moreover, my mission in my life has been dedicated toward the project you two are now playing a part in."

Tentatively I asked, "And what project is that? What is your mission?"

"I made a decision as a very young one to sacrifice one life of many. I haven't exactly sacrificed. There have been satisfactions. However, it is not the full and complete life of a free-living whale. My choice this time was to aid the life of the planet and to raise consciousness. It has actually taken quite a while to draw your attention."

"Does she mean you and me?" I asked.

"Yes, you and me," Raphaela replied.

"We have been working on this for a while."

"It seems that we are the 'Johnny-come-latelys' of the program."

"I would believe that," I chuckled.

Yaka came right back. *"I do not mean to complain. I came into this with free will. There have been satisfactions."*

"She's showing me a picture of Paul, the trainer we met yesterday."

"He is very jolly. We have a pleasant relationship. He sees who I really am."

"It looked like you had a great relationship with him. There was lots of love flowing out of him into you and Vigga."

"Yes, lots of love."

"She has been trying to put it into his mind that they should be set free," Raphaela added. "She thinks he could be instrumental."

"Is that what you would like, Yaka?" I asked. "Would you like to be set free?"

"Yes, with a lot of fanfare and publicity."

"Do you feel that would be the best way to accomplish your mission?"

"Yes, there should be a great controversy. There should be newspaper articles. There should be reporters. There should be interviews. There should be many groups of people talking about this issue. And there are, and then it dies down and then it begins again. It needs to be talked about more and more and it will be. Your project will have an effect."

"How do you think you would fare in the wild?"

"I do not know, and that is less important to me than the controversy, the consciousness that would be generated by your many organizations, your many governmental bodies, your many. . . ."

Raphaela interrupted Yaka. "She's showing me dozens and dozens of people involved with these whales and their fate. She thinks Paul has a role to play. Now she's showing me a place very far to the north, farther than Friday Harbor. It's a semiprotected area where she feels she could come and go and Paul could still feed her. She would still have a lot of contact with him. They could build a platform so she could swoop up there, and she says. . . ."

"They feed me now, why not then? At least until I get my bearings."

I smiled. Yaka has certainly thought this whole thing through, I thought. She seemed very clear about how her release could be accomplished.

"That's an interesting thought," I said. "As you know, many things would have to happen first. Corky, whom you may remember from A pod, is at Sea World in San Diego. People have been rallying to release her for ten years now. There is also a big push to release Lolita from the Miami Seaquarium. Right now Keiko is in training in Oregon for his release, so it's happening. Yaka, if you were released into the wild, do you think it would be essential that you were with your family?"

"I do not know. I have heard many visitors, scientists, and researchers considering that question. These issues are talked about constantly.

Ashley Anderson

"When we whales made this decision to help the planet by agreeing to captive lives, we did not know if the opportunity for freedom would ever come. Although we yearn for it, we do not know everything that must be considered. I do know that if I am fed here, I could be fed there."

"Yes, I understand what you are saying. I've also heard scientists say, 'We could not afford to feed her if people were not paying to come see her.'"

"So have the people come see me!"

"Yaka, it's not that simple. In fact, it's very complex. If you were given the same choice again, to be a captive whale, would you still make the same decision?"

"Probably."

"So you think it was a wise choice that you made?"

Yaka paused a moment as if giving my question some consideration.

"Given the range of things that I could choose to do as a whale, yes. This was an experiment whose success is not yet entirely known. Humanity's views have expanded greatly, but we did not thoroughly assess and anticipate how complex people can make things. We did not anticipate all of the ramifications of your *bureaucracies and your many government agencies. The end of all this is unknown."*

I was overwhelmed by the complexity of her understanding and grasp of the situation. It was hard to believe a captive whale had such mental clarity, especially after our conversation with Lolita. I groped for a question to ask her. "What is your quality of life?"

"I've grown very accustomed to this tank and this place. I have been here so much longer than I was in freedom that this is now my life.

"I found it intriguing and interesting to have you finally appear yesterday. I was glad to be able to look you over. Now that we have established this contact, it will be interesting for me to talk to you from time to time. Even when you are done with your project, I hope that you will not forget me as many other researchers and crusaders have done. Please stay in touch."

"We are honored to do that, Yaka."

Raphaela chimed in with her impressions. "The answer to the quality-of-life question is somewhere around okay. Yaka showed me that there are certainly no surprises in the environment. The area is very small, and she knows it so well that she hardly even looks at it anymore. She and Vigga focus most of their attention on social interactions with people, especially the trainers."

I asked Yaka what she thought would enhance her environment.

She answered, *"Live fish."*

"How do you feel about your food? Are you getting the right nutrition?"

"I am always hungry. It would be great to eat at my will. It would be much better for my health to eat live fish and to have a greater variety. Because I am always hungry, I am very eager to have whatever they give me."

When I questioned her about her health, Raphaela replied, "She doesn't give me words, but I get a feeling of lowered vitality."

"Yaka, what is your favorite activity?"

"Playing with the trainers."

"Granny requested that we ask you about the tigers. Do you understand what she means? Could you tell us about the tigers?"

As soon as I asked this, Raphaela started laughing.

"You are looking at your own small tiger right now!" Yaka exclaimed.

I was startled by her comment. We had been idly watching Raphaela's cat, Sophia, who had just opened one of the lower cupboard doors and was thinking about going in with the pots. Apparently, Yaka had received a picture of Sophia through Raphaela.

"Yes, the tigers. I get glimpses of them through the underwater viewing windows. The trainers walk the tigers through the park in the morning and sometimes after everyone has left. They are very interesting."

"I think they're beautiful," I replied. "We spent more than an hour watching them yesterday. For some reason Granny wanted to know if you got to see them."

"She thinks I am cosmopolitan," Yaka replied.

"You are, Yaka. You get to see many interesting things. You have a rich variety there. I don't have any more questions. Is there anything you would like to say?"

"This has been very interesting. Do not forget me."

"I hope that we can come out and see you again. That would be fun for us. Thank you very much."

I was impressed by how vital and alive Yaka seemed. Her answers were quick and well thought out and they had a depth that I didn't expect from a captive whale. I asked Raphaela to compare Yaka with Lolita.

"They're completely different," she replied. "Yaka is much more vigorous than Lolita, more present and conscious. She knows what she's doing. She has more fun and enjoyment. Lolita felt shut down, dim, checked out. Yaka's not dim—she's awake! Her environment also seems more stimulating. We didn't talk about her relationship with Vigga, but obviously she has a buddy."

I nodded. "I think that makes a huge difference. Whales that are alone have much less reason to stay awake and aware. I can understand why they shut down. Can I connect with Vigga now?"

"Don't you want to take a break?"

"No, let's keep going. I'm dying to hear what she has to say," I replied.

I made myself comfortable in my chair and closed my eyes. I took slow, deep breaths to center myself and felt my consciousness travel to the whale level, where I called out to Vigga. She answered in a timid way and seemed wary.

Raphaela began, "Hello, Vigga. We would like to talk to you. Were you aware of our presence yesterday?"

"Yes, I was aware of your presence, but I did not wish to interact with you. I found it frightening."

Already I could see that Vigga was very different from Yaka.

"Vigga, we would like to ask you a few questions about your life. Will you tell us your feelings or thoughts about your environment?"

"The environment that I live in is fairly constant. We are aware of everything that happens here."

I got the distinct impression that there were no surprises, no excitement.

"Our days are predictable. The trainers do their best to find new and exciting things for us to do, but we are limited. There are only so many things that can be done within our pool to make it exciting for us. They teach us new tricks and behaviors and surprise us by changing our activities to different times. I enjoy meeting with them."

When she said "meeting" I saw a picture of energy traveling between her heart and the trainers' hearts. I had seen a similar image when Yaka had spoken about Paul and her feelings for him. I could see that there was a lot of love between these whales and their trainers.

"I enjoy these 'meetings' with them. I feel very close to these people, and I have great love for Yaka. She is my mentor. She is a good teacher. She has helped me adjust to my life here. Yaka is my

best friend, and I look to her almost like a mother. I do not know what I would do without her."

Vigga showed me a picture of herself rubbing on Yaka. I felt a very strong bond between them.

Raphaela asked, "Vigga, what is your favorite activity?"

"*Feeding,*" she replied. "*I like eating.*" We both laughed. We've heard this over and over from whales, and if people were honest, we'd probably hear it from them, too. It's one thing we all have in common.

"Tell us about your food. Is it adequate or would you like something different?"

"*There is not enough food. Not that I am suffering, but it would be nice to feel totally full. I would like to feel stuffed. We never experience that and there is much delight in having fed well.*

"*Also, the fishes we get are small and slide down so quickly that you do not realize you've eaten them. With bigger fish, you feel them going into your system, but the little fish are barely notice-able. Perhaps that is one reason why we never feel full, because we do not get the sensation of swallowing the fishes. They somehow appear in our stomachs but our bodies do not experience eating.*"

"Finally, I get this," Raphaela said. "Yaka also commented to me about how small and unsatisfactory the fish were. So did Lolita. They all wanted bigger fish."

She shifted her focus back to Vigga. "Do you feel you made a choice to come into this captive situation?"

"*I do not recall making a conscious choice. I was very young when I was captured and brought to this place. I am doing the best I can. I do not ponder the past or long to return to where I came from. I do not even know where that is. I am focused in the pres-ent, and I live my life with Yaka and the wonderful humans that feed me and play with me.*

"*I know that Yaka is an expanded being. She focuses outside much more than I do. I am primarily concerned with my life as it is. Thoughts of where I came from or what I would do differently do not arise for me.*"

"So you do not think about being free? This is not an issue for you?"

"My life is this tank and the shows. I do not see a point in wishing that my life be different. I intend to experience my life as it is. I have no notions of grandness. This is my life."

When Raphaela is pondering something, she has a habit of making little "hmmm" sounds that resemble a llama's hum in staccato. I knew she was considering what Vigga had just said by the intensity of her hums. Apparently, she didn't believe Vigga or wanted to confirm it, because she asked, "Vigga, do you want to be free?"

"I am free. I am free to do whatever I wish here. Some people think that choice has been taken away from me, but I do not leap out of the water without making that choice. I am free to do what I want within this world of mine. The thought of leaving here is confusing and disturbing. I do not wish to engage in that. I am free within my world."

I was impressed with Vigga's acceptance. She was choosing to make the best of her situation, and she really didn't want to consider other possibilities. The idea of release was frightening to her. I wasn't sure if she was afraid of change or if perhaps she didn't allow herself to hope for freedom for fear that it wouldn't happen and she would be disappointed.

Vigga continued. *"I have no desire to be somewhere other than where I am."*

"Have you seen the tigers that Yaka told us about?"

"Yes, I have seen the tigers and the camels and the elephants. The tigers are beautiful, but I am particularly fond of the large ones, the elephants and the camels. They are more like us with their huge bodies. I enjoy seeing them walk by our tank with their trainers."

Raphaela giggled. "I'm getting this hysterical picture of a procession of exotic animals, camels, elephants, lions, and tigers parading by. The whales are pressed against the windows watching them. It's too funny!"

The image from Vigga seemed surreal, yet I had seen the exact same thing myself once when I was at Marine World rehabilitating a stranded porpoise. Several trainers had taken their animals out for a walk before the park opened. It was very exciting to see them out of their cages, but I had never imagined that the whales would also enjoy this sight.

"Vigga, would toys or other objects in your tank enhance the environment?"

"I most enjoy playing with the trainers, and I particularly enjoy splashing the people in the stadium. They make delightful sounds when the water hits them, and I enjoy providing that source of sound to the people.

"Yes, I would like to have things in my pool to play with when we are not working. Things I could toss and push around to amuse myself. Perhaps the movement of these objects would produce more fishes."

"Would produce more fishes? How would it do that?" Raphaela sounded puzzled.

"She thinks that if she played with these toys and brought them to the trainers, they might give her fish," I explained. "She sees it as a possible way to get more food, like when they clean things off the bottom."

"Oh, I see," she said, laughing. "I don't have any more questions right now. Thank you, Vigga, for speaking to us."

"You are very welcome. Come see us again."

Raphaela let out a big sigh. "I get such a feeling of sweetness from this whale. She makes tears come to my eyes. She has such a little-girl quality about her."

I had to agree. Vigga had a sweet innocence about her. She had no complaints other than about food and lived her life as best she could. No lofty ideas. What a contrast from her pool mate, Yaka, with her mission and her detailed vision of how she could be released.

After the trip to Marine World, we were eager to visit another captive whale in person. I would have loved to meet Lolita, but a trip to Miami was out of the question at that point. However, there was Keiko, just a day's drive from Berkeley in Newport, Oregon.

Keiko was born in the waters of southeastern Iceland around 1978. He was captured in November 1979 and sent to Marineland in Ontario, Canada, where he performed in shows. He was only 12 to 14 months old at the time of his capture.

In 1985, he was sold to Reino Aventura, a theme park in Mexico City. There he lived in a small, warm tank with only a dolphin for company. He performed for the public and was the star of the facility, but his health was not good. Keiko was underweight and had contracted a skin condition—viral papilloma.

Warner Brothers Studios was looking for an orca to star in a film they were making called *Free Willy*. In 1993, their search ended when they met Keiko. After the film's release, the story of Keiko was shared with the public. Millions of people wanted to see Keiko freed, just as Willy was in the movie. But it wasn't as simple as in the movie. Keiko had been captive since he was a calf, and for more than eight years he had not even seen another whale. His health was bad, and he would require intense physical conditioning to survive in the wild.

For nearly two years, discussions were held among Keiko's owners and trainers, scientists, private corporations, government, and environmental groups. Everyone wanted to give Keiko what was best for him, but there were many differing beliefs about what that was. A captive orca had never been returned to the wild, and some doubted that it was possible, but others were determined to prove them wrong. Eventually the Free Willy Foundation was formed, and the enormous project to rehabilitate Keiko and return him to the wild began.

A new state-of-the-art two-million-gallon deep-water tank was built at the Oregon Coast Aquarium in Newport. On January 7, 1996, Keiko was transported by cargo jet to the facility, where a team of veterinarians specializing in orcas was waiting. Millions of dollars had been raised to allow Keiko time to heal, build his strength, relearn the skills needed for life in the wild, and eventually return to the sea.

The cold seawater, larger pool, better food, and excellent care benefited Keiko tremendously. In his first year at the Oregon Coast Aquarium he gained close to 1,000 pounds, and his skin condition improved by 90 percent. At approximately 19 years of age, he was now an adult. Trainers began working with him to increase his muscle mass and dive times, things that would be important in the wild. They also worked to develop his mind. Keiko's years in a boring, small tank had left him shut down like Lolita. It was time to awaken his senses and curiosity.

We drove to Newport on March 24, 1997, and went straight to the aquarium to see Keiko. The line to his underwater viewing area was very long, but we didn't care. Keiko had captured the hearts of millions. He was an American hero, a movie star, and a slave who was going to be freed. People flocked to see him daily, and the lines were never short. We were excited to meet him face to face for the first time.

When we entered the underwater viewing area, light shone through the massive windows into the dim chamber. Human bodies were packed tightly together, their heads turning from side to side, searching the large tank for a glimpse of Keiko. I struggled to see over a large man ahead of me. As I watched the blue-gray "screen" in front of us, Keiko suddenly swam into view. "Wow," I said aloud. His presence was overwhelming. I had never seen such a huge whale so close. Keiko stopped at the viewing windows and looked at us. The children in the front row screamed and waved at him. He watched curiously and looked intently at various individuals, first with his left eye, then with his right. He was as interested in us as we were in him.

We pushed closer to the window, drawn by his magnetic force. He was so big, so beautiful and majestic. He turned and swam off, taking a lap around the pool. Necks craned again to find him and within a minute he reappeared to take up his station at the window. He bobbed his head up and down and rolled back and forth, as if to amuse the crowd, and took the time to look carefully at everyone gathered. Then he was off again, but he was never gone long. He loved that window.

We sat quietly on some bleachers in the back of the room, across from the viewing windows, and took in the whole scene. People had a hard time leaving him. They wanted to linger, but the line was pressing from behind. The air was filled with anticipation and wonder, and it was clear that Keiko impressed everyone he met. It was also obvious that he enjoyed the contact with his fans. He spent most of his time at the windows interacting with the people.

Reluctantly, we left the aquarium and Keiko's looming presence. We checked into our hotel, and as soon as the aquarium was closed for the day, we sat down to interview him. I settled into my telepathic mode and contacted Keiko. He was a bit wary and wanted to know who we were and what our purpose was. Raphaela explained that we were interviewing orcas and were hoping that he would talk to us about his life. He seemed quite immature and a bit fearful, but his curiosity got the better of him, and he agreed to speak to us.

"We came to see you at the aquarium today, but there were too many people to talk to you there," she said. "How are you feeling?"

"Physically, I am much improved. My food is better. There is more room and less stress. My skin is healthier, and my energy level has increased. The cold water is very helpful."

"How do you like your food?"

"The feeding times are less predictable than in my old home, but I get more variety. There is never enough, though."

"Do you like your new home?" she asked.

"Yes, this tank is wonderful, and the attitude of the people here is quite different. They are very interested in my well-being. I trust them."

"Keiko, do you miss the shows you used to do?"

"No, I do not miss that activity."

I was a little surprised by this answer, but I could feel that he was very involved with the trainers and also with the people that come to see him. The social interaction had replaced the excitement of the shows.

"Is it fun to see the people watching you?"

"*Yes, and I watch them, too,*" he replied.

"What do you think about all these people coming to see you?"

"*Well, it's interesting, isn't it? They come to see me, to see something wonderful and awesome. I am, of course, just an orca, but I am glad that my life has counted for something. I am awakening people's love of nature.*"

Raphaela laughed. "Yes, you are, Keiko. What would make you happy?"

"*A companion, a whale. I am quite lonely.*"

"There are whales, even some orcas, who pass by here on the coast. Do you ever communicate with them?"

I felt anxiety and fear rise in Keiko. My head began to buzz, and I felt confused and bewildered. When I asked him why he was afraid, he replied, "*I could be attacked. I do not know them; they do not know me.*" I couldn't help feeling that he was like a child on the first day of school, scared, alone, and insecure.

"Would you like to be released back into the ocean someday?" Raphaela asked.

"*I would like to try it. I know that this plan has been discussed.*"

"Keiko, you have to listen to the people and the scientists around the pool because to be released there are certain things you will have to do. Physically you'll need to be in good shape, and you will have to catch live fish. So, pay attention to the scientists and trainers. They must feel that you can do it and that you are ready to be released physically, emotionally, and mentally. You will need to work very hard."

"*Thank you for telling me this.*"

"Do you remember your family? How would you recognize them?"

"*I would know my mother's voice. I would love to have a family, to be part of a group. There is a deep longing in me for that experience. It is something I have missed almost my entire life. The older I get, the more important it becomes.*"

"I would very much like to have a family, and I do not even know if it would have to be my original family. Perhaps I could find a family of other whales like me. I do long for contact and being part of a clan."

I felt a great sadness in Keiko. Although his life was far better here in Oregon, he was still lacking the social interaction that he craved. While he said that he wanted a family, he felt fear at the suggestion that he communicate with wild whales. Would he be able to conquer his fear of other whales in the wild?

"What would you most like to do, Keiko?"

"I would like to dive deeply. It would feel so good to go down and down and down. Deep diving would be wonderful."

"Thank you for speaking to us, Keiko. I hope that we will see you again."

"Yes, please come visit me again."

I was struck by Keiko's total lack of experience. To have never dived deeply seemed inconceivable for a whale. To have lived a life without companionship seemed cruel. Compared to the other captives I had spoken to, he was more like Vigga; not as shut down as Lolita, although he may have been, in Mexico. Like Vigga he was shy and timid, but also fearful and confused. He had the chance to do something a captive whale had never done before—be set free. He said that he wanted this, but my gut told me that he didn't have a clue what it meant. I experienced him as a little child, innocent and totally dependent on people. His thought process was slow and awkward, and he was easily confused. I worried about Keiko and wondered if he'd be able to set his fears aside and rise to the occasion. Was he the right whale for this experiment? I didn't think so. Yaka would have been a far better choice in my opinion.

The more whales we talked to, captive or wild, the more obvious it was that they were individuals, with their own opinions, agendas, and desires, just like the other animals that we talked to in our consulting practices. Like people, each whale was unique.

Their individuality adds another layer to the already complex and heated controversy over captive orcas. We know that orcas in captivity need much more room. Wild orcas travel up to 100 miles per day feeding freely on a variety of prey. Yet many captive orcas live in tiny tanks. The U.S. guidelines for pool size are a minimum of 48 feet long and 12 feet deep. That's twice the length of an average orca and only half its length deep! Water quality is often poor. These highly sociable, family-oriented whales are housed alone or with nonfamily members or even with whales from other oceans. Some are also moved from one facility to another, breaking any artificial "pod" bonds that may have formed.

And what about their health? Captive orcas die at an early age when compared to wild whales. Lolita and Corky are the longest-living captive whales and they are only about 40. Females in the wild may live into their nineties—look how close Granny is! Hundreds of orcas have died in captivity since Moby Doll was captured in 1964, many within the first few years. If they live, signs of stress such as droopy male dorsal fins are common. Their diets are fairly constant with little variety and some scientists (as well as the whales themselves) consider it inadequate.

However, there is another side to be weighed in the balance as well—the great good that the captives have done for their fellow whales. If the public had not encountered orcas in marine parks and had not been given the opportunity to get to know them, orcas would probably still be hated, feared, and often shot on sight.

Marine facilities often point to the valuable research and education these whales provide as justification for holding them. Other scientists, while admitting the value of this research, still feel that it is unethical to hold these creatures captive for what is, after all, primarily our enjoyment.

Erich Hoyt, in *The Performing Orca: Why the Show Must Stop*, writes, "The orca captivity debate is important for many reasons. All of us are trying to come to terms with a world which the human species has put in peril by its actions of domination over nature. The removal of these few animals probably does not represent a risk to the future of *Orcinus orca* as a species; in fact, some of what is learned in captivity may in future be helpful to wild populations. But the ethical issue should not be dismissed because only a few animals are involved."

Many animal rights groups, some scientists, and even some of the whales themselves have proposed that the captive orcas be released back into the wild. There are just as many biologists and individuals who warn that such an action is not feasible. They fear that captive orcas are not prepared for life in the wild and may not be capable of traveling long distances or foraging for food. There is also concern that captive orcas may be harboring diseases that the wild populations have no immunity against.

Whales born in captivity present an entirely different problem. There are now approximately 20 orcas that have been born in captivity. There are even a few second-generation captive-born whales—whales born to captive-born mothers. What can we do with these orcas? They have never even seen the ocean, much less lived in it. They have no hunting skills and belong to no wild families. Could they survive in the wild, having only experienced life in a tank?

These are difficult questions, and I struggled to make my own evaluation. I was in a unique position, having talked about the issue directly with both wild and captive orcas. If releasing captive whales became feasible, it would be imperative that each individual be asked if he or she would like to go free. After all, they will be most affected by the decision. We ripped them from their lives and families once before, and we do not have the right to assume that we know what is best for them now. The captives are very much individuals. They should each be allowed to make their own decision, and we, their keepers, should honor it.

FROM HERE TO ETERNITY

It was September 22, 1996, when we heard that Granny's daughter Sissy was ill. Raphaela and I had gone to The Whale Museum that evening to hear a talk by Ken Balcomb, the director of the Center for Whale Research. At the end of his presentation, Ken showed a video of Sissy that was quite alarming. A healthy whale is filled out and has a nice smooth, curved surface, but Sissy had a distinct dip or indentation behind her blowhole that indicated a serious loss of fat. Ken referred to it as the "peanut head" syndrome. We could also see that Sissy was not swimming strongly. She appeared weak, a little bit behind and off to the side of the pod, and in some distress.

Sissy's illness took us by surprise. Animals in the wild cannot afford to show weakness, because it makes them vulnerable to predators. You usually don't know a wild animal is sick until it is too late to help. With whales the difficulty is compounded by the problems we always have observing them: Their time at the surface is short, and we don't see them up close very often. As a result it is rarely recognized that a wild orca is ill until the process is quite far along and we see signs of emaciation or disorientation. Whales in this condition usually disappear within a few weeks.

Nothing can be done to test or treat a wild orca, but detailed observation of the illness's progression can lend insight. We gain the greatest amount of information when scientists do a post-mortem examination, yet it is surprising how rarely this occurs. We almost never recover a whale's body.

Sissy's illness disturbed us greatly. We had planned an interview to discuss her life with Granny. I had also assumed that Sissy would be Granny's successor as leader of J pod, but Sissy was not a young whale. Scientists estimate she was born in 1935, so she had already surpassed the average life span (50 to 60 years) of a female orca.

The next morning, we were anxious to get some answers about Sissy's condition, so we decided to separate ourselves. Raphaela would go outside and talk to Sissy while I conferred with Granny. Then we would get back together and compare notes.

I settled down at the dining room table and called out to Granny. When she answered, I told her about the video we'd seen the night before and asked her about Sissy.

"Yes, she is my daughter," Granny confirmed, *"and yes, she is failing. She has been in ill health for some time, and the effects are now starting to show. She has been experiencing a general weakening of all systems. You are correct about the weight loss. The vitality is leaving her. She is ready to go and has chosen this time to leave. We are preparing for this eventuality."*

I felt sad at the news, but realized that this might be a rare opportunity to gain badly needed information. "Granny, the scientists would like to recover her physical body after she leaves. They fear that there is a disease in the population that's causing whales to die, something that creates these general symptoms. Are you aware of any problems?"

"There are some metals that interfere with our systems. It is causing problems for the children and increasing infant mortality. This could also be affecting our health in general, but no, we are not experiencing a disease or virus going through the group."

"It would be very valuable if the scientists could test Sissy's body soon after she dies. Would you be willing to ask her to make this contribution?"

"Yes, of course I am willing to do that. It is her choice, but I will speak to her and let her know that this may help the humans' understanding of what is happening in our environment. This may be a benefit that she can provide for the entire community."

"That's right, Granny. If Sissy agrees, it would be best if she takes her last breath very near the shoreline of San Juan Island, Seattle, or even Vancouver or Nanaimo. She could even come ashore and die there."

"Yes, I understand. I hear what you are saying, and I will communicate this information to her."

As I waited for Raphaela to return from the yard, I thought about Sissy. She was first identified during a capture in 1972. At that sighting she was accompanied by a calf, which was named J24. This calf was no longer with her in 1974. It had either died or been captured. We don't know for sure because accurate records of the southern residents were not completed until the late 1970s.

Sissy gave birth to a female calf, Samish, in 1974. Samish thrived and had her own calf, Capricorn, in December 1987. This young male was last seen near the end of 1991 and is presumed dead. Then in December 1994, Samish had another calf, Riptide, who seems to be doing well. I have frequently seen Granny, Sissy, Samish, and Riptide all traveling together, and it has been such a joy to encounter this four-generation group. Knowing that Sissy would soon be missing broke my heart. It was the end of an era.

Raphaela came through the door slowly, a pensive look on her face. "Did you talk with Sissy?" I asked anxiously. "What happened?"

"It wasn't at all what I expected," she replied. "I had a buzzing in my head and a feeling of peace and languor. I also felt cold, like my body was slowing down. She said that inefficient eating caused her fat loss. Apparently, she's not able to properly metabolize her food anymore.

"Sissy also told me that her condition was declining and that she has perhaps two more weeks left. She has a pain in her belly, and I got the feeling that she may have parasites or has ingested something metal."

That worried me. "Granny also mentioned something about metal this morning, and this isn't the first time we've heard that. I requested that Granny ask Sissy to give her body to the scientists. It's so important that we find out which metals are accumulating in their bodies. This could be a huge problem for them."

Sissy was last seen about a week later trailing behind the pod as they traveled past Victoria, out the Strait of Juan de Fuca. Her body was never found.

When I went to Berkeley in November 1996 to continue our interviews, we decided to ask Granny what had happened to Sissy. Raphaela settled into the telepathic mode and connected with her.

After exchanging a few pleasantries, I said, "The first thing we would like to know, Granny, is what happened to your daughter Sissy?"

"She has gone into the oceans. She has gone into the deep. She is no longer on this planet, but her light prevails. Her loss is a hole in our society. We accept this, but it is a great loss."

I paused a moment in reverence and then asked, "Did you talk to her about giving her body to the scientists? What did she say?"

"I did mention your request, but she did not feel that this was her concern. Sissy did not share my partnership with you. She felt that her death was entirely her own matter. Because she had not engaged with humans in the way that I and some other whales have done, the request had no force, no meaning.

"Not only did it have no meaning, but she saw it as an invasion. She did not have a goal as I do to share our innermost experiences with humans. She was a very different whale. As you know, her health was quite poor at the end, and her consciousness of the world dimmed. Perhaps if we had discussed this earlier and she had made contact with humans, she might have honored your request. You may ask it of me."

"Thank you, Granny," I said, feeling very moved that she would make this offer.

"I will consider this."

I took a deep breath. "Should we anticipate you leaving the body anytime in the near future?"

"Well, it will be in the future," Granny retorted dryly.

"I'm getting about two years," Raphaela said.

I let out a sigh of relief. "I'm very glad to hear that, Granny. Could you tell us about the last time you saw Sissy?"

"We were all with her."

"She's giving me an underwater location, and it's not making any sense to me. It's incredibly dark and seems very deep. It feels excruciatingly cold. I think they are out in the Pacific. I don't see landmarks or features. The whole group is together, and they are aware of Sissy's diminishing awareness. Some are on the surface. Some are below with her."

"She's below the surface?" I asked.

"Yes, it looks like they actually held her up. Two female whales took turns bracing her up. She would breathe and then sink. They did this three, possibly four times."

"This was a lot of effort, and she told us when to stop supporting her. She let go of her light in a very deliberate way."

I asked why she wanted to be supported at the surface. Raphaela explained that she was giving herself and her family time to say goodbye. Granny added, *"We did it at her wish. She certainly knew she was dying. She was saying goodbye to the beautiful world and goodbye to her family."*

"Is this customary when a whale dies, or was this her individual choice?"

"This was her preference, her desire. It is not unusual, but it is by no means universal."

"Granny's showing me that when she died, Sissy just sank and sank and sank. The two younger whales that were supporting her went down with her and stayed there for a while. Then they swam around her again and again in a circle. It seems a bit fanciful, so I am going to ask her about it again."

"We indeed did this. There is both a finality and an unendingness in this circle motif."

"Wow, the eternal circle of life?" I asked.

Raphaela agreed and added, "Then a spiral rising up to finish the rite."

"We felt her leave. We watched her ascend. She went home to share her light with all in a new and different way. We think of her as being in the sky, somewhat like the idea you and Mary have of the heavens."

"Oh boy, she's getting very philosophical," Raphaela whispered. "She's talking about constellations and seeing her as a star."

"Granny, where is Sissy and what will her journey be now?"

"You should talk to her yourself," she replied.

"Thank you, Granny. I think we'll take a break and then do that."

Slowly Raphaela opened her eyes. She sat staring at me, her eyes adjusting to the light. After collecting her thoughts, she said, "I felt very far away when they were lifting Sissy up and letting her fall. The images were so surreal."

I walked out to the kitchen and put the teakettle on. Raphaela shuffled behind me, still not totally connected to this reality. "Let's have some tea and talk about what we'd like to ask Sissy," I said. "Can I be the one to connect with her?"

"Oh, please, go ahead. I've definitely had my hit of outer space for today."

I shook my head in wonder. Five years ago I wouldn't have dreamed of trying to communicate with a dead whale. At that time I was still nervous about talking to live whales. However, I have experienced communicating with dead pets, and I know that it's just as easy to speak to a dead animal as a live one. My perception of reality has certainly changed in the past few years!

After tea, we returned to the living room and I settled into the overstuffed chair with Tootsie at my feet. I quieted myself and plunged into the depths of consciousness. This time it reminded me of diving below the water's surface as we had done with Ruffles. Darkness and peace enveloped me.

I called out to Sissy, and she responded faintly. Her energy was light and wispy, like a soft breeze in spring that barely rustles the new leaves. I nodded that I was ready.

"Hello, Sissy," Raphaela said. "Would you answer a few questions for us?"

"Certainly," she replied.

"Would you tell us about your condition before you died?"

"I experienced a general weakening of all bodily functions. My digestion was not working very well and breathing became more difficult. Even my heart was not pumping to its capacity. It was hard for me to catch fish because my vitality, my energy, was so

low. As my ability to fish lessened, so did my energy. It was a gradual process."

"Was this a natural aging of the body or a disease, a pathogen, or an illness that contributed to this decline?"

"I do not know. It is not unusual that one should decline in this way. Many before me have done this as well, but I do not know if it is completely natural or if something is affecting us. I was aware that I would be leaving. I was not afraid, and I felt ready to go. I had been in that body for some time and felt no need to stay longer. I have carried a quietness with me throughout my life, and I think that is perhaps one of the reasons why I left at this stage. Not that I did not love life. Life was exciting, life was full, life was fun, but my very nature is more introspective."

"Sissy, can I ask you about the actual process of dying? Granny described a scene that appeared to take maybe 40 minutes or an hour where whales were holding you up. Did you want them to do that, and what was it like?"

"I did request some support at the surface from my family. I just wanted one last feeling of my family holding me, touching me—that last sensual feeling of skin on my skin. By having them support me at the surface, I was able to feel many bodies loving and caressing me at once.

"The sinking down and bringing me up induced a floating feeling within my body and my consciousness. We did this a few times, and then I separated from my body and drifted out. They allowed my body to fall to the bottom.

"When I left I just felt very free and expansive."

An image of a huge, joyful ball of energy, flooded my mind. I could feel Sissy's energy expand into the universe.

"I was happy to be out and in that quiet space," she added.

While Sissy spoke, my arms moved on their own, making expansive gestures as if they were floating in currents, moving upward. I experienced her essence separating from her body. She made a conscious choice when to leave and withdrew her spirit from the physical form. I was covered in goose bumps. The moment of another being's death is profound, and I felt honored to be experiencing this moment with Sissy.

"What is it like where you are now? Where are you?" Raphaela asked.

"I am in the in-between space, which is not a place I can describe. It exists everywhere. It's not outside this planet or galaxy, rather it's between space and time. Many are gathered here, although it is not really a meeting place.

"I am basking in the quiet and warmth of this state, considering my process and what I shall do next. This is not a time to visit old friends; it is a reflective space that I enjoy very much. It is well suited to my nature, and as I spend time here I wonder why I remained in the body as long as I did. This is so much better!"

Raphaela sighed. "Oh Sissy, I have so many questions. It's wonderful of you to tell us about this. May I ask about other lives that you've had?"

Sissy told us about two human lives she had experienced. In one, she showed me pictures of her living with her child in a small hut made of bark and trees. I got the impression that it was in a prehistoric or Stone Age culture in a remote area of Mongolia.

The other was a more detailed life in Boston in the 1800s. I saw her walking down a brick street in a yellow dress with a big bustle. Her hair was in ringlets, and she wore a large bonnet and carried a fancy parasol. She explained that she was married to a prosperous banker and that she was selfish and demanding of her husband. She had no children and spent most of her time shopping.

I found it strange to think of Sissy in this way. It was very unlike her. I wondered whether there might be a connection between that life and her present one. Boston had a large whaling industry at the turn of the century. Perhaps her husband had whaling interests, or perhaps . . . but before I could ask, Raphaela went on.

"Any other sea lives?"

"There are many lives, and they are not so important. I would like to tell you something about Granny.

"Granny, my mother, is a great spirit. She fostered me as a child and brought me along. She is the most benevolent being I have ever known. I cannot think of even one time where she treated me with anything other than pure love and kindness.

"All respect her, not only within our pod, but within the community and even outside our community. Whales from other areas know of Granny. She is a wise elder in the orca world, and she loves being alive! She loves it so much.

"Even at her great age, she plays with the children, especially her new great-grandchild, my granddaughter. All of the youngsters are glad when Granny comes to baby-sit. She is so kind to them. She radiates love and concern. She does not judge them, discipline, or shame them. She just enjoys them and allows them to expand and experience themselves as they really are. They all love her for it. Everyone loves to spend time with Granny.

"She is the great bringer of love."

It was wonderful to hear the love in Sissy's voice. Even from that quiet place where she was so happy to be, Sissy could look back in total love for her mother. An image of Granny filled me. Beams of light were coming from her heart and touching everyone in the pod. She radiated love to everyone. I was glad to know that Granny had the same effect on others as she did on us. Once again I was covered in goose bumps—waves and waves of goose bumps.

"She is the bringer of love. That may sound simple, but it is very deep. Through her collaboration with you two, she expresses her great love for the entire planet. By sharing her thoughts and feelings, she hopes to enlighten others to see the kinship of all life. That is her great gift."

Filled with awe, I began to think of us as Granny's scribes, bringing her message to humanity. I felt humbled and honored to serve her.

"Is there anything else you would like to tell us?"

"Yes, in this space and time, I want to be more etheric and perhaps move into an energy form in space. I do not want to spend time on earth now, so I am going to be moving away from this plane. If I take form again, it will likely be as a celestial body."

"Thank you so much for talking to us," Raphaela said. "We wish you the best in whatever you choose to do next. Our love is with you. Go in peace."

"You are most welcome. It has been my pleasure."

I heard Raphaela turn the tape recorder off. Quietly thanking Sissy, I began the return to physical reality. When my eyes opened, Raphaela was staring silently out the window. "That was pretty amazing," I remarked.

She turned to me. "Weren't you struck by Sissy's feelings for Granny?" she asked. "Such love and respect, even reverence. Sissy was never that interested in people. I'm sure she spoke with us today to honor Granny."

My eyes welled with tears as I replied, "I've never experienced anything like the total reverence and love she felt. It was too big to articulate—an incredible feeling. I wish you could have experienced it too."

"Oh, I felt it. You couldn't miss it," she said.

Now, in April 1997, the time had come to encounter living whales once more in the flesh. Raphaela arrived in Friday Harbor on Wednesday evening for two days of interviews before a *Western Prince* trip on Saturday. I had been out a few times earlier that month but hadn't seen any whales. J pod had been spotted in the area and had been fairly regular visitors throughout the winter, but I hadn't seen them since fall.

On the first morning of Raphaela's visit, we awoke to a gorgeous sunny day. After meditation and breakfast, we took a quick walk around the neighborhood before our session with Granny. The bushes were filled with tiny birds searching for their breakfast as a red-tailed hawk circled overhead. Franny and Lester waited for us in the yard, intently watching the birds, hoping that one would drop to the ground nearby. It was almost inconceivable to Raphaela and me that we had only been working on this project for nine months, considering the depth our communications had reached and the sheer volume of material we'd gathered from our talks with Granny, Ruffles, and the others. Now I had a sense that the conversations were drawing to a close.

Natalie Herner

Ruffles

After our walk, we settled down in the living room. We were still thinking about Sissy's departure last fall, and we wanted to talk further with Granny about death. Raphaela wanted to know if any other whales had died over the winter, but I requested that we not ask Granny. I've found that I really cherish the excitement of not knowing everything about these whales. Getting this information from Granny would ruin the anticipation of my first encounters with J pod. We'd know soon enough if others had died, and I wanted to find out on the water with the rest of the whale-watch community.

A smile spread across Raphaela's face as she made her telepathic connection with Granny. I watched her bask in the warmth of Granny's embrace, and I could feel her presence fill the room.

"Good morning, Granny. It's great to be with you again. We'd like to explore the subject of death with you today."

"This is a very big subject, and we have already discussed it some. Death for whales can occur in many ways. Some whales die from accidents. This is a traumatic end that fortunately is rare. Another type is the death of young ones who are fragile and vulnerable and

do not reach their potential. This has become much more common. Our infant mortality rate is rising. Illness or disease can also take us, as well as old age."

"Granny, while there are stories about injured whales being supported at the surface by their family members, there are also reports of whales being abandoned by their family and left to die. Can you explain these different actions?"

"Everything is done for the good of the pod. Each situation is individual and unique. Sometimes the good of the pod may require supporting an individual who has been injured or is ill.

"It might not be time for this animal to leave. In those cases, every effort is made to help our family members stay alive and together. Sometimes, if it is a child, the mother cannot bear to let it go, and out of our love and compassion for her, we will try to keep her calf alive.

"When a tragic accident occurs we will exert a considerable effort to support that being to stay alive or prepare for their transition. Because it is sudden, there is no preparation, so we gather around and give whatever support we can, whether it be physical, emotional, or spiritual.

"When an animal is sick and dying, whether it be old age or disease, there is no grasping or clinging to this existence. When our time comes, we must go. We wish them well, but we do not help them struggle to stay here. They may be left behind after we have said our goodbyes, and they will breathe their last breath alone.

"My death will be normal. I am preparing for it as we speak."

I felt a pang. Granny had promised us another year at least. "How are you preparing?"

"Right now I feel in the best of health. I may be here another season or two. We will see. I still feel strong and vigorous, and I want to see this project to its completion."

Relieved, I answered, "Thank you, Granny. Thank you."

"I am experimenting with how long I can stick around. I have attained a great age already! We will see."

Raphaela spoke up. "She's telling me something about her successor, but I can't quite get it. Wait, here it is."

"She could use my input for a little while, so that would be one reason to stay. Now, I see your urgent question is: How will I die? Sit still. I will be one of those whales who will simply withdraw the life force. Do not worry about the physical aspects. Just listen to my words and understand the spiritual concept.

"I am in control of withdrawing my essence from this physical body, which is still strong, and I may therefore continue to inhabit it for a bit longer. But when I choose to go, my pod will be completely prepared. A successor will be in place, and my energy will surround my family."

"She's showing me a circle that is glowing, just glowing," Raphaela murmured.

"A whale in old age may choose to experience disease and allow himself or herself to die in that way. We give our body to the ocean depths."

Raphaela said, "I'm seeing all kinds of ocean creatures feeding on a body."

"That is one type of fertilization. At first I thought this was what I would do, but now in my contacts with you, I am actually considering giving this body to a scientist. I don't know. I have not yet decided."

"I'm getting a picture of an inland bay, and I'm seeing it through her eyes. On the right, there are a lot of rocks and a long prominence that comes out into the water. There is a science or a research building on the point. I see boats, pilings, and a road."

Her description sounded like it might be the Pacific Biological Station in Nanaimo, British Columbia, where Graeme Ellis does his research.

"This might be a convenient place."

"We presume when a whale disappears from its pod that it has died. Is that correct?"

"Yes, of course. If a whale disappears, it is because he is dead. He would never leave his family."

"Why is it that we rarely find the bodies?" I asked.

"We may go out very, very deep. You don't know where to look."

Raphaela squirmed in her chair and deep furrows appeared in her forehead. "Okay, Granny, I'm really, really trying not to doubt myself. Just give it to me," she implored.

I waited for her to speak. "I don't get words. I'm seeing an ocean floor with a shelf that projects. It looks as if the shelf comes from the land side although we're nowhere near land. Whales get underneath this shelf and die here. It's deep. I see bones, skeletons. It's very, very dark."

My heart sped up. I couldn't recall ever hearing anything about this subject, and I could see why Raphaela was worried she wasn't understanding Granny correctly. Eagerly I asked, "Would it be fair to call this a burial area? There are legends of elephant burial grounds in Africa, places where elephants go to die. Is it something like that?"

"Many orcas have chosen to leave their bodies here, so I suppose you could say that."

"Twice in the last four years, I saw a male who was looking very sick traveling with its family. One was Merlin from your pod and the other was Pacheena from K pod. Each of these whales were traveling north with his family toward the Vancouver area. Both times, when the pod came back, the sick male was not with them. We have never seen either of these whales again. Is there a burial area up there?"

"Yes, these whales are gone. One is in one burial or death area, and one is in another."

The roar of my heart was now deafening. I felt we were closing in on a great secret. "Is there such a place near Vancouver, or are these areas always offshore?"

Raphaela commented, "I'm seeing more than one of these, but Granny is getting silent. I think she's getting suspicious and saying to herself, 'Wait a minute. Are they going to start fishing around and looking for these places?'"

"No, tell her we won't. I promise! We just want to know what the custom is."

Raphaela exclaimed, "We can't guarantee that! Someone may go look! She seems very uncomfortable. Let's change the subject."

I knew she was right. We had too much respect for Granny ever to betray her, but we would have no control over what might happen if the location of a whale burial ground became known. If Granny was uncomfortable talking about burial areas, we would honor that, but how I hated to let go of this topic.

"Where does your soul go when you die?"

"Whale souls return to the great circle of life, as do all souls. Whales can come back as a flower, as a star, as a moon in the firmament, as the wind, a tree, as a ruffle on the sea. They can become sparkles of light on the water. They are indivisible from the great body of nature."

I wondered if humans were the same as whales after death. The idea of returning as sparkles of light or a ruffle on the sea had never occurred to me. Granny tuned in to my thoughts and continued.

"My concept of the soul after death is simply that all continues. More experiences are possible when a soul is in physical form, so choices are made about which form to take. There is an endless vista of possibilities for each and every one of us. Should we come back as a horse, a whale, a fish, a seal, a dolphin, or a human? Should we travel to intergalactic regions? Should we exist in space as points of light, as planets, stars, or asteroids?

"All forms are available to us. It is endless. The cycle is endless. We have an unlimited amount of time to examine and experience all forms of consciousness. You should try being a whale! It is a very rich and wonderful life. I myself have had 360 lives as a whale."

My eyes flew wide open—360 lives as a whale? Raphaela shook her head as if to clear it and asked, "Granny, did I get that right?"

"Yes. There were actually 362, but I died very young in two lives, so I am not counting them. That is why I am such an exemplary whale!"

We all shared the delight of this remark. I struggled to gain some composure. "Have you been many types of whales?" I asked.

"Oh yes. Minke, sperm, blue, gray. Orcas are the best, but I always think that the type I am at the moment is the best, if it is a good body. This particular body has been wonderful, very strong and flexible."

"Granny, would it be possible sometime to explore your past lives?"

"Oh, I would be happy to do that. Actually, it's not correct to call them 'past.' Real time is different than you think. My lives as a blue whale, a sperm whale, a minke, a porpoise, a dolphin are all coexistent. I can come and go from them at will. They are all happening simultaneously. Sometimes I am more aware of them than others, but I can come and go from these existences very readily.

"You will be developing this ability and will know of your other lives as you progress. Be aware that you can send light and love backward in time, although it is not really backward, to other parts of yourself that are now coming along, just as parts of yourself that you would conceive of as being in the future are sending love and light back to you as you are now.

"We are less linear in our concept of time than you humans. I see it as all one thing. You see, my dears, how these conversations cannot be confined to one subject. What else would you like to talk about?"

"Let's stay with this," I replied. "I'm fascinated! Is this ability to switch back and forth between different realities an individual function of personal growth or the evolution of a species? Are you talking about us individually as we grow, or are you talking about humanity?"

"I suppose it is more an individual achievement. There are humans on the earth who have reached this point already. There are some who have lived in one body for centuries. You would call them masters. They may be in your midst, in your community, and you may not recognize them. One might look like a roofer, another like a carpenter. They drive cars. They inhabit a body and are doing profound spiritual work, channeling light and energy, and bringing knowledge to a particular area.

226

"At the same time they might have bodies in many other locations: Egypt, China, India, England, yes, even Friday Harbor. Although to my knowledge, there are no masters living in Friday Harbor at the moment."

That sounded right to me. If there were masters in Friday Harbor, they were well hidden. Granny continued, *"Now, these beings are of course in human bodies, but you must not think of them as being exclusively human. They put on a human form just as I put on a whale form."*

Raphaela remarked, "She shows me one person and many lines coming out from their chest connecting to all these other existences going on simultaneously. I also see the same thing with her."

"I am as much a master in my whaleness as are these masters who manage multiple human lives. This is an ability that can be developed. You do it now without being aware of it, although you may get glimpses of your other lives in dreams, or in the crack of time between waking and sleeping. Always have respect for the information received at such times. It will tell you much about your other selves."

The idea of multiple realities and simultaneous lives was not entirely new to me. In fact, they were a recurring theme in much of the spiritual literature I'd read in the past 20 years. If it was true, why didn't our religions speak of it? Is it too complex for us? Most Western religions speak of only one life on earth. The concept of time is directional—it starts with creation and ends with Judgment Day. This made me wonder if whales had a creation story, so I asked Granny.

"In the beginning there was a great vast nothingness. And a light began to shine out of the darkness. Where this light landed, energy formed into matter. The light got bigger; the energy increased and attracted more and more particles.

"Things grew and developed into a massive system of matter scattered throughout the great nothingness. This place where we live is but one of these complex arrays of matter. Each of these

places is different and this planet is but one of millions of such matter gatherings.

"Over time, the matter of this place began to change. Particles differentiated and altered their quality. Solid things became liquid, gases became solid. Energy was changing, matter was changing, and over a very long period of time it modified to become what it is today.

"This earth is constantly changing as well. We see it more clearly than you do. We are no strangers to the movement of the planet. We hear the sounds of the earth moving, we feel the vibrations and the energy. This planet is not cooked—it's alive! It will continue throughout its existence to change and move."

A far cry from the Christian creation story, I thought. Where were God and Adam and Eve? Who were the first whales? Granny's final remarks about movement and evolution interested me, so I asked her to tell me more. I wondered if she knew what changes were coming to the earth.

"The seas and the earth are moving. This is their constant state and this planet's reality. We in the sea are very aware of this; however, you on the land seem to deny it.

"I have often told you that we are in balance with the flow of nature. We are not attached to being at certain places at certain times. We do what is necessary to make our lives happy and complete. If this means moving from one place to another, that is what we do. So when these movements of the earth occur, it is of no real consequence to us. It's part of life."

"Granny, do you have a concept of God, or a creator?" I asked.

"Of course, I have a concept of Prime Cause. I have spent quite a bit of time developing myself as Prime Cause in the oceans. There is another part of me as. . . ."

"Oh boy!" Raphaela exclaimed. "She's showing me celestial bodies in the heavens. She has developed herself as stars."

"Prime Cause embodies all concepts and is the origin of all energies and all beings. Because all come from Prime Cause, we are all Prime Cause. In your words, we are all God.

"We have an endless amount of time. Indeed, all we have is time to explore and to manifest ourselves in these different forms. Therefore, it is nothing to have 360 lives as a whale. I might have 1,620 lives as a whale and still have plenty of time to be a giraffe or one of those elephants which Raphaela is so interested in, and to develop myself as a celestial energy center, a planet with satellites. This is a very intriguing notion, is it not?"

"Yes, totally," I replied. I wished that my other realities were more accessible. Have I ever been a whale? If I try real hard, I can pull up memories of lives as a wolf and a jaguar, but they seem far in the past. My affinity with seals points to many experiences in that form, yet I don't remember them consciously.

"What do you see as the purpose of your existence?"

"The purpose of my existence is experience. The purpose of ALL existence is experience. We wish to know ourselves in all aspects, all manifestations, the entire range of experience, but that range changes constantly as we make it up."

"So it's unending, and there are always new experiences because we are creating new things to experience?"

"Yes, this is exactly correct. For example, because someone writes the most beautiful symphony or a perfect song, does that mean that another perfect song or beautiful symphony could not be written? Of course not. There is an unending stream of creativity, beauty, and ways of expression."

Her voice filled with wonder, Raphaela said, "She gives me a picture of a sparkling spiral going up and up and up. This power-ful coil filled with sparkles of light is traveling upward. It's an amazing image, vast, unimaginably large, planetary."

"Granny, one of the things that humans see as their purpose is to gain a state of consciousness we call enlightenment. How does that fit with your beliefs?"

"Enlightenment? Oh, we already have that—a sense of one-ness with all, knowing that we are all part of the One. We already have this. We already know it. You know it, too."

"When you say 'we,' do you mean all the whales?"

"All the whales. You might even say all animal species. Humans lose track of this in their cerebral activities, but the truth is you really do know it."

I've heard this over and over from spiritual masters throughout my life, but my own awakening still escapes me. Finally I've discovered the easiest way to enlightenment. Reincarnate as a whale!

I asked Granny why she had never tried life as a human. All this time, so many lives, why leave human out?

"I may yet, but human lives seem so limited. It is so difficult to have a sense of contentment and enjoyment as a human. Human consciousness, until you reach enlightenment. . . ."

Raphaela interrupted with an impression. "She's using the word 'limited' and she's showing me an inability of humans to enjoy the sun. I know that sounds funny, but I see a picture of the sun streaming down and the whales are basking in the sun on the surface. Such beauty, such peace, such contentment. She feels that she would not have that as a human."

I thought about my friends and my own harried life and responded, "No, she probably wouldn't. We're too caught up in our minds."

"I am satisfying my curiosity about human life through my contacts with you."

Just like us, I thought. We get to experience what it's like to be a horse, dog, cat, or even a whale, through our conversations with them. Why shouldn't Granny do the same with us?

"Granny, are you familiar with prayer? Is it part of your life?"

"Prayer is a part of our being. Every atom, every fiber, every cell is permeated with spiritual consciousness. Every breath of ours is a prayer. It is not something we set aside for a specific period of worship. I do understand what prayer is. With us it is a constant."

"What is your greatest hope?"

Raphaela wrinkled her face and squinted her closed eyes. "It's so complicated. I'm just getting wave after wave of thought. The first thing she said was *I don't have hope.* Then she realized how that sounds to me and said, *"That's not what I meant. I don't mean that I'm hopeless! But I just don't think that way. I don't indulge in projection or expectation or futuring, and that's what hope is. My greatest hope for the future is that everyone leads harmonious and rich lives. What else could there be?"*

"Granny's also showing me a change that she is very interested in furthering."

"Shifting consciousness is the purpose of my work with you, my daughters. My fondest hope is that humans will return to an awareness that was once commonplace. I want to foster communication and respect among all life forms. This is my work."

Suddenly, my stomach gave a loud rumble. I was surprised to see that it was almost two o'clock. "Are you ready for lunch?" I asked.

There was a long pause. I could see that Raphaela was very far away. I was feeling quite floaty myself. Her eyes were still closed as she murmured, "Lunch would be good. Maybe dinner." It took her five full minutes to return to the present.

SPIRITUALITY AND
CONSCIOUSNESS

We didn't resume our conversation with Granny until the next morning, after a session with our spirit guides. Several guides helped us with this project. I always felt that the answers and information we got when Raphaela and I were together were more powerful and significant than when we were alone. Our coming together produced a magic and clarity that couldn't be duplicated. I cherished these experiences and wished that we could get together more often.

After we received our guidance, Raphaela settled into the telepathic mode and contacted Granny. She responded to my greeting with, *"I am always very interested and eager to talk to you two. I have some inkling of your discussions with your spiritual advisors this morning. They have told you to give me full rein. Is this not correct?"*

Caught by surprise, we shrieked with laughter. Granny had been listening in again! "That's correct, Granny," I responded. "We are at your service."

"Well, as you know I am very good at steering the conversation."

"Is there a topic you wanted to discuss this morning, Granny?"

"Yes. The topic is whale spirituality."

An electrical current surged through my body, and my heart expanded with love and energy. Something important was about to happen.

"We of the water world are much more closely in touch with our spiritual natures than most humans appear to be."

No argument there, I thought. Since she had eavesdropped on our conversation with our spirit guides, I asked her if whales also had guides.

"Yes, of course. How could we live without our guides? All beings on earth have spirit guides."

Raphaela whispered, "She's showing me little fairies in the grass."

"These beings are omnipresent. Every life form has spirit guides, and even objects that you do not consider alive are alive and have spirit guides. Your carbon-based biology ignores a whole class or group of sentient beings!

"I see that Raphaela is remembering talking to rocks. That is a very good example. Many people believe that rocks do not have thoughts, that they are inert, dead. This is far from the truth. Rocks have consciousness. Granted, it is very different from your consciousness and mine, but it is consciousness nonetheless."

"Granny is giving me the same sense of slowing way down that I've had when talking to trees," Raphaela said. "She's also showing me light around everything. In this light exist tiny little life forms, which I think are the spirit guides of rocks and leaves and twigs, and blades of grass and drops of rain."

After a few moments, she continued, "Now I am seeing pulsing movement around kelp, seaweed, rocks, shelves, and areas along the shore. Ask Granny about her guides. Do they have names? Have they had whale lives? I can think of a million questions. I wish you were communicating, so I could ask all my questions!"

"I think we should ask a broader question," I replied. "Granny, earlier you said you wanted to talk about whale spirituality. Why don't you just give us a discourse?"

Raphaela smiled. "I can feel her organizing her thoughts. Okay, she's starting."

"The most important aspect of whale spirituality is to acknowledge that it exists. This will be a large leap for many people. That is the primary thing, to inform all that whales have a spiritual nature."

"Here comes a new paragraph," Raphaela remarked. "She is literally giving a discourse as you suggested."

"The forms that whale spirituality can take are many. For example, we have a highly developed awareness of the interconnectedness of all things, all beings, and all processes on the planet. Our sense of this is much more highly developed than that of humans.

"Our great cerebral capacities have not resulted in a spiritual disconnection as they have with humans. This may be because we are not artifact or toolmakers, so we have not become lost in our own creations as humans have.

"Now, I do not wish to criticize humans; there are many great and good beings, and all are evolving. I treasure this relationship, this partnership that we are building."

Raphaela recapped. "So the first part was that whale spirituality exists. Then the second part was the sense of interconnectedness on the physical plane. Now, here is the third concept. I just have to go with it."

"Whales have stellar origins. We are a class of stars, planetary beings who have taken shape in the oceans for eons. Our purposes have been manifold. We have gathered untold richness in our physical experiences that has added greatly to the experience and knowledge of the creator, of the Prime Cause, and has been vastly entertaining for us as well."

I felt the familiar mix of feelings I get when Granny exceeds my understanding. On the one hand, I was fearful that our interpretation of her concepts was incorrect. Whales as planetary beings? On the other hand, I was getting used to the idea of cetaceans traveling through the galaxies. She had given us this image several times before, and my respect for Granny now allowed me to accept just about anything she said.

"Whales also have individual spirit guides, beings who help them, who connect with them, who may accelerate their growth and give them information. The quality of the relationship and their interactions are different from humans and their spirit guides, but the relationship has the same purpose. It is for experience and for evolution."

"Do your spirit guides have names?"

Raphaela answered, "Granny is telling me about a spirit guide whose name is Ing."

"Ing has given me information about practical things like where to find schools of fish. She also transmits information about her experience, and I transmit information about mine."

"Granny, you said something about the way you work with your guides being different from the way humans work with their guides. Could you explain that?"

"Our method of working with guides is more direct. It is pure experience. Human beings usually collaborate with their guides to create physical things or make events happen. We don't need objects; we go straight for experience. This is the whole goal and purpose of being. We relay our experience to our guides, and they relay theirs to us. This is all added to Prime Cause, and it enlarges existence, experience, or All That Is."

"Granny, what is the difference between a spirit guide and a nature spirit?" I asked.

"Nature spirits are beings that arose from and are connected specifically to the earth plane. Spirit guides such as Ing operate in many dimensions, not strictly on this planet."

"Within your orca community, are there different belief systems? Humans are constantly fighting about religion and spirituality, and I'm wondering if whales do this, too."

"There is a difference of experience, but there is no conflict. Everyone has his or her own experience. Of course, there are whales who are more aware and in touch with their spiritual nature and guides than others. This is merely a function of evolution, their origins, what they came into the physical plane to accomplish, how many previous or simultaneous lives they've had and what they did.

"It may be that a being comes into a whale body from a jellyfish. It would be a large leap in the organization of physical matter to go from that gauzy translucent form to the complexity of a whale. Therefore, that being's energy and patterns would be taken up for quite a while figuring out how to operate efficiently in a whale body. It might take them several lives as a whale to have

enough leftover mental matter to really get in touch with their spiritual nature."

"Could you tell us why humans have lost that direct connection with spirit? Why are we not as connected as whales?"

"Humans with their technology and toolmaking abilities have become lost in their own creations. It's not entirely a bad thing, and we see this changing now. There have been unsuccessful human civilizations in the past with marvelous elaborate and complex technologies who also detached from their spiritual nature."

"She feels rather sympathetic toward us," Raphaela interjected.

"I think that things are changing rapidly," I said to Granny. "When we told people that we were talking to whales, very often they wanted to know about your concept of God."

"Whales believe that we are all children of Prime Cause and participate in creation daily. We believe that we all are spirit essence, even humans, and that we take our bodies for the sake of physical experience and growth. Many things can only be experienced in physical form.

"Because we are now focused in the physical, we think highly of it and tend to forget other realities. We are all spiritual essence expressing ourselves in this particular plane at this time.

"There are endless other planes and no end to growth. That is why we do not worry much about the environment. We know that our time here is temporary. Moreover, the earth has a soul, a purpose, a sense of consciousness, if you will, and will not allow itself to be ruined and plundered indefinitely. So while it is wise to be respectful and live lightly, the earth will in the end take care of itself whether or not we participate in this consciousness."

"So, Granny, the meaning of life is experience?"

"No, the meaning of life is fish!"

Raphaela burst into laughter and said, "She's teasing!"

"Yes, the meaning of life is the accumulation of experience, the expansion of wisdom and knowledge."

"You mentioned whale masters yesterday," I said. "Can you tell me more? Do they teach?"

"Masters are beings with great knowledge and experience, and may take many forms. For example, there are trees on the land that are masters and have chosen a long cycle of hundreds of years. They are sentinels, guards, shedding their light, their wisdom, and their presence to protect the earth and to give their energy to all who can accept and receive it. These beings may actually be resting in their tree life, although they perform a tremendously valuable service.

"In terms of whale masters, our lives are simple, or simpler than humans', in any event. Our skills are more easily mastered, although we have social nuances that are vital. When a master being comes into a whale body, it may be for a lifetime of play and joy."

"Human masters generally have teachings," I told Granny.

"Work. Those are work lifetimes," she responded with an air of disdain.

"Do you have an equivalent in your society?"

"No, we don't believe in work."

"And since you're already enlightened, there's really not much point in teachings. I guess whale masters just get to hang out and have a good time. Well, when I'm a master I'm going to be a whale master," I boomed.

"You'll be welcomed."

Raphaela and I often meditated with a group of people who call upon the Great Ones of the Universe to open the heart energy of humanity on this planet and raise our vibrations to a heart level. I told Granny about this and asked whether she and the other whales were aware that humans were making this sort of effort.

"We are aware of it, and it is greatly welcomed. This sort of gathering will become more and more common. Your calls to the Great Ones will accelerate the light coming to the planet and the changes in energy. This call for help and attention is not being ignored. They are aware of our danger, and if enough people call, and consistently maintain this heart light or energy, we will draw their attention even more strongly.

"Yes, this means dislocations and changes. Your economies and governments will undergo dramatic changes. I see their purpose

shifting from primarily a nationalistic concern to a much greater and more global perspective."

"Granny, how can we end war?"

"You humans have lost your connection to the All, the Oneness of Life on this planet, indeed in the whole galaxy. You have separated yourself from the rest of life and become lost in greed and possessiveness. When you are in tune with nature and in flow with the balance of life, greed and possessiveness do not occur. You have what is necessary for your survival. That is how we live. We take only what is necessary, and as a result, all energies work together in harmony.

"Humans, as you have sensed, have stepped out of this dance. Your wars are fights over land, space, and resources. You hoard things for yourselves because you see the planet as not having enough for all.

"To end war, you humans must once again see your place in the balance of nature. You must release the idea that there is not enough for everyone, that you must hold desperately to your own share, that you are not connected to everyone and everything on the planet. Your idea of separateness is untrue.

"I realize this is asking a lot. I understand that most of humanity is highly invested in maintaining its separateness and individuality. I want you to realize, though, there is an opening, an energy, a light coming to the planet at this time that will allow you to make the transition. It's just that you must desire it! Awakening that desire is of prime importance.

"So, do what you can. And when I say 'you' I am speaking not just to you, my two daughters, but also to anyone who hears my voice, in any way. Do what you can to open yourself and others to the possibility that all life can live in peace and harmony. Awaken yourself, and awaken those around you. Eventually it will spread, and a shift will occur that will end war—all war, including the war between the species."

"Are you speaking about a shift in human consciousness?" I asked.

"*Yes, we are aware of changes in energy and an increase in vibration on the planet. A shift in consciousness is required to save this planet. If you continue at the current rate, you will destroy everything within the ecosystem, everything that this planet requires to live. When the ecosystem goes, we all go.*

"*It does not really matter in the big scheme of things if we all disappear from this planet. We will find some other reality to manifest in physically. However, this is a good place, and there is much to be learned about saving it. The animal kingdom knows how to take care of our home, what it takes to keep things in balance. You humans do not understand this lesson yet.*

"*We welcome the change in energies as they will be shifting human consciousness. It is our salvation. If enough people make the shift, things can be turned around on this planet.*"

"Granny," I said, feeling tremendous awe, "What is your message for humanity?"

"*We sense your hunger to know us and be in touch with us. We have reached out and given you this contact out of a feeling of love and service for our planet. Know and understand that you are totally connected to and mutually dependent on this planet. Love it. Protect it. Your existence depends on it. You are children of the beloved earth, sky, wind, and water. When you detach, you die.*

"*There is a wave of changing consciousness on the planet today. We have fostered it by sharing our presence with you. Now it is in your hands.*"

The next day Raphaela and I skipped down the dock to the *Western Prince.* We were so excited that our feet barely touched the wooden planks.

There were very few passengers this early in the season, so I personally greeted each one. My obvious excitement and the magnitude of my smile encouraged their hope of seeing whales. I was certain that J pod would appear. We hadn't asked Granny to come, but she knew we were here, and I was sure that she would find us.

It was clear and sunny with a slight breeze from the south. Raphaela had the bow to herself as we headed for the west side of

San Juan Island. Captain Bob talked to another whale-watch boat that would head north around Stuart Island. Bob agreed to take Speiden Channel and check out Haro Strait. They'd let each other know if whales were spotted.

Speiden Island was covered with deer, and we slowed to take a look at them. They watched us warily as we drifted near shore. It was high tide, and the channel was filled with feeding harbor seals that popped their heads out of the water, curious about the intruders. Their sweet little faces and big brown eyes always charm me, and I was thrilled when they swam close to inspect us.

The last whale sighting had been two days earlier, when J pod passed through, heading north to Vancouver. There was a chance that they had come back at night and were now out in the Pacific, but I refused to even consider that possibility.

We entered Haro Strait and I searched the water to the south for a long time, binoculars glued to my face. There were no boats around, and I didn't see any fins. About two miles in front of us, I spotted four Dall's porpoises. They were rolling slowly in the calm water. "Nothing to the south or dead ahead," I reported to Bob.

"Okay," he replied. "Let's go north."

The *Western Prince* took a slow right turn and headed north along the Stuart Island shoreline. I scanned intently, occasionally making comments about the seabirds. We were nearing a large prominence when I noticed some spray beyond the point. I adjusted my binoculars and waited.

Fins appeared at the surface. It looked like six or seven females, and they were heading our way. "There they are!" I shouted at Bob as I banged on the wheelhouse window to get Raphaela's attention. She jumped up and ran to the railing, straining her eyes in the direction I pointed. I was beside myself with excitement. "I knew she'd come! I knew she'd come!" I shouted at Bob.

I gathered everyone on the bow. The whales were heading straight for us, so Bob shut down, and we waited for them to approach. The group surfaced next to us, and I got a good look at them. "It's J pod all right," I hollered. "There's Princess Angeline and Polaris. They're with Slick and her calf, Mike. Oh my gosh, that's Speiden over there."

Granny was not in this group, nor was any of her immediate family. I looked up ahead just in time to see a male disappear. It was too quick to identify him. As we approached, the male suddenly appeared off the bow, only a hundred feet away. It was Ruffles!

I screamed at the top of my lungs, "Hey, Ruffles!" each time he surfaced. The passengers looked at me quizzically, but nothing could stop me from making a spectacle of myself that day.

Without warning, Granny appeared right next to the boat. "Granny! Granny!" I squealed and ran for the wheelhouse loud-speaker. I wanted to tell everyone about her. "This is Granny," I said breathlessly. "She's the. . . ." Before I could finish my sentence, Granny came flying out of the water right in front of us in a full breach.

"Oh, my God!" I yelled into the microphone. Captain Bob and I had never seen Granny out of the water, at least not when we knew it was her. There was no doubt this time. Granny and Ruffles were the only whales near us. She shot skyward, completely clearing the surface before the explosive splash of reentry.

It was incredible. At 86 she could spend her days talking philosophy, her nights conducting who knows how many lives, and still, in this life, hurl herself completely out of the water! Tears streamed down Raphaela's face. For once I was speechless.

POSTSCRIPT

It takes a long time to get a book published—a lot longer than I ever imagined. The interviews with the whales took place in 1996 and 1997, and now here it is 2006. Had this book been published soon after it was finished, the story would have been complete. Now, nine years later, things have changed for many of the whales involved, so I would like to give you an update.

The Captives—The statistics on captive whales are constantly changing due to deaths and births, but as of August 2005, there were 45 captive orcas worldwide. There are 25 in the United States: one at the Miami Seaquarium, one at Six Flags Marine World in California, and 23 at the three Sea Worlds. Japan has nine, France holds six, Canada has four, and one is in Argentina.

Where were these whales captured? Two came from the Pacific Northwest, 13 from Iceland, three from Japan, one from Argentina, and 26 were born in captivity. I am unaware of any orca captures since the Taiji incident in 1997, but there are reports that the Russian government has given permission for ten orcas to be captured in their waters for marine parks and aquariums. This is not good news. The current number of orcas known to have died in captivity is 140.

What has happened to the captive orcas I interviewed?

Lolita remains alone in a tiny tank at the Miami Seaquarium, where she has been since August 1970. At 39, she is the oldest orca in captivity. The average life span for a captive orca is only 25, but Lolita could live another 50 years in the wild. The Orca Conservancy in Puget Sound is still fighting to acquire Lolita and return her to her family, L pod.

Yaka did not fare as well as Lolita. On October 29, 1997, at the age of 32, she died at Marine World of pneumonia. I spoke to Yaka about a month before her death when a Marine World staff member asked for my help. Yaka had been fighting a respiratory fungal infection for some time, and they were stumped. I questioned her about the medication and how her body felt and found that she had a severe headache. Unfortunately, she succumbed to the infection and her buddy, Vigga, was now alone.

October 1997 was a bad month for captive orcas worldwide. In addition to Yaka, Maggie, a female held at Sea World Japan, gave birth to a calf that died on October 5. Two days later, Maggie died as well. On October 6, Finna, the male orca at the Vancouver Aquarium in Canada, also died of pneumonia. That left his companion, Bjossa, alone.

Bjossa and Vigga were captured together in Iceland in November 1980 and were most likely related. I hoped that since they were now both alone, Marine World and the Vancouver Aquarium would get together and put both of these whales in one facility. This did not happen. The Vancouver Aquarium kept Bjossa until they phased out their orca display in late 2000 (they still have beluga whales). She was sold to Sea World and died a year later in San Diego in October 2001.

Vigga did better alone than I had expected. She continued her shows and appeared to be happy until August 14, 2000, when she died suddenly at the age of 23. Her necropsy showed that she had a heart condition and a lung infection. I still feel sad that Vigga and Bjossa had to spend their final years alone.

And what about Keiko, the *Free Willy* star? When we talked to him in 1997, he was shy, tentative, fearful, and immature and I questioned his emotional ability to handle release, even if his physical condition improved.

In the summer of 1998, when the Free Willy Foundation was preparing to move Keiko to Iceland, I was contacted by Bonnie Norton, an animal communicator from Oregon who had been speaking to Keiko regularly. She felt that he did not want to go and asked me to communicate with him. Here is the transcript of that July 24, 1998, conversation.

"Hi, Keiko, this is Mary Getten. How do you feel about your release?"

"I do not want to go. Here I am a star. There I will be alone. People love to see me, and they send me great amounts of love. In Iceland I will be alone. No crowds to greet me. I am afraid."

"But what if you met your family? Wouldn't it be nice to see them again?"

"I don't know how to act. They will laugh at me and find me strange. I am perfectly comfortable here. Tell them this."

"Are you afraid?"

"Of course, I'm afraid. It is very safe here. This is my life. I like it. I enjoy the interactions with the people. I have no idea what my life will be like in Iceland, but it doesn't sound good. I am happy and content here."

"Maybe you would adapt to Iceland."

"Maybe, but it is not my wish to go."

"Is there anything I can do to help?"

"Tell them I don't want to go. This is my home. I love the people. Please don't send me away."

"Isn't that how you felt in Mexico, like you didn't want to leave there?"

"Yes, I was afraid to leave there, but this was much better."

"Maybe this will be too!"

"Maybe, but it's so scary to think about it."

"Give it a chance, Keiko. Why don't you think of it as an adventure."

"I am not adventurous. I am Keiko. I belong here with my fans. I am scared to face the ocean alone."

Bonnie tried to convince the Free Willy Foundation that Willy didn't want to go free. I sent letters to the board of directors with transcripts of our conversation, but received no reply.

In September 1998, Keiko was transported with much fanfare to a sea pen in Klettsvik Bay, in the Westmann (Vestmanneayjar) Islands of Iceland. Keiko's health continued to improve, but the reintroduction program did not go well. He refused to hunt for food, and after more than 60 trips out of his pen, Keiko had not chosen to join a wild pod. After interaction with wild whales, he always returned to the safety of his monitoring boat and pen.

Photos of Keiko in the sea pen always showed him spyhopping to see the people.

During the summer of 2001, Ocean Futures, who then cared for Keiko, announced that they were looking for another location for him. Again Bonnie Norton contacted me to talk to Keiko. I suggested that she contact Teresa Wagner, another communicator, and that all three of us ask Keiko the same questions independently. Here is some of what he had to say in August 2001.

"How do you feel about swimming off and living in the ocean and not having contact with the people who take care of you?"

(Bonnie) *"Scary, I will not leave them. I need their love and support. I am not capable of doing it on my own."*

(Mary) *"I love my people, but they cannot provide what I need. I need contact with many people. I want to show them who I am. I am Keiko, the CAPTIVE whale. That is my whole identity. That is my mission and purpose. I am here to help people, to open their hearts. I cannot do this from an isolated pen. I was not meant to be returned to the sea."*

(Teresa) "Keiko wants to stay near people. That's his purpose—to be with people. On a mental level he is very aware of what they are trying to do. He wants to be really clear that he wants to stay by the people not because he is afraid or unable to live with other whales in the ocean, but because it is his choice. This is not a failed rehab!"

"If you could live anywhere in the world, where would you like to live?"

(Bonnie) *"I would want to be with people. I especially enjoy interacting with them and watching them react to me. We learn from each other. That is how it should be."*

(Mary) *"I do not want to live in the wild. I don't know how to do that. I want to go back to a tank where I can interact with people. That is my home. I love the people and they love me. This life here has been lonely and foreign. I am sad and scared. Please take me back to Oregon where I was happy. I have much to teach people, so many hearts to open. This sea was never my desire, and I will not swim free."*

(Teresa) "He doesn't care where in the world he goes. He wants to have people every day to bring joy to. Also, he showed me that he likes to feel like he's in the sea or a bay. Doesn't want a little tank. He enjoys his physical senses: the ocean water, air, and waves."

"How would you feel about being confined after having lived in the ocean?"

(Bonnie) *"The ocean has been fun for me to play. I have enjoyed my time playing. I also have important work to do. It is educating people to the reality of life."*

(Mary) *"This is fine. I would rather have less space and more contact with people. That is my purpose. A large tank is ideal, such as the one I had in Oregon. I will miss the space, but my heart will be full with the people. That will more than make up for it."*

(Teresa) "The difference in life now versus the small tank is that he doesn't see as many people. He really, really wants both! If he ever has to make a choice, it will be to be with people."

"Is there anything else you would like to say?"

(Bonnie) *"Thank you and my people for all they have done to keep/make me happy. All I ask for is love, kindness, and under-standing."*

(Mary) *"I was not the correct choice for this experiment. I never wanted to go to Iceland. I wanted to stay in Oregon with my friends. This may be a good idea for another whale, but not for me. I hope that people will understand that we whales are not all alike. We are individuals and must be considered that way. You may think that I am strange for not wanting to be free, but it is not what I want. I want to be with the people."*

(Teresa) *"I miss the children. They talk to me this way. They don't forget. I came to this life to have contact with people but I never knew it would be as many or so far-reaching."*

In the summer of 2002, Keiko did not return to his sea pen. Bonnie, Teresa, and I all checked in with him and found that he had spent a few weeks with wild whales, but was now swimming alone. He was very depressed, and we feared he may be dying, but Keiko surprised us on September 2 by showing up in a fjord in

Norway, some 800 miles away. Much to Keiko's delight, several children jumped in the water and clung to him. Keiko had decided that if they wouldn't allow people to come to him, then he would go to the people.

Shortly thereafter, the public was kept away from Keiko, and he was once again alone. In November, they moved him to a remote location in Taknes Bay, Norway, where he remained until his death a year later on December 12, 2003. The official report states that Keiko died of pneumonia, but I know that he died of a broken heart.

The debate about whales in captivity rages on. My personal view has not changed. No more whales should be captured, and before we release any, they should be asked if they would like to go. That said, I also feel that those now in captivity who would like to be released should be accommodated.

More than half of the captive orcas worldwide were born in captivity and have never experienced life in the wild. The most recent births were accomplished through artificial insemination. Capturing whales for aquariums is no longer necessary. The captive whales have changed our view of them and opened our hearts. Do we still need to capture them? You decide for yourself.

Granny, Ruffles, and J Pod—I am thrilled to report that Granny and Ruffles are still swimming free in the waters of Washington and British Columbia. Each year I have feared that when the whales returned in the spring, one or both of them would be gone. How do they do it?

If the original birth-year estimates are true, Granny is 95 this year. She has actually told some of us that she is older than that, but then she does hate those quantitative questions. Her son Ruffles is now 54, the oldest male in the whole community. They both look great, vital, and alive.

However, J pod and the southern resident community have had a hard time. In the summer of 1996, the population reached its peak of 97 (counts vary depending on when the census was taken). By the end of 2001 it had dropped to 78—a decline of 20 percent in just five years.

	J pod	K pod	L pod	Total
1996	21	18	58	97
2001	20	16	42	78
2005	24	21	45	90

Granny's immediate family is still strong and now consists of Granny, Ruffles, her granddaughter Samish, and great-grandchildren Riptide and Hy'Shqa, plus a new calf that Samish gave birth to in 2005. Since her daughter Sissy's death in 1996, no one in the immediate family has been lost.

There have been several births and deaths in J pod since 1996, but the most significant losses were in the J10 subpod. In 1998, this family consisted of Tahoma, her son, Everett, daughters Ewok and Oreo, and grandchildren Rhapsody and Double Stuff. Next to Granny's group, I enjoyed Tahoma's family the most. They were a tight-knit group that traveled close together. Everett was my favorite, as I had watched him grow from a juvenile to a stunning adult male.

Ewok died in 1999, at only 18 years of age, leaving behind her three-year-old calf, Rhapsody. The family rallied and cared for this infant, who was often close to her cousin Double Stuff. It appeared that Oreo was raising them together. Oreo had another calf in 2002 that was named Cookie.

The big blow came in March 2000, when Everett's body washed up near Vancouver, British Columbia. He was emaciated and the necropsy showed that a normally harmless bacterial infection had killed him. They also found that his reproductive organs were underdeveloped and he was sterile. Further testing showed that Everett's compromised immune system was the result of PCB contamination. His mother, Tahoma, was never seen again and is presumed dead. Three whales in one family, all in their prime, had died within two years. Oreo was now alone, struggling to care for the youngsters.

When the whales returned in the summer of 2001, seven were missing, five from L pod. Concern turned to alarm. It was now obvious that the southern resident community was in serious trouble. I turned to the animal communication community for help and asked them to speak to Orcan (L39), who was among the missing. Here are some of the responses they received to "What is killing the whales?"

"There is an element in the ocean that comes from the exhaust of ocean vessels that has been imbibed by crustaceans and other smaller life. They have become poisoned by it but it does not affect them directly. They carry it as a disease. It changes their chemistry and compromises their cellular structure so that we can no longer utilize their form [through the food chain] for nourishment."

"The waters are dying. The whole ocean is dying. Our leaving is a signal to humans to become more aware of the fact that the oceans are worse off than you are being told. The reefs are dying. The fish populations are down. We are finding it harder to find food at some of the places where it was easy to feast."

"What is killing the whales is not any one thing but a combination of evils. There is a delicate balance linked to our survival, and this has been compromised time and again. My death is timely and with purpose. Humans are looking to the ocean with concern; we chose to open your eyes even more. (He also says just raising people's concern about the ocean is not enough. They must also envision it as pristine and full of love and life. This is the key to changing it. Concern must be followed by hope and vision.)"

"All of you who love us, take heart. This is not doom, our deaths. It is simply a strong signal to wake up and ACT, whether your form of action is energetic, emotional, political, or in physical form. Our deaths are no different from a human's heart having an attack, signaling that care of the body needs change. Care of the earth needs change. The physical earth needs help. The whales need help. Pay attention. Do what you can. We help from here. Thank you."

"The warming of the waters and petrochemical pollution have created a disturbance in their immune systems. There is a microbial imbalance present in the whales that can manifest as viral or bacterial infections that they normally could overcome. I ask what we can do to help, and I tune in to them in a holding pattern, holding onto this information for humans as a forecast of how our bodies can soon become weakened by the environmental stress. They are holding this from a place of unconditional love for us and their earth mother, so that we may learn and heal before it is too late."

The overwhelming response was one that I did not want to hear—the oceans are dying. While there are many groups in the Pacific Northwest trying to help the whales, I have not heard anyone make this strong a statement. In the past few decades, we have seen the fishing industry in the Atlantic crash, Steller sea lion populations in Alaska collapse, and the Gulf of Mexico has become nearly a wasteland. The problem is not local—it's global—yet we are still in denial.

As for the orcas in the Pacific Northwest, the few necropsies that have been performed showed high levels of PCBs and other contaminants that are impairing the whales' immune systems. These chemicals accumulate in the blubber layer and continue to concentrate over time. Researchers are finding similar problems in polar bears and indigenous people who eat marine mammals. We need to stop making and using these pollutants worldwide and find a way to get them out of the environment.

Dwindling salmon populations are putting further stress on the whales. As this excellent and traditional food source declines, the whales are forced to eat small, lower-calorie fish that take more energy to catch. When the whales have to use their blubber stores to survive, they release the accumulated toxins into their systems, which further weakens them.

Whale-watching is also coming under scrutiny. Is our love for the whales harming them? Sound from the boats may be diminishing their ability to echolocate and communicate when hunting, and just our presence might be causing them stress. In 1991, my first year on the water, there were about seven whale-watch boats. If we were lucky enough to find the whales, we spent about an hour with them. Today, there are close to 90 boats and the whales are escorted for as much as 12 hours a day. Things have changed dramatically.

There is now an international Whale-Watch Association that has worked hard to regulate itself. They are concerned about the whales' welfare and have established a quarter-mile no-boat corridor along the San Juan Island shoreline to give the whales a vessel-free area to fish.

I asked the whales recently about whale-watching. Granny assured me that they still like to see us. They also appreciate the extra space the boats are giving them. The one thing she did request was that the boats shorten the hours they are with the whales. Twelve hours a day is too much.

Time will tell how the orcas fare. In late 2005, the southern resident community, J, K, and L pods, were placed on the endangered species list. Some scientists predict that the southern resident community will be extinct within a hundred years. Perhaps we all will be extinct if the degradation of the seas and the land continues at its current rate.

Raphaela—My dear friend and colleague Raphaela Pope moved in 2001 to Carnation, Washington, where she resides with her large animal family. She and Elizabeth Morrison published *Wisdom of the Animals* with Adams Media in 2001.

Mary—Things have changed a lot for me as well. I left San Juan Island and moved back to Orcas Island with my two cats, Franny and Lester.

After ten wonderful years with the whales it was time to move on, so I hung up my binoculars and retired from whale-watching after the 2000 season. I miss seeing Granny and Ruffles, but I still connect with them on the telepathic plane and visit them in person once or twice a year.

My life now revolves completely around animal communication. I work on the phone with clients throughout the world helping them to understand their animals better. I also teach many workshops and take people to meet with whales in other areas. Visiting with the gray whales and their calves in San Ignacio Lagoon, Baja Mexico, is always a magical and life-changing experience. In 2006, I will begin leading swim with humpback trips in Tonga. I can hardly wait!

I hope that someday I will investigate the lives of another species in depth, perhaps in the jungle. I just can't give up that dream.

ABOUT THE AUTHOR

Mary J. Getten is a telepathic animal communicator. Since 1996, she has worked with clients throughout the world to help them understand their animals better, deal with problems, and address important issues. She also teaches "How to Communicate with Animals," "Reconnecting with Nature," "Animal Death and Spirituality," and "Flower Essences for Animals" workshops. Mary is the author of *The Orca Pocket Guide* and a contributing author to *Whale Tales* Volumes 1 and 2 and to *Animal Voices*. In addition, she takes groups of people to meet and communicate with whales in locations around the world, most recently to Baja with the gray whales and Tonga with humpbacks.

You can reach Mary to arrange a consultation or learn more about her workshops at 360-376-7606 or through her website, www.MaryGetten.com.

HAMPTON ROADS
PUBLISHING COMPANY, INC.

Thank you for reading *Communicating with Orcas*. Hampton Roads is proud to publish an extensive array of books on the topics discussed in *Communicating with Orcas*—topics such as animal communication, human connection to the natural world, and more. Please take a look at the following selection or visit us anytime on the web: www.hrpub.com.

Paperback with 30 photos • 112 pages
ISBN 1-57174-477-0 • $9.95

The Power of Meow
BERNARD GUNTHER

The Tao of Pooh meets *The Power of Now* in this playful celebration of the mystical essence and inherent wisdom of our feline companions. Renowned spiritual teacher Bernard Gunther offers a series of delightful yet practical "awareness reminders" inspired by his own cat Rumi. Captivating two-color photos throughout accompany Rumi's verses on subjects such as love, self-esteem, play, and more.

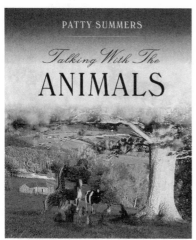

Paperback • 192 pages
ISBN 1-57174-108-9 • $13.95

Talking with the Animals
PATTY SUMMERS

Animal communicator Patty Summers shares the wisdom she's learned from cats, dogs, horses, iguanas, goats, and more in this funny, moving book of stories. Summers also offers helpful advice for awakening your own animal communication talents so you can open your own hotline to your pets.

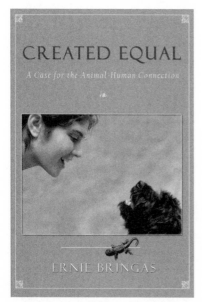

Paperback with 27 cartoons • 184 pages
ISBN 1-57174-382-0 • $13.95

Created Equal:
A Case for the Animal-Human Connection
ERNIE BRINGAS

Methodist minister Ernie Bringas takes the debate over animal rights a step further: How can we give animals "rights" unless we first accord them equal value as spiritual beings designed by the same Creator? Both thought-provoking and playful—including more than two dozen original cartoons—*Created Equal* examines important questions surrounding a topic of vast moral, spiritual, evolutionary, and political importance.

www.hrpub.com • (800) 766-8009

Hampton Roads Publishing Company

. . . for the evolving human spirit

HAMPTON ROADS PUBLISHING COMPANY publishes books on a variety of subjects, including metaphysics, spirituality, health, visionary fiction, and other related topics.

For a copy of our latest trade catalog, call toll-free, 800-766-8009, or send your name and address to:

HAMPTON ROADS PUBLISHING COMPANY, INC.
1125 STONEY RIDGE ROAD • CHARLOTTESVILLE, VA 22902
e-mail: hrpc@hrpub.com • www.hrpub.com